Charles G. Leland

The development of memory

Increasing quickness of perception and training the constructive faculty

Charles G. Leland

The development of memory
Increasing quickness of perception and training the constructive faculty

ISBN/EAN: 9783742846679

Manufactured in Europe, USA, Canada, Australia, Japa

Cover: Foto ©Thomas Meinert / pixelio.de

Manufactured and distributed by brebook publishing software
(www.brebook.com)

Charles G. Leland

The development of memory

PRACTICAL EDUCATION.

TREATING OF

THE DEVELOPMENT OF MEMORY,

THE INCREASING QUICKNESS OF PERCEPTION, AND

TRAINING THE CONSTRUCTIVE FACULTY

BY

CHARLES G. LELAND,

LATE DIRECTOR OF THE PUBLIC INDUSTRIAL ART SCHOOL
OF PHILADELPHIA,

And Author of " The Minor Arts," " Twelve Manuals of Art Work,"
" The Album of Repoussé Work," " Industrial Art in Education,
or Circular No 4, 1882," " Hints on Self Education,"
And of a Series of Articles on Decorative Arts published in
the London Art Journal

Third Edition.

LONDON: WHITTAKER AND CO.,
PATERNOSTER SQUARE, E.C.
1889.

CONTENTS.

CONTENTS.

APPENDIX.

PREFACE.

EDUCATION as it exists consists of storing the memory, developing the intellect, and training the constructive faculty. I propose to go a step beyond this, and show if possible how memory may be created, quickness of perception be awakened, and the constructive power formed, so that the mind, when it begins to acquire knowledge, may do so with confidence and strength. I think that before learning children should acquire the art of learning, or, to use the words of ARTHUR MACARTHUR, we should *intellectualise* them before attempting to improve their intellects.

My suggestions are based on what the history of mankind shows to be four truths. Firstly, that every human being possesses a memory which may be easily increased to what would seem to most persons a miraculous degree. This is proved by the fact that in every country in Europe before the invention of printing, as in the East at the present day, thousands or millions of men have had such memories, which were formed by a very easy system of development, which may be introduced to every school. Secondly, that quickness of perception may also be brought forth to an astonishing degree in every mind, as is also proved by research and observation, and that by so doing any undue preponderance of mere memory can be effectually avoided. Thirdly, that there is a faculty of visual perception, or eye-memory, by means of which we may bring before us vividly anything which we have ever seen, as FRANCIS GALTON has shown by exhaustive experiment. This third factor is a subtle blending or combination of memory and quickness of perception. It was first well experimented on and proved by ROBERT HOUDIN and the artist COUTURE. I venture to say that my own inquiries have added something to what is known of it. Fourthly, we have the constructive faculty, by which children of from eight years of age, and even younger, to fourteen, can be taught original design, and that not of an inferior quality, and to work it out by what I call the minor arts in modelling, wood carving, embroidery, inlaying, &c.

Memory, quickness of perception, and "visualising" meet and blend in art or manual industry. By means of the latter alone, as it is now taught in certain schools, children are easily and pleasantly trained to take up any kind of work. That is to say, one does not make artisans of them, but they are prepared in the best possible way to become artisans. A very great artist, when complimented on his skill, said, " I began to draw at fourteen years of age, and every day of my life I realise the fact that I should draw twice as well if I had begun at seven." Here was a great truth. From seven to fourteen years of age a certain suppleness, knack, or dexterous familiarity with the pencil or any implement may be acquired which diminishes with succeeding years. This is precisely the case with memory and quick perception.

It is strange and true that this latter faculty may be awakened in extremely dull children by merely mechanical methods or tricks, and these may be so improved as to lead to an awakening of intelligence This also is proved by observation. All of these assertions have in fact been perfectly and abundantly proved. What I now assert is, that the time has come to combine them all, and practically utilise them in the school. If this be resolutely and earnestly done it will entirely change our whole present system of teaching. It would be the height of vanity and presumption to believe that I have shown how this can be perfectly effected. What I hope for is that the attention and labour of others may be drawn to the subject. It is evident enough that the time has come —it is no longer in "the dim and remote future"—when science must either develop the mental faculties or else the schoolmaster must stop cramming—to go on with the old systems is no longer possible.

Though it should logically be the last, I have made the division on Industrial Art Education the first in the series. I did so because it is at present being earnestly studied, and is of great popular interest. It is probable that nineteen out of twenty will consider that it has "something in it," while they will regard the remainder as "unpractical." There is also this consideration. When I began nearly thirty years ago to seriously study education, and evolved the whole system laid down in this work, and resolved that if I ever should be in a position to do so I would devote my life to practically working it out, the only part of it which caused me doubt and fear was this—whether mere

children could be taught hand-work while attending
school. To resolve this I learned the minor arts, and
taught them till I found that they all resolved themselves into one art—design. The pupil who can
design and model can confidently work in all the
arts. I published a book, entitled the Minor Arts,
on this subject, which was read by Mrs. JEBB of
Ellesmere. While I was engaged for four years in
introducing industrial art work as a branch of education in the public schools of Philadelphia, Mrs.
JEBB established in Great Britain the Home Arts and
Industries Association, which has now, in addition to
its central point in London, more than two hundred
schools or classes in successful operation. From it the
teaching of the minor arts of every kind has extended
to the People's Palace for the Poor, to the East End
Working Men's Clubs, and to many other institutions.
In America, the attention of the Central Government
was attracted to the system, and General EATON, the
Commissioner of Education at the Central Bureau of
Education in Washington, requested me to write a
pamphlet setting forth how industrial education could
be taught in schools. From the literally thousands of
letters which I have received, I have learned that it
resulted in the establishment of as many classes. That
the system was well received is shown by the fact that
it was warmly commended in contributions in *The Nineteenth Century, Good Words, The Times, The Standard,
The Saturday Review, The New York Tribune, The New
York Herald, The New York School Journal, The Century*
(illustrated), *The Saint Nicholas* (illustrated), *The New
York Home Journal*, and in scores of other journals. The

first article ever published on my school in Philadelphia was in the *New York Herald*, in a leading editorial of a column. For this purpose the editor had sent a reporter expressly to examine the classes. The *New York Tribune* also constantly manifested great interest in the undertaking, and more than once gave a long account of it. Notwithstanding the great encouragement extended to me, there was a great deal of opposition and miscomprehension of the work by many who regarded the idea as Utopian. There are now, however, thousands of pupils in the public schools of New York who are studying the minor arts and industries. Two very important points have been established in this connection. Firstly, that art-work, instead of adding to overpressure in school study, relieves it, because it is regarded by all children as play or relaxation. Secondly, that it was ascertained by careful inquiry that the pupils who attended my classes were in advance of others in their usual studies. I myself ascertained that such work quickened their general intelligence.

I have also delivered more than a hundred lectures on this subject before the most varied assemblies in England and America, always followed by free discussion, and answered the same objections, till new ones ceased to be put. But now the system is a success. I believe—nay, I am sure—that there are now in both countries many more people who will believe in the possibility of creating memory and quickness of perception than there were ten years ago to put faith in industrial art-work in schools. The world moves. The hardest part of the reform has been tested and tried, and it has succeeded. There will be the same objections to what remains, and they will be worked down.

I have added to the chapters here described another on the art of awakening interest in subjects. It was inspired or aided by Mr MAUDSLEY'S remarkable comments on the possibility of attracting or creating attention. There is also a translation of a long review of the Washington pamphlet published by KARL WERNER in the Vienna *Morgenblatt* This was regarded when it appeared as a remarkably able paper, and it excited much comment.[1] Since it appeared the Austro-Hungarian Government have introduced industrial art-work to their public schools, and I was deeply gratified a few months since at finding in Buda Pesth, in the Normal School of three hundred pupils, classes in operation which reminded me of my own in Philadelphia. The work executed was under the direction of able artists, and the results were magnificent. I have also added an account of the British Home Arts and Industries Association, in the hope that it will induce my readers to visit it and see for themselves what it is doing.

I will add, in conclusion, that I will cheerfully answer any questions relative to the subjects treated of in this book, especially from those who are desirous of establishing classes, of introducing art-work into families or public institutions, or of undertaking it themselves.

---

[1] It was considered as of so much importance that by special request of Commissioner General EATON I executed a translation of it for the use of those consulting the papers of the Bureau of Education, who did not understand German. It contains a comprehensive account and critique of all that has been done in manual or industrial education in Germany.

There is no part of North America so wild that I have not in this way been instrumental in successfully establishing classes there. I have within two days received applications from ladies in Alaska and South Africa asking me for advice as regarded teaching native classes, and I have given and received instruction from Red Indians who were the quickest pupils to learn whom I ever had

It is only within a few weeks that I learned for the first time anything of the very excellent Swedish Slojd system. I wish it every success, but may be pardoned for remarking that while it teaches admirably a great variety of arts, no person who reads the following pages will say that it has anything like the same principle on which I have taught, or which I follow. Nor does it teach anything which is not to be found in the English system.

I have been on many occasions warmly encouraged or otherwise aided by many gentlemen distinguished in literature, philanthropy, science, journalism, indeed in every work of culture both in England and in America. I can never sufficiently express my gratitude to them. It is said that we lose friends and feelings as we grow older. It has been my happy fortune to experience the contrary.

PRACTICAL EDUCATION.

———————

Part I.

INDUSTRIAL ART IN EDUCATION.

Treating of the study of Industrial Art as first tested as a branch of Public School Education in Philadelphia, and since extended to the Schools of New York. According to the system recognised by the Bureau of Education, Department of the Interior of the Government of the United States of America, and set forth in the Official Circular, No. 4, 1882.

INDUSTRIAL ART IN EDUCATION.

"All men are artists if they did but know it."

·THE great question in education at present is. Can children while at school be trained to practical industry? Can their minds be more fully developed? Can they, while learning to read, write, and cipher, be taught a trade, or fitted for some calling, so that on leaving school they may be prepared to work, and if possible gain a living? This question has risen so recently into importance in Europe and America, that while it already boasts a literature, and is the cause of

A

much official and private discussion, it is as yet far from being solved.

It was very natural for the "practical" man, when this question rose, to attempt to settle it in a practical manner.   It seemed to be a very simple thing to teach a boy to read or write for three hours, and then keep him for the same time at shoemaking, carpenters' work, or printing   It was tried, but with very little success   It is remarkable that so much money and labour should have been spent, and is still being spent, to prove that mere children cannot perform men's work, or even be trained *directly* to most trades. The farmer knows that a colt cannot be put in harness or worked, though even during colthood the animal may be prepared in Arab fashion by gentle care or culture for training   But it does not seem to have been known to most men that a human colt is subject to precisely the same conditions.   The result of the faith in teaching trades to children was the establishment of technical schools.   And the result of the teaching has been that so far as the training in these has been *purely practical*, technological, or aiming at a mechanical calling, it has only fully succeeded with vigorous boys at least fourteen years of age   And it is no great discovery that a boy can' begin at that age as an apprentice to *any* hand-work. It has also been found that the industrial or technical school proper costs a fortune to establish, and is only available for the youth in cities or large towns.   And the problem to be solved is: "By what system can, *all* children, girls as well as boys, both in town and country, in school, or possibly at home, be trained from infancy to industry?"

According to the method of FROEBEL, the founder of the Kindergarten, the youngest child can be taught the beginning of hand-work of many kinds. It can learn to observe, its quickness of perception can be stimulated, it can be taught to draw and model in clay, and in short "begin to prepare" for serious work. No one would think of training it then to make a living, but its mind may be diverted into a channel tending in that direction And it is in this *attracting the attention of a child to the rudiments of industrial callings*, and in making them easy and attractive, that the whole solution of the problem consists.

Has the reader ever thought seriously what it is to have *thought* about a thing until it has become familiar in many details, and a subject of interest? He knows, we will suppose, that carpets are made of woollen thread on a loom, but let him go through a carpet factory and examine the process of weaving in detail, and about the same time read a cyclopædia article or a book on carpets. He will be, so to speak, in a different frame of mind on the subject, for he will be informed—perhaps he will feel himself quite capable of going into the manufacture as operative or manufacturer This *thinking* on a subject as a preparation is as applicable to a child as to a man. There is not a single department of industry known to culture for which a child may not be, to a certain degree, prepared at any age, by having its attention properly called to it.

It has been, I think, fully demonstrated in the system of industrial art which I have practically carried out in application to the public schools of Philadelphia and elsewhere, that all the *minor arts*, such as modelling in clay, carving in wood, sheet leather-work, simple cabinetmaking, stencilling, mosaic, inlaying, and repoussé or sheet metal-work, are only applied design, worked out with other implements than pencils, and that the degree of skill in outline decorative design requisite for this may be acquired by all children from nine or ten years of age, or even younger. The real importance of this principle has been fully recognised by CARL WERNER, an eminent German writer on education,[1] and an inspector of schools in Austria "In no European school," he says, "has the importance of design as a basis for practical education been so recognised as it has been in the American system" Now be it specially observed— for it is the clue and key to the entire method of culture which I propose — that the attraction of attention in tender minds to industry in any form corresponds to design in all the arts—nay, it is design. For design, far above all arts, consists of will brought to bear on or influencing attention.

It seems a very simple thing to say that design-drawing is the root of all art, and everybody will freely admit it. And yet it is so far from ever having been understood, that a great writer boldly declares that all Europe has hitherto utterly ignored the real importance of this principle. Perfectly understood, it reduces all the arts to one, and abstract as it may seem, mere children enter into it and act on it. "You only want to know how to design your patterns to do all these things," said a boy of fifteen in my school to another. By "these things" he meant modelled faience, wood-carving, and a dozen other arts. And he also meant

---

[1] See Appendix.

that by design there is a great deal more implied than a pattern to copy.

We will suppose then that it is desired to train a child to industrial pursuits These are broadly and generally to be classed as agricultural, artistic, economical, and commercial. Under "artistic" I include all manufacturing or technical work whatever; under "economical" all housekeeping and administration of affairs, and under housekeeping again all that pertains to the domestic support and comfort of life. In a broad sense there is no human occupation for which some prevision may not be made in education. But I am writing now especially of hand-work, and I would declare that there is no division of it which may not be made to a certain extent familiar to the young, and the key to it is simply to call attention to and awaken interest in an industry. It is to make the pupil *think* about it. This sounds extremely commonplace, but it is as far from being generally understood or appreciated as any idea can well be.

There are many boys destined to become farmers who are made to think of the *details* of agriculture, such as ploughing and sowing, but very few who think of it as a study, or as a whole. Very young children easily get an idea of arithmetic as a science, of which addition, subtraction, and division are only the details or branches, and those who are trained to thus regard it as a whole excel in mastering the parts. The same is the case with grammar. I have, though rarely, met with teachers who excelled in giving this general idea of a study, such as arithmetic or grammar, to boys and girls, and the result was a progress far beyond that of those who worked at details only.

Now I venture the assertion that if the boy who is to be a farmer were induced to study a manual written in the simplest attractive style, teaching of farming *as a whole*, he would study the practical details with greater interest   Experimental gardens or farms would in many places aid in such education, but where this is not possible the farm itself would serve as well, and as many would think, even better.   The initial point lies in making the boy feel that farming is an art allied to science, that it is interesting, that it does not consist in tending cattle or ploughing, or in any details, but in all of these, and the difference between the farmer as a leader and the mere labourer consists of really understanding this   The false ideas of the dignity of being above work, or the indignity of labour, are due in a great measure to the fact that industry has never been properly taught as an art or as a science.   To the man taught only to dig, without a hope of rising by his general knowledge above this detail, farming appears naturally enough low and coarse.   Train him to regard it as a career with many stages which he comprehends, and which, because he comprehends them, he may surmount them, and his calling equals in " dignity " any other.   This is therefore that which corresponds to design in the industrial arts, that boys in country schools shall be trained to think of farming as a study, and this primarily by means of manuals of agriculture.   For design, as its very name implies, is *fore*-thought.

Everybody may be said to know that the difference between a housekeeper and a housemaid lies in this that the former understands housekeeping as a whole. Her administrative capacity is the result of her grasp of the relations of all the details of the *ménage*. Now is there a mother of a family who doubts that little girls would be made incipient housekeepers by having their attention and interest directed to or centred in domestic economy ?[1] Here again a manual of house-keeping, or an elementary work devoted to making the young understand it as a whole, would be the point of departure on which verbal instructions should be based The boy or girl who has had this beginning of thought can be trained to plan for himself a farm, or for herself a home. He can be taught, if a certain number of acres of a certain productiveness be given, to determine what labour, what receipts, and what expenses may be anticipated in connection with the land. And the little maid may in like manner calculate what may be done with a certain income. There are many ultra-practical people who will find many ready arguments to prove that all such farming and housekeeping would be simply " theoretical," a word which is, strangely enough, a synonym among the ignorant for idle and unprofitable. And I will even agree with them as to direct results if they will but grant that the attention of the child can be thereby drawn to the subject, and its interest awakened. For this is really all that *design* in drawing effects—it leads the pupil to the minor arts, and from these to the higher, by making him *think* about them. I have often been told that my system of teaching art was all " a theory," but the practical results have spoken

---

[1] Girls have indeed a great advantage as to their future mission as mothers, nurses, and housekeepers, in their playing with dolls. There is no reason why a part at least of a boy's recreations should not to the same degree be a preparation for future work.

for themselves, and any theory which results in profit thereby becomes practical.

There is no industry which is without its rudimentary design. At present nineteen boys out of twenty go into "business," or to shops or callings of any kind, without the least previous training It is not always possible while at school for the intended grocer to sell tea and sugar, or for the apothecary to learn anything of medicines. But he can be taught something more than arithmetic as a preparation. He can be made to take an interest in any industry His attention may be called to it Let those who object to this first try the experiment If the method has succeeded in industrial art, I do not see why it should fail in agriculture and commerce, or in housekeeping.

There is much needless confusion at present as to Industrial Education We hear of cooking schools here, art schools there, farm and mechanical and wood-carving schools everywhere. What is needed is a co-ordination of these forces, a recognised principle and point of departure. This will be found in mastering certain principles which this book is intended to set forth. The first of these is that from the very unfolding of constructive ability in the Kindergarten method, which is too generally known to require explanation, up to the industrial school with its advanced technological training, there are successive steps, and that these are, firstly, design, or the attraction of the attention of a pupil to a calling as a study and as a whole; and secondly, his or her preparation, not so much to at once make a living on leaving school, as to be a preferred junior workman or qualified beginner or learner in a factory, or in any

" business." The public expects a boy to be able to make a living or be fitted to begin some practical calling when he leaves school, let us say at fourteen years of age. And it can very often be done. I have had a class in my school in Philadelphia of thirty boys and girls engaged in carving wood, and every one of these could by application to carving alone, and by selling directly to consumers, make eight or nine dollars, or nearly two pounds a week. But generally speaking, all that I expect of my pupils is that the foremen of factories would give them the preference to other applicants for place. This always means more money for wages And this is as much as should be expected for about one hundred hours of tuition, at an expense of from five to ten dollars, or from one to two pounds, according to the branches taught. ✓

To arrive at this co-ordination certain rules must be followed. We begin in my schools by teaching design. After this every pupil takes up one or more applications of it, as they are guided by circumstances. One thing is certain, that after working, seeing others work, and becoming familiar, or at least acquainted with half a dozen arts, their taste is cultivated, and all realise that they can, if they choose, turn their hands to and master many things—in fact they have acquired that confidence in their own abilities which makes them sure to succeed in any kind of work. When a boy, or even a grown person, unfamiliar with the processes, sees large under-glazed coloured faience vases covered with garlands or monsters, carved and inlaid panels in cabinets, brass plaques, mosaics, and intricate arabesques, he or she is often almost awed at the genius supposed to be needed to produce this. In a few months or weeks the youth moves in this little art-world with the utmost indifference, and criticises the works closely. He is quite sure that if he now tried he could make or even design any of these fine things. It is a great deal in practical education and in beginning life to have attained to such confidence I do not exaggerate when I say that for every kind of work this gives the beginner a great advantage over all rivals Now the basis of all familiarity with all industry, be it agriculture or art, is to first set the pupils to thinking about it as a study, and then to show it to them in practical operation. They must first learn a theory, or general principles, for example *design*, and then its application. Those who think that because we work from design that our work is necessarily of an " æsthetic " sun-flower kind greatly err. For when a boy can use his hands and brains to guide them, or in fact becomes a practical workman in any form, he can work if he will in many ways—I may say in *all*. In every school in the country, every teacher should make industry a theme for instruction. From industry and its importance he may proceed to its sub-divisions—to agriculture or art, business or household economy. When this beginning shall have been made, the practical teaching of all branches of manual labour will follow in due place, time, and course How one of the most important can be realised (I refer to industrial art), I will now explain.

Many years ago I began to think seriously on the question of training the young to hand-work while yet at school The possibility of teaching " trades " to children was dismissed almost as soon as I considered it. PESTALOZZI had attempted it; it had been tried in every country in Europe, and very earnestly supported in America, and it had nowhere really succeeded. The cause was not hard to find Had it been a success, the employment of little children in factories would also have been a success It is true that this infamous branch of human sacrifice, prohibited by law in England, is still common in Massachusetts, and, I am told, in other American States, but it is none the less inhuman on that account That something could be done, in a small way, in this direction, no one can doubt.   But it was always a forced growth.

It was during a visit to the school of Miss WHATELY in Cairo, and in Egypt, that it suddenly occurred to me that very young children could, however, profitably and pleasantly master the decorative arts.   I there saw little Copht and Arab girls and boys, apparently only six or eight years of age, executing such works in embroidery as I had hitherto associated only with the efforts of accomplished adults   The next day in the bazaars I found even more striking illustrations of the discovery.   I saw very small children, with a single frame between them, working both sides alike of beautiful, highly elaborate designs in silk, without a pattern before them   I saw in the jeweller's bazaar mere boys, with tools as rude as those of an English tinker, making jewellery of the kind so highly praised by CASTELLANI; that kind which, while it lacks the machinery finish of Western work, excels it in originality and character   Then I found day by day, on inquiry, my interest having been aroused, that most of the lighter ornamental work of the East, or such as does not require great personal strength, is executed

by women and children.   I had seen before, as I have
since this visit to the East, what the young can do
in wood-carving in Switzerland, South Germany, and
the Tyrol   I found that in Italy wood-carving and
repoussé and shell-carving, of a far more elaborate
kind, is executed by boys, and that in Spain these
youthful workers make pottery of a highly artistic
nature.[1]   I also found, and this was the most important discovery of all, that in all these countries
these children did not by any means merely follow
the designs furnished by artists.   In most cases they,
like the grown-up workmen around them, had no
patterns at all, but worked like birds or bees by
sympathy with the rest, modifying or varying it
according to the aim of the work   When elementary
drawing formed a part of the work, they picked it up,
just as many men in factories picked it up, and were
soon able to produce designs.   The result of this was
certain conclusions which I have given elsewhere in
the pamphlet entitled "Industrial Art in Schools,"
which the Bureau of Education in Washington issued
as Circular No 4, 1882, and which the reader may
obtain *gratis* and post paid by application to the
Commissioner of Education.[2]   These conclusions were

[1] The reader can find a very interesting account of an industrial
art school in Smyrna, in "Pen and Pencil in Asia Minor," by W.
COCHRAN   1887

[2] I have in this chapter borrowed very freely from the pamphlet
here referred to   The latter contains practical details as to establishing industrial art classes, while in this work the general theory is more
developed   As repetition of certain ideas would have been in this case
unavoidable, I have, to save much labour and time, simply extracted the
passages in question   I am indebted to the kindness of General JOHN
EATON for permission to do this, as for many other courtesies on all
occasions.

to the effect that constructiveness, or the faculty of making things which are useful or ornamental, is in man innate or instinctive. Even in the beginning of the struggle for life, or in the rudest pre-historic times, people made ornaments, though they were only beads, of shells or dried clay While the mammoth yet existed, man etched with taste and skill his likeness on his own bones As the flower precedes the fruit, decorative art is developed in a race before it attains proficiency in practical work. Long before men had good axes, knives, or any kind of decent tools, they made jewellery and embroidery superior in design or character to anything produced in modern times. During the infancy of almost every race, the ornamental is developed before the useful, and the same principle is reflected in the individual. The child who cannot make a shoe, or file metals, or master a trade, can easily learn to design decorative outline patterns, mould pottery, set mosaics, carve panels, work sheet leather for a hundred purposes, and emboss sheet brass. He or she can cut and apply stencils, model papier mâché or *carton pierre* (a mixture of composition and paper-pulp), inlay in wood, with ivory, and in short master a hundred minor arts. For the child corresponds to primitive man All children like to *make* something, mud pies and spontaneous chalkings on walls being generally the first manifestations of this impulse. A box of paints, an apparatus for printing, or tools, are generally very welcome gifts. Now if the child is almost universally capable of executing valuable works of simple or easy decorative art before it can produce much that is *useful*, and has moreover manifestly an *instinct* for it, should not this fact be considered in education ? One thing is absolutely certain : that with the progress of education as a science, we must and will eliminate from it the repulsive and severe. Young women may be forced to work in coal-mines, and mere infants in factories, but it is wrong. It is not really right that children should ever be employed at uncongenial pursuits. Even reading, writing, and ciphering may be made attractive, and every school pleasant, and under these conditions the young will acquire learning more rapidly.

Having formed the theory, I proceeded to put it in practice. I had to labour at great disadvantage. I knew very little indeed of drawing at school I had never distinguished myself in it, and beyond a few weeks' independent practice at panel carving in wood I was entirely ignorant of every minor art But I immediately perceived that all these arts were in reality only *one*, and that this *one* was simple outline decorative design applied to different materials Carving a panel is drawing it in wood with chisels and gouges , repoussé work is strikingly like it, as is leather-work. In all three, as in drawing, the pattern is brought into relief by outlining, and the ground "matted," or indented with tools. As PANINI the Indian had reduced all grammar to a simple single system of inflection, as GOETHE reduced the plant to the leaf, and his successors the leaf to the cell, I saw that there was a single principle in art-work which would render all its branches comparatively easy to the one who grasped it If I had at this time read much of what I have since perused, I might have found that OWEN JONES and his school had in many respects preceded me, and should probably have let the experiment drop. As it was I proceeded to work without teachers, without reading, and without example When I published the manuals of brass work, of wood carving, of leather work, and of stencilling, I had never seen a man in my life at work at any of these. I simply obtained the materials, and went to work teaching myself. After I had written the manual of repoussé work, I asked my friend, Mr KARL KRALL, of the firm of BARKENTIN & KRALL, of Regent Street, London, metal workers to the Ecclesiological Society, to revise and correct it. He laughed on returning it, and said " It is all quite correct and practical; but I see that you have evolved the whole out of your moral consciousness, as HEINE'S artist evolved the image of the camel. If you had ever seen a man at work on metal, you would have used the tracers and matts in a different order. It comes to the same thing, but it is not the usual way." It was through ignorance that I hit on the idea of simply hammering the work out on a piece of soft pine board, instead of "foxing" it on cement and annealing it. This very primitive invention, followed hitherto, I presume, chiefly by the natives of Nubia, who make their silver jewellery with a nail and a stone for a hammer, had, however, one remarkable effect. It was possible by means of it, and by cold hammering, to make a plaque in low relief, rude, but not devoid of beauty, for very little money. The ordinary apparatus would cost from £5 to £20, but by this means tools, board, and brass would cost, perhaps, only six shillings. This is, I may add, partly due to the fact that the modern brass appears to be softer than most of the old, and it certainly has a more gold-like colour.[1]

Having experimented in several arts, and satisfied myself of the truth of my system, I began to teach, *en amateur*, a few young girls, who, almost without exception, learned so much in a lesson or two as to be able to go on by themselves and turn out creditable work.[2] I had a fixed idea before me, and I pursued it. I observed closely in myself as in my pupils what the average *child* could probably do. I became convinced that by an extraordinary law almost every decorative art is *easy*. It is about the same thing to an ordinary girl of ten or twelve whether she works at mud-pies in the road or at modelling a vase in a studio. One soon becomes as easy as the other. This led to many conclusions One was that this principle had been extensively carried out during the early ages in Greece, Rome, and the East, as it was in all Europe during the Middle Ages. In such eras decorative art-work had not only been abundant and cheap, but,

---

[1] The result of the publication of this manual, and the teaching of repoussé in the Industrial Art School and Ladies' Art Club of Philadelphia, was startling Tens of thousands of workers, chiefly ladies, took up the art all over America It was introduced as a branch of study into many schools, and soon assumed the proportions of a great art industry One of my pupils, a schoolboy of seventeen, saved forty-three pounds during his summer vacation of two months by making 16-inch plaques It was said by experts or professional metal chasers that simple *cold*-hammering had never been brought to such perfection as it was in my school in Philadelphia

[2] A Miss L M of Weybridge, having had only a single lesson in wood-carving, but who with great quickness grasped all the principles of the art, took, during the year after, two prizes for bas-reliefs at two exhibitions I must state in fairness that I never knew her superior in cleverness so far as learning anything (*e.g.*, languages and literature) was concerned.

what was more, it had been original and human, and
not ground out by machinery. Machinery a generation ago promised to increase art by multiplying cheap
copies, and the result has been that it has almost
extinguished everything original in it   But the vast
increase of culture has of late brought cheap duplicates into disfavour. People are beginning to learn
the great truth that no real work of *art* can be made
by machinery. That is most artistic which most
shows the hand and soul of a maker. When this
principle shall be firmly established as a canon, as
it certainly will be, there will also be a demand
for much labour which is now without employment
Work fully equal to the mosaic pavements of Roman
villas, and all the exquisite ornament of the Middle
Ages, could all be *designed* and made by women,
children, and a vast army of men who by some
fatality cannot succeed at more prosaic employments.
That machinery can aid art is true, for every tool
is to a certain extent a machine, but that a copy
made and multiplied entirely by machinery is artistic
is false. The vulgar and ignorant call everything
which is beautiful and artificial "artistic;" the educated know that the term is only applicable to a work
which shows the direct art of a maker and the action
of a mind. With the increase of culture there will
come not only an increased demand for decoration,
but also for that which is hand-made, and then a very
large proportion of those who are now idle will find
easy work to do.

As I have written in my pamphlet on Industrial
Art in Schools, the question as to what children could
make has risen just at the time when there is spread-

ing all over the world a demand for decorative and hand-made art. " The developments of capital, wealth, and science during the present century have naturally led to luxury and culture. With them learning and criticism are teaching wealth what to do   Culture has awakened humanity or benevolence.   It is a fact that children can, while at school, profitably practise decorative arts." By profit I do not mean merely making money, as the very great majority of the public at first misunderstood my promises, but the qualification of the pupil for future employment. This study, far from interfering with the regular branches, aids and stimulates them. While the minor arts, guided by even a slight knowledge of decorative design, are so easy as to be regarded by all children as a recreation, they are at the same time of practical value in training the eye and hand, and awakening *quickness of perception* They aid all studies and all work. I would here call the attention of the reader to the chapter devoted to this, as a separate branch of education. There have come under my observation many instances in which I have found that beyond all doubt children who have been regarded as dull in everything have shown great aptness and ingenuity in designing, modelling, or carving. When such skill is once awakened, there comes with it greater cleverness in those studies or pursuits in which the pupil was previously slow, *because he has begun to think about himself* and believe that he can do something. It is a great truth, too little studied, that sluggish minds can be made active even by merely mechanical exercises. And the practice of the minor arts by children effects this to a remarkable degree.   Yet while everybody is

quick to observe mental ability or activity when it
is transmitted from progenitors, very few notice the
innumerable instances in which it is incidentally
developed by education or circumstances. It is a
matter of fact and observation that children who practise decorative arts, or any manual arts, are thereby
improved mentally and morally The consciousness
of being able to make something of value inspires
pride and confidence in their ability to master other
studies. For these reasons I believe that industrial
art should rank in education next to reading, writing,
arithmetic, and geography, or rather *with* them, since
it conduces to mental development, and that it should
precede music and the other studies which are urged
as "essential."

It is a law with but little exception, that all the
minor arts, or such branches of industry as are allied
to taste or ornament, are very easy, and can generally
be so far mastered at a first lesson, when properly
taught, as to produce a perfectly encouraging result.
For this reason art should form the beginning of all
industrial education, because it is the *only* work easy
enough for mere children. It should be the first step.
And as it rapidly trains the pupils to understand that
several arts are really but a single art, or to regard
them as a whole, it is a good preparation to induce
them to consider the subdivisions of farm or household
labour, or of a commercial business, as parts of an
unity There are many who will say that this is "too
theoretical" for children, but I am sure that it would
not be too much so for such children under fourteen
years of age as I have had from the public schools of
Philadelphia. But industrial work, to be taught even

to the very young, should not be limited to the ornamental Design-drawing should precede everything,
but when this is understood, carpenters' work, or joinery
in its rudiments, or any branch of easy industry, suited
to circumstances, may be taken up as soon as the pupil
is fitted for or desires it.   It has been from the
beginning a source of annoyance or of serious im-
pediment to me, that certain editors and other critics
have represented that I aimed only at teaching
"æsthetic trifling," "sunflower nonsense," and "playing at art," when it was impossible for me, owing to
circumstances beyond my control, to go beyond the
first steps connected with design.   *Therefore I here
state plainly, that the system as I understand it, embraces
every conceivable branch of practical industry suited to
a child's brain and hands, that it begins with design
and with teaching pupils that arts are only applied
or developed design, and that in like manner all other
industries not artistic are each a "many-in-one," or
an unfolding of a single principle.*   Industrial art in
schools—and it should be in *all* schools as well as
families—covers the ground or fills the time inter-
vening between the Kindergarten and the industrial
school, but it blends with and includes the latter.
And it may be observed that the system is capable
of being introduced into any school or family or circle
whatever, great or small, where there is a preceptor
who has some little knowledge of drawing, with intelligence enough to apply it, according to the easy rules
laid down in certain elementary handbooks of art.   To
aid such teachers I prepared a series of cheap Art-
Work Manuals, embracing the following subjects :—
Ceramic Painting, Tapestry Painting, Outline Embroi-

dery, Filled in Embroidery, Decorative Oil Painting, Drawing and Decorative Design (outline), Wood Carving, Repoussé Work or Embossing Sheet Brass, Leather Work, Papier Maché, Modelling in Clay and Underglaze Faience Decoration, and Stencilling. Each manual is accompanied by a large pattern sheet of designs in outline, ready for tracing or copying, specially appropriate to its special subject. These design sheets have been prepared so that they are generally applicable to all the arts taught by the manuals. Being full size they can be readily adapted. Finally, the Messrs. Whittaker have in the press and will soon publish a very carefully prepared series of manuals on a much greater variety of subjects of art and industry, including those needed for commercial, agricultural, and domestic education These works will be strictly adapted to the practical training of even the youngest children. The greatest pains have been taken to simplify the method of instruction, so that any teacher of ordinary intelligence may, by studying one lesson in advance, conduct a class. The first, on drawing and design, is already issued.

DESIGN

DESIGN is here the invention of original patterns. It may be taught simultaneously with drawing, which is the practical realisation of the design. The one is quite as easy as the other. It is popularly believed that to produce any kind of an ornamental design, however simple, a peculiar gift, talent, or genius is required. But there is no person who is capable of learning to write who cannot learn to design and draw, so as to produce useful or elegant work. Of course in the higher stages of such work, genius or culture and taste with learning manifest themselves. But to learn to design well enough to invent or execute modelling, carving, or repoussé metal work, &c., requires only ordinary capacity.

If we were to give any child, let us say twenty or thirty dried and pressed ivy leaves, and tell it to arrange them so as to form a wreath, on a flat surface, it would find this a very easy task (fig. 1). If a sheet of transparent paper or a pane of ground glass were now to be laid on the leaves, and their outlines required to be drawn or traced on it, this would also be easy. If the child were to do this twenty times it would gradually become accustomed to using the pencil.

22

Then it would have taken the first step both in design and drawing Reflect a little and it may occur to us that the best decoration consists of simple ornaments arranged at intervals, and that in doing this the mere savage often surpasses the civilised artist Now the average *savage* is not, as regards innate artistic capacity or *intellect,* superior to an English schoolboy.   And it

Fig 1.

is remarkable that so few persons have ever made serious and numerous experiments to ascertain how much ability as regards designing patterns all children really possess.   If a single leaf should now be given, and the pupil required to draw a circle with a pair of compasses, and *repeat* the leaf on the circle so as to make another wreath, it would take a second step.

And if one or two or three ornaments or finials should be cut out of thin sheet brass or playing-cards, and given as *motives*, it would not be found to be a difficult matter to arrange these either in wreaths, or in a straight line, or border, or in a square frame The pupil could, by using a sharp pencil, draw lightly around the edges of these stencils, and thus in a very mechanical manner produce patterns. When the attention has been combined with interest, and the will to work awakened, it will be found that it is a very easy matter to thus construct simple designs. This may be the first stage, which amounts to merely becoming familiar with the handling of the pencil.

The pupil should now be taught to draw a clear light line with accuracy and confidence.[1] "It should be a line like a hair or a spider's web, on rather smooth paper, with a sharp, long, and hard pencil. There should be no re-drawing on the line, no stumping, rubbing, or sketching in breaks. Be it remembered that it is really easier to learn to draw well than to write well, and there is no child that would not do both admirably if it were obliged from the first hour to use *free hand*, that is to say, to control the pen or pencil from the shoulder, allowing the arm to rest on the table just enough to prevent fatigue. The whole difficulty of drawing lies not, as is popularly and very ignorantly supposed, in composing and inventing figures, but in drawing simple lines. Now, let the teacher in every school, however humble, bear in mind this great truth, that if a child acquire true free hand in writing, it can not only *draw* well, but do almost anything well which requires perfect control

[1] Industrial Art in Schools, p. 21.

of the hand. This wonderful faculty enables the possessor to almost at once feel, as it were, the chief difficulty of wood-carving—the light, artistic touch—and to overcome it So is it with all other arts. With this power they can all be literally mastered The younger the pupil who acquires it, the sooner in life will he make it his own, and the greater will be his manual skill in all things when older grown. There are very few teachers who fully realise this, few parents who ever think of it, yet it is the main-spring of all manual art. For the sake of this it would be worth while to make industrial art a part of the education of all children—the younger the better. Therefore all who propose to teach or learn art in any form should seriously consider *free-hand* as the true key to all its practice. It is a great stimulant to quickness of perception."

One object in drawing a light line is this. The most experienced artist in making sketches for patterns must necessarily use the indiarubber freely. Therefore he must make lines which can be easily effaced. Having learned to draw curves with confidence and accuracy, and made progress with stencils and tracings in the simple manufacture of patterns—and this may be carried so far as to produce really elegant and even *original* designs—the pupil may be instructed in the principles of construction lines. He should be shown how to change a circle into a spiral, and that a spiral consists approximatively, though not exactly, of semi-circles (fig. 2). Then he may learn that there is a simple law on which all decorative design involving curves may be based. If from a circle, a spiral or any sec-tion of these, that is to say, from any curve whatever, other external and internal curves be thrown, at any point or points, the result will be the construction lines or a skeleton of what must in all cases be a *perfectly*

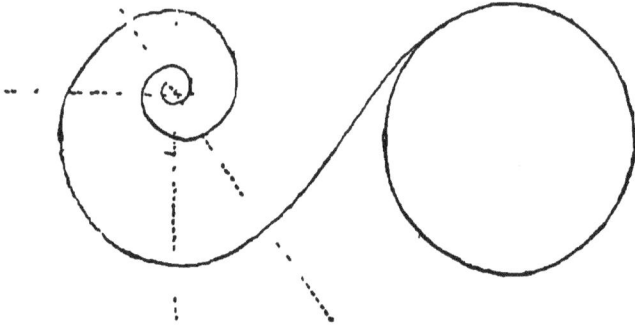

FIG 2 —Rough Free-hand Spiral and Circle

elegant design. This virtually amounts to a vine or creeper with its branches, and a very large proportion of the best and more advanced decorative design of all ages is based on the *vine* (fig 3).

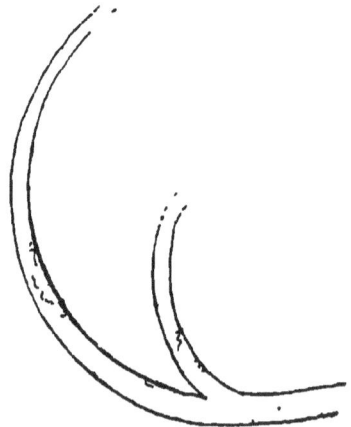

FIG. 3.   FIG 4

These tangential offshoots are of two kinds, the inner and outer, and their elegance is generally increased when they, but especially the outer shoots, are drawn as *lines of beauty*, that is to say, in a form approximating to an S. These outer and inner offshoots may be described as forming a $\mathcal{D}$ or an $\mathcal{C}$ without a cross line. When the pupil understands this, and can draw a curve, and throw off other curves from it, he should be taught to double these lines, either as parallels, or so as to form gradually diminishing vines or cords, and then ornament them Ornament is chiefly effected by applying *finials* or end-ornaments, such as buds, flowers, card-spots, &c, and *crockets* or side-ornaments, so called from *croche*, a crook or corner, as they generally form angles with the stem [1] A rosebud at the end of a twig is a finial, the thorns or leaves on the stem are crockets. It will be found necessary that the pupil should get by heart and be able to draw from memory as soon as possible a few definite simple ornaments, such as trefoils, leaves, or buds, and to learn to make these in due proportion to the stem. It is a rule with singularly few exceptions, that if there be a wrong way to design anything, the beginner is sure to adopt it. He will always make an offshooting twig smallest next to the parent stem, and he invariably makes the finial too small for the pipe or stalk. Yet there are reasons for all this, and the teacher should know and explain them. The child draws the twig too small, because it seems to him that there is at the point of

[1] JAS. K COLLING (Examples of English Mediæval Foliage) limits crockets to the ornaments of pinnacles and canopies, but adopts the French term of crochet for all spiral heads of foliage as used in capitals, &c , that is to say, when crockets are expanded into leaves forming the greater part of the design, or filling up the space, they are crochets I specially commend the work of this writer, also those of Professor HULME, and for straight line designs The Anatomy of Pattern, by LEWIS F. DAY.

junction an unduly large swelling. This may be rectified by teaching him to begin the double lines from the *other side* of the stem. The dotted portion may then be rubbed out (fig. 4). All of the ornaments used for stencils are applicable as finials. The making finials too small is the result of that tendency to the petty and trivial which manifests itself in all children, and in adults of feeble mind who cannot carry art beyond the literal imitation of flowers, or similar "fancy work." The cure for this is very free-hand drawing, and designing *en grand* or large. The first designs should all be large. Anything like the literal imitation of small leaves and petty flowers, or any use of heavy lines or *show* in little detail, should be avoided. As a rule nothing should be drawn for many weeks which cannot be perceived by the naked eye at a distance of fifteen or twenty feet   Children left to themselves will always make petty figures. They will draw scores of diminutive buds and leaves on a small page. Just so in the infancy of a race: it perfects the fineness of illuminating manuscripts before designing grandly. Now it is always easy for one who can draw "large" to come down to petty patterns, but it is impossible for the petty worker to rise to great execution.

Practice in curves, such as circles and spirals, should precede that in straight lines. This may seem a heresy, but I think it is a reform   It is as easy to draw a circle around a cardboard disc as to rule a line, and the very simplicity, rigidity, and palpable accuracy of straight lines makes them as difficult to draw as curves. This is certain, that after a little practice in correctly throwing off free-hand spirals or curves, and examining or copying a few examples of decorative art, even young children design with taste and skill, and when they once begin their progress is rapid.

I would say something here as regards rubbing out and altering. There is an old-fashioned popular theory that pupils should be trained to such exactness as to be able to draw without using indiarubber The invariable result of this is a timid care and a striving towards mere finish which is utterly at variance with all free and characteristic design. Let the reader examine the sketches of any kind in pencil or crayon or pen by RAPHAEL or MICHAEL ANGELO, or any other of the great masters, and see how utterly they ignored the system of attempting to produce "perfection or nothing" at a first effort. How they drew, rubbed out, and altered again and again! Yet these advocates of first sight accurate designing expect from school children what RAPHAEL himself never dreamed of achieving. The truth is, that of two children, the one trained to design freely and alter freely, and the other to be rigidly accurate from the first, the former will in a few months *far* surpass the latter in correct drawing. An exact parallel may be found in two pupils trying to learn a language—one being instructed never to utter a sentence which is not perfectly correct in every detail, while another is encouraged to chatter freely. It will always be found that the latter has to all intents, as regards the *use* of language, the superiority, and that in the end he will converse more correctly, so far as custom is concerned.

When a pupil can draw a spiral or volute, and throw off curves from it like a $\mathcal{Y}$, parallel and ornament them, he should be taught the great fact that as a rule to *double a design is to more than double its beauty*, for this is the first step in symmetry, which, according to F. W. Moody, "is a law of higher order than *even distribution;* it is a form of repetition, the result of doubling or repeating twice." Any form, even the ugliest, when balanced by its double, will become ornament, and this symmetrical doubling is one of the causes, and certainly not the least, of the beauty of two-thirds of the works of art in the South Kensington Museum[1] Let the pupil draw a design, and then put a looking-glass upright by its side He will see it doubled, and it may be doubled from several sides. It may also be trebled and quadrupled. If two pieces of looking-glass, let us say six inches by six, be joined by a piece of muslin pasted over their backs, so as to form a book or folio, as it were, to open and shut, and this be placed up and down on any pattern, and opened at different angles, it will multiply it from three to twelve times, and thus by shifting its position an infinite number of *original* designs may be obtained.[2] The student may now form from semi-circles wave-lines or any other combinations of curves, double or parallel them, and apply ornament as before

[1] Lectures and Lessons on Art By F W Moody, instructor in Decorative Art in South Kensington Museum, London George Bell & Sons Lecture IV Dresser and Day have also fully illustrated this law

[2] This extremely useful article for all designers was re-invented about twenty-five years ago by Mr Journet, of 25 Great Portland Street, London, by whom it is still sold. He calls it the folding kaleidoscope. By means of it one can form an infinite variety of patterns. It was originally described by Baptista Porta and Kircher, but was then old. It should be in use in every art school. It costs six shillings

In learning design, the pupil may freely use not only compasses and rule, but circles, curves, and ornaments cut from tin or card, to be used as stencils. The youngest soon learn how to draw, repeat, and combine these so as to form borders or centre-ornaments. The art of invention is not only rapidly developed by this short-hand method of drawing, but there is also developed with it a greater interest and confidence—the feeling, in fact, of creativeness, or being really an artist Now, if with these merely mechanical aids we combine constant practice in free-hand drawing from the shoulder, it will be found that the pupil soon abandons the former and relies on the latter. No one swims long with bladders after he can dispense with them. This method is, therefore, a union of technological and free-hand drawing applied to that merely outline decorative design which has a place between the two.

Too much stress cannot be laid on the importance of teaching a child to draw with a really *free* hand, and on a *large* scale. Designs which are large and simple are the most saleable. There should never be more space occupied by beginners in a pattern than by the ground, and *vice versâ*. The principal reason why pupils draw petty leaves and mean details, and crowd them confusedly together, is because they do not design with a free hand.' They rest all the weight of the body on the hand which is occupied in drawing. In this position there is not more than a square inch of sweep or play for the point of the pencil, so that the whole arm must be pushed or moved to enlarge this compass. Resting lightly on the wrist gives an enlarged sweep of perhaps two or three inches, this being an extreme maximum. When only the fore-arm touches the table, the wrist-sweep is again doubled. But those who draw with a free hand from the shoulder can with confidence cover a space of three feet diameter And every child may be trained to do this TURNER, the great painter, always painted without a maulstick. It gives not only greater freedom of execution, but much more accuracy. We have all been told not to bear down *too* heavily on the drawing arm, but I say do not bear on it at all. Rest the body on its own centre, or rather bear its weight on the left arm. It is impossible to do the latter without giving great freedom to the right arm. The reader may test this for himself. If he will press the left arm on a table, he will find that he can write much more freely or with a far easier sweep than if he threw his weight on or pressed with the other hand. I need hardly say that I regard drawing with chalk on the blackboard as useful practice. Indeed, I am not sure but that if all children were first taught to write and draw in this manner we should have better chirography and drawing. Writing is ten times as much of an art among the Arabs and other Orientals as it is in Europe, the chief cause being that by them it is executed either with freely flowing reed-pens or brushes, and that it is done so lightly that it is an axiom that to write really well the paper must not be laid on a desk or table, but held in the left hand while being inscribed.

The principle of one thing at a time laid down in the first chapter on memorising is as applicable to design. No person not familiar with the practice can have any idea of the extraordinary rapidity with which children learn to draw and design when they are confined to simple outline patterns for decorative work, under the stimulus of invention. It is because there is no shading or "effects" or "picturesque" mingled with their drawing to bewilder their brains that they advance so quickly. As soon as they have a few lines and finials by heart, and know how to set the latter together to make circles, &c., they begin to design and combine boldly. The extreme degree of free-hand sweep, and the bold dash which result from making branching curves, give a character to this system of drawing which is not found in any other with which I am acquainted. As the pupil is step by step familiarised with a great variety of curves and ornaments, he finds that to combine and vary them becomes easier and easier. As a rule, with very rare exceptions, or in my experience with almost none, the child from twelve to fourteen years of age who can draw a clean, light, free-hand line can be taught in a few weeks, at the utmost in a few months, to design beautiful original patterns By this I mean patterns worth executing in art, or patterns worth money. When this is acquired all is acquired Either technological or artistic drawing may then be learned in half the time usually demanded for their mastery.

When the pupil can make a good design, and is desirous of advancing to simple decorative painting, he is taught to fill in the ground with India ink or any flat colour, and from this proceeds to varied monochrome or to large illumination. According to the old methods, by which everything was taught at

.   C

once, such as drawing and shading, outline and blending, the mere beginner painted flowers in all tones and hues. I believe, with TURNER, that it is through monochrome or single colours alone that a true colourist can be made. If we take two children, and teach one to draw and shade together in the old style, and then to "paint flowers" or to mix colours from the first, and then train another through free hand, outline, and monochrome to blending, it will be found that the latter will, at the end of the year, be far in advance of the former in every respect. I have tested both methods, and found that the superiority of what may be called the single method is incredible. Simple decorative art is the best road to high art, and it has this advantage, that those who stop by the way at any stage have at least learned something useful or valuable in itself.

THE PRACTICAL APPLICATION OF DESIGN.

When design is mastered to a certain extent it may be practically applied to many arts. Of these the cheapest, easiest, and most practical are modelling and embroidery.

NEEDLEWORK.

In this art some knowledge of design is of primary importance. Simple embroidery may to great advantage precede plain sewing, though this is far from being generally recognised as a truth. For good plain sewing is really a difficult art Experience must teach any one that simple crewel work and outline embroidery are much easier. The child who begins with easy work may be led to hard work in half the time in which the latter, by itself, can be learned. This rule constitutes the beginning and the end of the whole system of industrial art. Now, the girl who can invent and draw her patterns always "outlines" and "crewels" much better than the bungler who has to rely on begged or bought designs. Few would believe at what an early age little girls who try can make their patterns. It does not take a child long to learn that with a tea-cup, a coin, and a pencil she can draw a semicircle stem with from one to three grapes at the end, or that the stem may be made double or with two lines. It is no harder for her to learn to arrange these sprigs in a circle or in a straight border. With a very little practice in such stencilling she learns to draw. Those who object to such a method as mechanical have never tried the experiment of urging pupils to trace or use the compasses, rule, and stencils. If they will do so, and teach them at the same time to draw free-hand lines, they will find that boys and girls soon become impatient of using what are still in most schools surreptitious and forbidden aids. Perhaps if man were given all he wants in this world he would want much less than he does. The class of girls in needlework may begin with outline embroidery, or filled-in work, or crewel, as taught by manuals. There is a very easy and effective kind of work made by stencilling or painting flowers in flat or dead colour on brown holland, light canvas, or any similar stuff. The colours may be either dye-stuffs or water-colours. When the flowers or other patterns are painted they may be surrounded with an outline in corresponding colour of woollen or silk needlework. This is very easy work, yet rich and effective. The beneficial result of making even little girls in this class draw their own patterns will show itself from the first in all. With very little management, all that is made in this class can, in most places, be sold at a profit; if not on the spot, by sending it to "depositories" or art stores in the cities. From two to ten pounds' (or from ten to fifty dollars' worth) of materials will suffice to establish an ordinary school class in needlework.

MODELLING IN CLAY.

The next branch of industrial art study is modelling in clay. If a teacher can draw or design even a little, he or she may, with the aid of a manual, confidently undertake to conduct such a class successfully. Clay fit for the purpose is to be obtained in most places at from three to five cents (halfpence) a pound It should be kept in a waterproof cask or box A very large box with a lid is best, as it serves not only to hold the clay, but also for a depository for the work, which must be kept damp from day to day. With this certain tools are requisite, the forms of which are given in the Art Work Manual for Modelling. Any boy with the ordinary gift for "whittling" can reproduce them in pine wood. The fingers are, however, the principal tools Some artists produce very good work with such adventitious aid as old spoons and any chance piece of stick cut into the form which the need of the moment may suggest. A pair of carpenter's compasses are, however, indispensable. As mud wasps occasionally make raids on sculptors for material, so in our school the youthful modellers now and then appropriate the tools of the wood-carvers for certain mysterious purposes, a bent gouge being a favourite implement wherewith to make scales on fishes. Where there is a will there is a way, and pupils should often be told to *think* how effects are to be produced.

Modelling is drawing in clay. Any child who can copy an old shoe with a pencil can make it from a plastic material. More than this, it is easier to model anything than to draw it. A little boy can make a mud pie much better than he can copy it on paper. An old shoe, or a plaster cast of a rabbit, life size, forms a perfect model for imitation. When jugs, jars, or vases of green or wet clay can be obtained from a pottery, it is easy for the children, after a few days' practice, to ornament them with flowers, lizards, fishes, crabs, leaves, or other figures. When the jars cannot be obtained, they may be made by hand; thus, cylindrical cups are easily formed around a broad pipe of pasteboard. Baskets of clay are often made in beautiful forms. A corrugated ground is produced by breaking a stick in two and pricking the clay with its jagged end. When finished and dried, articles may be sent to a pottery and fired. The process of colouring and glazing such work is not more difficult than rough water-colouring. It is fully described in the Manual of Modelling. All the requisite materials for it may be had by express on sending an order to any dealer in artists' materials in any city.

Let it be remembered that in modelling those who begin by drawing well shape well. Their inventiveness has been awakened. Nothing conduces to inventiveness so much as design. I incline to believe that any man who can invent a machine could have been an artist, and that every true artist is only an inventor on another road. It is not theorising when I say that the pupil who can design immediately shows his superiority in modelling in clay. All children in modelling follow a leader or go in a crowd. If they are set to making little balls and birds' nests, and miniature fruit, and similar petty trifling work, they will keep on making feeble things. It is a mistake even in the Kindergarten to give children *petty* patterns. In the modelling class, if one gets a new idea, such as making a cat following a mouse on a vase, or a giant frog, all the rest will take to cats, mice, and frogs. If one makes something great which is admired, they must all do the same. And after the mere rudiments of manipulation are mastered, it is better that the pupils should work on a large scale in great variety of subjects than be kept to petty devices. It is the fault of too many current systems of drawing that they limit the youthful mind to *small* inventions. The boy or girl who can design has in a way learned to invent, to seek for original devices, and what is learned in the lead pencil expands in the clay. With design and modelling all the minor arts may be regarded as mastered.

WOOD-CARVING.

As a beginning in industrial art in a school I commend design, embroidery, and modelling. Yet in some places wood-carving may be preferred by pupils or parents to modelling, as I have known it to be the case in England; or it may in time be added to the three branches already described. For wood-carving a very strong common table and about two dollars' (eight shillings) worth of good tools and fifty cents' or half-a-crown's worth of wood to each pupil may be called an outfit. The steps in wood-carving from drawing to cutting may be very gradual. It is to be desired that children in schools should be confined to "flat cutting," which is easy and profitable, and not be led at once, as they are in many schools, to ambitious and difficult sculpture "in the round."

With a competent teacher the pupil in wood-carving learns sometimes from the very first lesson to make a valuable or successful piece of work. I have never known a pupil of Professor HERMAN UHLE, teacher in the Public Industrial School, and also in the Ladies' Art Club of Philadelphia, whose first or second panel was not fit to make up. Of a class of twenty-five boys and girls, from twelve to fifteen years of age, under his teaching—as I have already written—there is not one who could not earn eight dollars (£1, 12s.) a week by steady work. All of these children have learned to do this while attending school, and while keeping up high "averages" in their other studies. When a good teacher cannot be had, one or two well-carved panels, costing from $1.50 to $2 each, may be had from the school or from *any* carver, to serve as models. Wood-carving is an open door to cabinet-making; the two go hand in hand, and the boy who can handle gouges and chisels to produce ornaments, and whose eye is thereby trained to patterns and propoitions in wood-work, is already half a carpenter. Carving requires beyond all other arts a knowledge of design and modelling. I have had several coloured pupils who were expert in it.

With *design, embroidery, modelling,* and *wood-carving* a school may be certainly said to be fairly established as to industrial art. They may all be learned in the rudiments by book. When well practised in these rudiments, pupils can advance themselves to the higher branches. What I have described may be made a part of the course in every village or private school. When *design* is acquired, *every* art is acquired for those who want it When these four branches are familiar to teacher or pupil, all other varieties of the minor arts are really trifles, so far as acquisition is concerned.

STENCILLING.

This is the cutting out of patterns in cardboard, which is then varnished, or in thin metal of any kind, and painting through the spaces thus cut, with either paint or coloured washes, thickened with glue, *i.e.,* "distemper."

The advantages of stencilling are but little understood. By means of it every whitewashed wall in the country might be made to look much better than it would when covered with ordinary wall paper, which paper, by the way, has been proved to be in innumerable cases, when damp, a fruitful cause of malaria. A well stencilled wall is artistic, since only a good designer can draw the pattern, and it requires artistic taste to combine the stencils in more than one colour. This would give profitable employment to thousands in every State It consists of nothing but drawing designs, cutting them out of cardboard or sheet-metal, and then painting the patterns thus cut with a broad brush and coloured washes or paint on walls or other surfaces. The art is as yet in its infancy, and the vast majority of all the stencils sold are of a very commonplace, old-fashioned character. The expense requisite for stencilling would be about 50 cents [1] a square yard for best cardboard; brushes, from 30 to 75 cents each; washes, best quality, 25 cents a gallon, paint, at the ordinary prices It may be executed in small size, and applied to chests, boxes, cabinets, panels in doors, and in fact to all plane surfaces.

PAPIER MACHÉ.

This consists of waste paper moistened with paste, and pressed in moulds or worked by hand into any shape It is a very cheap and easy art, little known, and capable of wide application. It is closely allied to modelling in clay and casting By means of it all flat surfaces can be decorated with permanent reliefs as durable as wood. Every kind of merely ornamental architectural moulding can be made of pressed and moulded paper. It is also worked by hand like clay. It is capable of being combined with paste, glue, clay, chalk, leather in fragments, pulp, and peat, according to many recipes which change it to as many different textures The number of practically useful as well as ornamental objects made from these combinations

[1] A cent is about a halfpenny.

is really incredible. I know of one man who by manufacturing a very simple object indeed from papier maché has within a few years made a fortune There is no person who, if able to design, and somewhat familiar with modelling in clay, could not make saleable objects in this material It opens a wide field to inventiveness, and can be practised by girls and boys at home as well as made on a large scale in factories, as is done in the case of plaques of this material.

CARPENTERS' WORK, JOINERY, OR CABINETMAKING.

Taken as an art by itself carpentry is much more difficult than when practised in a school in connection with design, wood-carving, and other arts. I find it hard, very hard indeed, to make most people understand this. They profess to be able to see how something "practical," such as the use of carpenters' tools, can be useful, but the "theory" that the application of design to "arts" can make a carpenter of a boy in less time than by the old method, they do not approve of. I have found in my school that it is very usual for a boy or girl to ask if he or she may not take up some new branch. "What have you been doing ?" is the question. "Designing, modelling, and a little carving." If the proposed class is not too full permission is accorded. I am always certain that the pupil who is at home in one or two branches will take up any other almost as readily as if it had been already practised. It would be precisely the same in carpenters' work, or printing, or shoemaking, after he had become familiar with our studio or *atélier*. It is not what is taught in an industrial art school to which I call attention so much as the fact that *anything* technical and practical can there be very easily acquired, if the right beginning has only been made.

SHEET-LEATHER WORK OR CUIR BOUILLI

This is an art which yields good results in proportion to its cost, but in common with stencil and papier maché, it is very little understood or practised. It consists of pieces of leather soaked in alum water or plain water, or in some work only wet with a sponge, on which patterns are then drawn by means of a toothed wheel pricking through a design drawn on paper. This pattern is outlined with a small hand wheel or tooling instrument, and the background put down and roughened with a common stamp or punch. When dry the pattern may be painted or stained with black or any other dye. Wet leather is capable of as much modification as clay or papier maché. Not only can sheets or skins be utilised in its manifold applications, but also all kinds of bookbinders' and shoemakers' waste. It can be applied to any surface, such as chairs, boxes, panels, tables, or cabinets. The sheets of leather used cost from two to four shillings per skin, according to the quality; some kinds for very elegant work are as much as from eight to ten shillings, that is to say, sheet-leather is about the same price as drawing paper or Bristol boards, or very little more. Very elegant work can be made with thick parchment. An outfit of tools which will serve for much good work costs about eight shillings. The Leather Work Manual contains full instructions for this art. *Vide* also "The Minor Arts" (Macmillan, 1880), also an article in the London *Art Journal* explaining Vienna Cut Leather Work. In this latter the lines of a picture are very slightly *cut* in the leather with the point of a penknife, and are then pressed in. They are then filled in with colour with the tip of a very fine brush

CERAMIC PAINTING.

Of ceramic or porcelain painting little need be said, if it meant no more than covering plaques or saucer plates with feeble pictures of flowers and dogs' heads, as it generally does, but there is a vigorous style of purely *decorative* tile painting in monochrome, or single colours, which is almost unknown to most painters, and which will yet become popular, and possibly extinguish the current debilitated imitations of ivory, water-colour, and canvas pictures. The tile, as a wall ornament, should as a rule be decorated in single colours, simply and boldly designed, so as to be clearly visible at a distance, in common with the architectural details of a house. Were this kind of tile painting commoner the art would be more legitimate than it now is, and be more respected not only by those who understand art, but by the ignorant. Single colour china or stoneware painting may be begun in stencil and carried on by hand. Those who have gone on from design to filling in the ground with colour will find it very easy. There is no certain sale or regular demand for such fancy work as is generally found on the plaques and tiles of art depositories and church fairs, but a single-colour tile painter who can work rapidly from good designs, and also make them, can always find a market. Therefore this form of industrial art may be introduced into schools, when artistically designed stencils may be used for tiles.

The teacher should beware of letting pupils choose too freely what they will do. Left to themselves, all the silly ones, and not a few of the wiser, would elect "to paint," probably to paint pretty little posies and dogs or Greenaway babies, in water-colour, oil, or china, which would be the positive end of all practical or useful art industry with them. If you would keep a girl from becoming an artist set her at once at flower painting. There is, it is true, a natural appetite for colour and flowers as there is for sugar, but this is no reason why people should be fed on it It should only be gratified after being well nurtured on design and monochrome Among the principles adopted by the Board of Education in Boston, I find the propositions concerning design by OWEN JONES. Of these No 6 declares that "flowers or other natural objects should *not* be directly used as ornament, but conventional representations founded upon them sufficiently suggestive to convey the intended image to the mind without destroying the unity of the object they are intended to decorate. This principle, universally adopted in the best periods of art, is equally violated when art declines."

I have said in the foregoing lines that if you would keep a girl from being an artist set her at painting flowers. This, when first published, caused great indignation. Now it is certainly true that there is not one instance in a thousand in which young ladies' flower-painting is above the level of "fancy work," and the same may be said of all the arts as taught of yore in fashionable schools   Fancy work is allied to that produced by machinery : it consists in manufacturing pretty and petty work without originality and without thought.   As in Berlin worsted work, and the making wax flowers or wax coral baskets, it is only necessary to know certain *rules*, so in the average boarding-school china and flower painting one pupil works as the rest work in the same way.   Thus I have often seen in an art school where all were free to do as they pleased, two or three dozen damsels in rows all painting flowers and dogs' heads, or perhaps even girls' faces, one as second-hand and amateurish as the other, and all characterised by ineffable feebleness   Not one of these painters could have made a decent outline decorative design, or achieved anything original.   Now the children in the school were above fancy work, for they were taught to make original patterns.   This led to so much grotesqueness that a literary gentleman who wrote a long article on the school observed in it that young people, when taught to design and urged to invent, produced work strangely like that of the Middle Ages.   This is very true.   There are in the school specimens of originally designed repoussé work which the best archæologist in Europe, seeing them photographed, would declare had been executed in the fourteenth or fifteenth century.   But they were strong and original, therefore works of art. Not only the designs, but the finish and touch on the metal were like those of *common* or second-rate mediæval work.   A few specimens of these were given in the *Century* and *St. Nicholas*   It is a healthy and natural beginning.   In due time the grotesque will be abandoned for other styles. There is much priggishness and affectation in the current "fashionable" detestation of the grotesque.

REPOUSSÉ OR SHEET-METAL WORK IN RELIEF.

Until within a very few years no art was so little practised by any save professional workmen as repoussé, and even with these hand-work had sunk to the lowest stage of neglect. I trust I may be pardoned for again mentioning, in this connection, that the revival of repoussé as a popular art dates from the publication of my work on the Minor Arts, and of my manual on the subject, and that this was due to the teaching that although elaborate and perfect work of this kind is expensive and difficult, yet that very beautiful and really artistic plaques or panels may be produced with ease by hammering sheet-metal on wood. This principle was generally recognised during the truly great eras of decorative art, that if the *design* was good it might be set forth cheaply and easily. At present there is a general tendency to believe that to even begin any art there must be an enormously expensive outfit. I have known women who had never touched a brush or pencil propose to begin china-painting with under-glaze, and to provide themselves for this with such a stock of expensive materials as SARDANAPALUS [1] or NERO the imperial *artifex* might have hesitated at treating himself to. They did not know that to make a real work of art, a tile, a single tube of colour, a penny brush,

---

[1] BULWER, "Children of the Night."

and a halfpenny's worth of turpentine are all sufficient. But these would-be artists, who have such hope in mere tools, seldom know much of design And it may be well to remind many people, teachers as well as editors, that it is only the veriest snob in education or in journalism who would sneer at any man for devoting himself to simply teaching the rudiments of any humble branch of learning or art.

It must be admitted that embossing sheet-metal, especially brass, though popular as an amusement for amateurs, is less generally *useful* than any of the branches already described. It requires a finished knowledge of design and a skill in tracing which few possess if really good work is to be done. By means of it sheet-metal is hammered into low relief by working it *cold* on a piece of board, or into much higher relief and more varied form by beating it on a bed of composition made of pitch, plaster of Paris, and brick dust, and annealing it. The tools used are punches, usually costing from 9d. to 1s each. They are generally either *tracers* for outlining patterns or *mats* for grounding. The sheet-brass costs from 1s to 1s 6d. a pound in small quantities. A full description of the art, in a readily accessible and cheap form, both in cold hammering and by annealing, is given in the Manual of Repoussé Work Annealing consists in warming the work from time to time as it becomes hardened from hammering It is easily done with a heater and tube from a gas light. It is all important in repoussé that the pupil before attempting to work patterns should learn to make or run lines, curves, &c, very accurately with the tracer. Unless this is done, no good work will ever result   This work is, however, admirably useful as a preparation for all who intend at some future time to work in metal.   Familiarity with the hammer, the punch, and stamps leads to a really practical knowledge of the properties of metal, and how to turn them to advantage.   There is, too, a growing demand for many hand-made objects of beaten brass.   Facings for fireplaces, finger-plates for doors, bellows, panels for cabinets, picture or mirror frames, and a hundred other objects, may be easily made by women and children.   But let it be remembered that neither sheet-brass nor any other kind of work is worth taking up unless it is preceded by a knowledge of design-drawing and perfect skill in the use of the tracer   Without such preparation it at once degenerates, as china-painting has often done, into frivolous fancy work.   This work can also be elegantly executed in sheet-iron, tin, pewter, copper, or silver.   The reader should be careful not to confound the hand-made or true repoussé work with the machinery-made plaques and bellows, become of late so common, which are stamped by thousands and by steam on dies.   The profits on these are enormous , more correctly speaking, they are profits on the ignorance of the public   I have known a machinery-made plaque to sell for seventy dollars, which, though sold as brass, was only of spelter   The maker, not satisfied with, perhaps, £12 (or sixty dollars) profit, after deducting the cost of the machinery, must needs make a few pence extra by a swindle and a lie.   To a true disciple of art a hand-made plaque, after a really good design, would be far more desirable than a cartload of these shams.

PAINTING.

There are millions of people to whom the word *art*, as human action, suggests nothing but painting pictures. Pictures are beautiful as flowers are beautiful, but those who care for nothing in art but pictures or flowers are like the French washerwoman who declared that "she would wear for ornament nothing but the most expensive diamonds—or their imitations" If you are not a genius—and it is not probable that more than one person in ten thousand is a "genius" in anything—or unless you have had a long and thorough training in art, do not attempt picture-making Without these qualifications you may produce excellent garnets, topazes, or amethysts, but not diamonds.

Painting in oil or water-colours, for the majority, requires a special teacher. Yet when the inevitable design-drawing is really mastered, monochrome or single colour presents no difficulty whatever to a person of ordinary intelligence, even without a master And after monochrome I see no reason why, with a good manual, any one cannot gradually and carefully mix colours and experiment and test and copy his way, with the aid of Aaron Penley's work on water-colour, without any real difficulty into skill Those who write a letter to an editor to know what colour would result from mixing blue with yellow would, perhaps, be too impatient to travel the only true road, which, seeming long, is yet the shortest Painting, though the most popular branch among all pupils, because producing such pretty results, is the last to be thought of in an ordinary school. In proportion to the time, trouble, and expense which it involves, it is of less practical use than any of the minor arts. Yet in one branch it is easy and commendable. I refer to mural or purely decorative painting of walls and ceilings. Here flowers have their place, and may be appropriately introduced. In a large experimental industrial art school decorative painting will of course form a regular part of the branches

And I would here emphatically declare, for the benefit of certain critics, that nothing can be alleged against flower-painting or picture-making as branches of art, save their great abuse by ignorant and untrained amateurs. Picture-making is the last stage, the crown, the summit and glory of art, to be reached only through long labour in *minor* arts, and yet nine out of ten of those who profess to teach art begin with this end.

TEXTILE FABRICS.

Weaving is not more difficult than much of the embroidery, macramé-work, or netting practised by many women, and it comes very near to the latter. There are many stages in it, from merely ranging rows of threads from corresponding rows of pegs, and working the pattern in by hand up to the loom. A cheap loom for small work is easily made or purchased. I have been in many houses in the Southern United States where every inmate was dressed in cloth woven on looms made by the men of the family with axe, saw, and knife. These looms could have been as well employed to produce elegant and tasteful work as linsey-woolsey—if the people had only known how to do it! It is not in the mere quality of the

materials, in elaborately finished work, or in expense
that true beauty and value in art consist, but in design
This may be seen in so simple a thing as a rag-carpet,
which any one can make. Sort the rag strings for
carpeting according to colour, and let them be woven
up singly. Thus you may have one which is black
or brown or blue. Take preferably a black for a
beginning, and work a pattern by running white tape
with a bodkin through the threads. Sew this where
needed If Etruscan or Greek designs are followed,
the result will be a rug or portière or hanging, cheap
indeed, but, if properly made, elegant enough for the
drawing-room of a duchess The simpler the colours
the better, but a variety may be employed according to
the subject. In the East at the present day the most
exquisite weaving is done without looms, the threads
being simply arranged between pins and drawn along,
the pattern being worked or drawn in by hand.

PAINTED EMBROIDERY.

This is made by painting or stencilling patterns in
water-colour or dyes on any suitable stuff. The flowers
or arabesques are often simply outlined in woollen
or silk. The name of this work is misleading and
false, and induces a belief that it is merely a sham
or imitative art. It would seem that dyed and
painted tapestry was made as early as the woven It
certainly can make but little difference whether a
decoration is made by weaving dyed threads or by
dying woven threads. The mania for making pupils
believe that no art can be practised unless a certain

expensive outfit and certain materials are used ha
been of great detriment to decorative dying as an art
If an American Indian can produce artistic result
with butternut, white maple, hickory bark, sumacl
golden rod, black tea, &c, with only alum as a mor
dant, I do not see why white people cannot do the
same, if they cannot afford to pay ten or fifteer
dollars for ten or fifteen cents (or fivepence) wortl
of patented dye in labelled bottles. The advantages
of dye-painting on a woven fabric is, that it has quite
a peculiar character and beauty of its own, that by
means of it any house may be easily, cheaply, and
elegantly decorated, and that it *will wash.*

MOSAIC SETTING.

This ranges from a microscopically minute art, as
seen in Roman jewellery, up to large inlaying with
stones of any size. What I here refer to is made
with cubes about the fourth of an inch in length and
breadth These are of two kinds—those made from
hard stone of every or any kind and colour, and
those broken from sheets or plates of terra cotta
The stone cubes for this work are sold in New York
as in London, but at a very high price. They may
be made with a little practice by anybody with a
sharp-edged hammer and an iron bar—or better still a
sharp-edged anvil or rest—from almost any kind of
marble or stone They are from a fourth of an inch
to a half inch square, set so as to form patterns in
cement; they make not only a durable and elegant
pavement, but also squares which may be used to

cover walls, or as panels in cabinets. For summer, mosaic floors are preferable to wood. They are specially suited to bath-rooms. Cubes of earthenware, though far inferior to stone, may, however, be used for mosaic. They are easily made in moulds, and may be baked or fired even by amateurs at a trifling expense. The stone pieces are to be smoothed down with stone, water, and sand. Much mosaic work is used in London for floors, walls, and façades. It corresponds to that of the Byzantine period, such as is seen in Ravenna. Like tiles, mosaic is very durable, and like dye-painting, it will wash There is a very easy kind of mosaic, known as Scagliola, made by taking coloured stone in fragments of any size, or in powder, and imbedding it in cement.

CROCKERY MOSAIC.

It occurred to me one day while in York that all broken china might be utilised for wall and ceiling mosaics. Dr. Coles of the Home Arts and Industries Association suggested that there is a tool in common use, which costs only half a crown, by means of which the fragments could be broken into squares, &c, with perfect accuracy. It proved to be a success, and such mosaics are now produced by the pupils of the association in many places in the kingdom. There is no reason why all the broken china or pottery of the world should not be utilised for this purpose, since the variety of tones, shades, and colours from it are far more varied than those of the ordinary cubes.

SCULPTURED BRICK.

Any brick and mortar wall may be sculptured.   It is a question whether after the relief is executed the mortar should be stained red to match with the bricks, or whether all should be left in primitive material Brick sculpture may be very elegantly executed on a small scale, from a single brick up to half a dozen. There is really no artistic reason why these should not be set in red mortar or cement.   A single sculptured square set under each window of a house, or between the stories on the front, will change the whole façade, and greatly improve it.   Large squares of brick of any size can be made to order at many kilns.   The work, after carving, may be painted, or glaze-painted, and again baked   By this means beautiful panels for filling spaces in the façades of buildings may be made.

VENETIAN MARQUETRY.

Take a panel of any hard white wood neatly polished.   Draw on it a pattern, as simple as possible. Outline this with a pen-knife or a small cutting wheel, which is a sharp-edged disc the size of a three-penny piece or less, set in a handle   Then paint the pattern with wood-stain dyes. (Manders Brothers, 165 Oxford Street, sell the best for this purpose in nine-penny boxes.   One box will, with *hot* water, make a pint of dye)   Fill in the cuts with a "filler," or with black putty.   Then cover the design with a thin coating of size, and this again with varnish.

METAL STRAP AND NAIL WORK.

Bands of sheet iron or brass from half an inch to two inches in thickness produce beautiful effects when applied as borders or in pieces to make crosses on chests, &c. Cut them in pieces with a file, and make holes in them with a two-shilling drill. Drive small or knob nails through these holes.

Nails (brass, steel, or silvered) may be had of all sizes, from those with a head like a pin, up to a bowl two or three inches in diameter. These, arranged in rows, diamonds, or other ornaments, produce a fine effect—in fact, the most elaborate designs may be executed with them, as may be seen in many of the old coffers of the Middle Ages.

BROKEN GLASS MOSAIC.

This is an exquisitely beautiful art. It is executed by taking glass of all colours and breaking it to different sizes, from fine powder up to a granulation like rice or peas. It is set in the cement like any other mosaic. The glass is not of course applied grain by grain, but is sprinkled on the surface and pressed. Larger cubes of ordinary mosaic and gold squares, such as may be bought at all Venetian glass shops, are also set sparingly in it. There is, I believe, a shop in Wardour Street where patterns and materials for this work, there called Ceresa, may be obtained.

IVORY WORK.

This is an imitation of ivory or of highly polished old leather and parchment binding It may be applied to any surface. Take a panel of carved wood, or a sheet of leather. Cover it with a good coat of varnish (*flexible* varnish for the leather). When this dries, give it one or two coats of white paint toned with Naples yellow. Then work the face with tracers or dull point and stamp A bodkin is preferable for the latter. Then rub dark-brown oil paint into the lines and dots thus made. When dry, apply two coats of best retouching varnish. In Vienna this work is executed not only on cardboard, but on ordinary paper. This work is very applicable to book-covers and albums. Though termed ivory work, it is capable of great variety. If black paint is used instead of white, a perfect imitation of ebony is the result, and in fact every colour thus treated looks well. Olive, with shades of light and dark green, may be so treated as to imitate old bronze. I am not aware that this last effect has been attempted by any "manufacturers."

GESSO-PAINTING.

This is one of the most curious and beautiful of the minor arts, admitting a very wide range of execution, from the coarsest to the most minutely delicate ornamentation. *Gesso* is the composition of powdered plaster of Paris, or any similar powder, such as baryta, whiting, &c, with size, glue, or gum, and as the mixture is applied and the pattern formed with a pointed brush or hair pencil, the process may be regarded as either painting in relief or modelling Mr. WALTER CRANE, from whom I acquired my own knowledge of it, says of gesso: " My own predilection in gesso is for rather free-hand work of a character something between painting and modelling, but the art is capable of endless development and variation" There are different kinds of gesso; the simplest is merely the powder mixed with glue to a proper consistency. A common water-colour brush is dipped into it, and the pattern is painted in relief. By using a size of one part resin, four of linseed oil, and six of glue, and adding to it whiting which has been soaked in water till all is of the consistency of cream, a very hard gesso can be made, which sets firmly, takes a high polish, and which will endure much wear and exposure It is admirably adapted to being *ivoried.* Should there be any cracks or shrinking in the work when set hard, they are easily remedied by the addition of more gesso Articles made from fine gesso cast in moulds are sold at a very great profit. Gesso can be applied or coated to articles made of wood, papier-maché, &c.[1]

There are so many more of these minor arts that the list might be indefinitely extended. Suffice it to say that there is no person, young or old, who has the time and will, who cannot master one or more of them, the materials being so abundant and generally so cheap and so accessible that it is not possible to think of a place without something useful for the purpose.

---

[1] *Vide* "Gesso-painting," by the author, published in the *London Art Journal* (J. S VIRTUE & Co), October 1887. With illustrations.

And here I have a conclusion to make which I earnestly beg the reader to seriously consider. The practical man will be very apt to say after running over the list of the minor arts, "This is all very fine, very pretty; but do you call this actually preparing a *boy* for the battle of life? Is this getting him ready for a trade?" To which I, after years of experience, reply with serious, sober common-sense, "*Yes.*" For it is the only way in the world to train all children so that they can in an emergency turn their hands from one trade or art to another. Thinking men have of late begun to be alarmed at discovering that the tendency of machinery and the organisation of labour is to turn men into mere unthinking machines themselves. Instead of becoming an artisan or intelligent mechanic, the worker is all the time turning into the ignorant maker of some sixty-seventh part of a shoe, or the ninety-ninth part of a lock, and nothing else, and caring no more for the rest than the actress Rachel cared to know what was in the fifth act of a tragedy since she died at the end of the fourth. And by and by when a new invention comes, the drudge on a fraction is thrown out of work [1] If his wits had

---

[1] The following extract is from the report of Mr JOHN BURNETT, the labour correspondent of the Board of Trade, on the "sweating system" at the East End of London, which was published as a Parliamentary Report, November 24, 1887. It illustrates a very great evil which is rapidly spreading.

"The system of tailoring has undergone a complete revolution since the introduction of machinery and the growth of a ready-made clothing trade, and the great bulk of the cheap trade is now in the hands of a class who are not tailors at all in the old sense of the term. The demand for cheap clothes, irrespective of quality, has continually tended to bring down the rates of remuneration of the least skilled among the workers, and has caused the introduction of the most minute

been trained in youth to design, his mind to form his fingers to some variety of manipulation, he would not in sheer dumb ignorance cry out, What can I do? He who can design and model a little, and knows, as every child in a minor art school knows, the infinite resources of materials, and how many ways there are of working them up, is actually provided with what is as good as a trade—and that is the capacity to readily find out and master a trade To such a "practical" man I would say : Do not let yourself be blinded by the stern vanity of your "common sense" into condemning these brass plaques, clay mouldings, embroideries, and carvings as mere trash, which have nothing in common with "staple" work. A boy or girl who can make these things has learned something which you in all probability do not in the least understand, for he or she has developed knowledge and skill of a kind which will enable him or her not only to learn anything practical with great ease, but to regard all branches of labour as possible.

When a boy or girl of from ten to fourteen years of age can look at all the arts which I have here

systems of sub-divided labour   Instead of there being now only the customer, the master tailor, and his journeymen and apprentices, we now have the customer, the master tailor, the contractor, and possibly several other middlemen between the consumer and the producer, each making his profit out of the worker at the bottom of the scale   Instead of the complete tailor, we have cutters, basters, machinists, pressers, fellers, button-hole workers, and general workers   The learning of any one of these branches is naturally so much easier than the acquisition of the *whole* trade, that immense numbers of people of both sexes and of all ages have rushed into the cheap tailoring trade as the readiest means of finding employment   The result has been an enormously overcrowded labour market, and a consequently fierce competition among the workers themselves, with all the attendant evils of such a state of things."

described in operation without any sense of wonder, and feel perfectly confident that he or she can execute any of them at once, is not that child in a more advanced industrial condition than if its skill did not extend beyond sawing and fitting boards, or filing iron in a small way Yet there are in the United States to-day scores of thousands of men who persist in ridiculing the former as "æsthetic," and praising the latter as practical. It is not long since the principal of a technical school (and of a very good one) politely informed the public in print that the brass plaques, &c, executed in my school were all *trash*. His ideas did not go beyond the market value of the articles. The same man had previously informed the world in the *New York Tribune* that there could be no greater wisdom than to send children to technical schools (*i.e*, to his), "and no greater foolishness" than to attempt to introduce work as a branch into public schools.

"Come to our shop—all others being impostors" Since this opinion was issued hand-work *has*, however, been made a branch of instruction in the public schools of New York, and it will in a very few years be found in the schools of every country in Europe.

After having had an industrial art school under my charge for several years, during which time more than a thousand pupils, mostly mere children, have been in the classes, I have arrived at certain conclusions, which are of the more value, since I conducted the undertaking, not to prove preconceived theories so much as to simply ascertain what children can do. To effect this I have in every way endeavoured to sound the average capacity of children. It is far greater than is generally supposed, but it lies in a different direction, and is based upon entirely different principles from those assumed as the conditions of adult labour, be it mental or manual.

The practical results of a combined knowledge of decorative design and modelling are these. The pupil learns to use the eyes and fingers in a way which will render *any work* easier. The boy and girl who can draw and model even tolerably well can easily find a situation wherever casting or any other kind of plastic work is executed. There is a great demand for boys with such knowledge I could, without exception, find paid places in a great variety of manufactories for nearly all the pupils in any Public Industrial School who have had from twenty to forty lessons in design and modelling

It may be well in this place to consider one or two of the popular objections to industrial art in schools. One is of those persons who, looking at vases with flowers or frogs, admit that they may be all very pretty, but that they cannot see in such " fancy work " any trustworthy means for getting a living Of another class are those who examine the work critically, ask its market value, and then inquire if it could not be made more cheaply by machinery, and, if so, whether it is worth while to set children to making it. Since this work was begun a distinguished reformer, who professed great interest in art in schools, began with me by saying, " I wish to see some of your children's work. I want to know its market value, and how much money it will bring.   You see I am a *practical* person." I did not see it, for it seems to me to be most senseless and unpractical to expect goods of average market value from mere children just beginning to learn.   There are people " deeply interested in education " who inquire what is the current shop value of the work of a child in its second or third lesson.   It is perfectly true that in the hands of competent teachers and directors the average art industrial school may be always made to meet its expenses , yet it is almost as unreasonable to reckon on this as to expect that reading and writing will " pay " from the alphabet onwards, or as Mrs JEBB has said, " that school copy-books should bring money " In the words of WILLIAM GULAGER, of Philadelphia, " Whatever is worth teaching is worth paying for " Meanwhile it is worth remembering that wherever ornamental castings in metal of any kind are manufactured, or wood, plaster, terra cotta, stone, or any substance whatever is made to assume shape, there the workman who can design and model even a little is wanted

I would say in this connection that I consider *exhibitions* of mere children's work as of very doubtful utility—where the public is very ignorant. That they are very popular, and that they serve to advertise teachers, cannot be denied, and that they stimulate an interest in art is apparent enough.   Their defect lies in this, that the public always look at the *work* exhibited as the end and aim and sum total of all that industrial education can effect.   They see brass plaques and designs, plates and panels, and either call them æsthetic frippery or " playing at art," or judge them as a Philadelphia newspaper did, by their inferiority to work executed in higher art-schools by adults who have a large corps of teachers to instruct them every day in the week. Where there is one person—even an editor—who reflects on what a knowledge of design practically applied to several arts can effect, there are a thousand who expend an ignorant admiration, or as ignorant criticism, on the mere experiments of the pupils. The only exhibition which I would willingly make is of the children themselves at work. This is really interesting. There the visitor may see how many, almost infants, in a few lessons have learned to design patterns, and how easily a mere child grapples with clay to make a vase, or manages the carving-tools. The true result of all this is not shown in the vase or panel—it is in the brain and fingers of the pupil, and it is not expressed by the thing worked on. But the majority, as yet, judge entirely and totally by the quality of the tangible *result*, and are incapable of understanding that it is no expression at all of the amount of power which its production involves. So at the university, a youth, in whose brain-cells and nerves is stored up the talent and power of industry derived from a long line of philological or mathematical ancestors, steps to the front and takes the first honour, while another who has worked ten times as hard, and produced in himself ten times as much relative mental development, gets nothing.

LARGER SCHOOLS.

I have, in what is previously written, considered the expediency of industrial art as a branch of education, and shown how it may be introduced to village or private schools I have, of course, only considered the pupils, but it is worth remarking that the teachers themselves, "learning while instructing," will also become accomplished, and in many instances fit themselves for a more congenial career as artists or teachers of art No one can doubt that if every teacher in America or England could practise one or more strictly industrial decorative arts of a more practical nature than are now taught in schools, there would be an immense impetus given to our national culture and industry.   There was very little really *solid* in old-fashioned drawing, watei-colour, theorems, wax flowers, and china flower plaques, but there is a great deal of real value in free-hand design, and in executing it in wood, metal, leather, and all other suitable substances. Not only does the teacher find in decorative art a means of making more money, but he or she is also provided with what to all is an agreeable change from other duties, for, while teaching, the instructor, in common with the pupils, can produce something saleable or valuable.

THE INTRODUCTION OF ART TRAINING.

Where it is proposed to introduce industrial art work to public schools in large cities or to whole communities, there will be either much opposition or great indifference to the innovation on the part of those who do not understand it.   The best way to begin in such cases is to establish on a small scale a single primary school of from twenty to thirty pupils, to be taught design, embroidery, and plain sewing,

E

modelling in clay, and wood-carving This school may be supported by private contributions and the aid of ladies and gentlemen who will give time and teaching for nothing, as many do in the Home Arts Association and East of London classes; or it may be entirely based on appropriations from School Boards, or the latter source may be eked out by the former When the school is established and well under way, all that is necessary to convince any rational man of its utility will be to have him inspect it while in session. If managed with any ability, it will speak for itself The sight of the girls and boys proving to the most prejudiced their ability to make a living on leaving school, is all that is needed to make converts. The walls of the school may be decorated with specimens of work, but I do not urge the appeal to these as the sole proof of the expediency of teaching children to use their hands As a rule without exception, it is the unreasoning and ignorant visitor who is amazed at plaques and panels made by children, and who cries at every indication of what is or should be only *ordinary* effort, "How wonderful ! Is not that child a genius ? Has she not extraordinary talent ? " The children themselves soon learn to laugh at this false estimate of their skill. They know that they can all do these things with practice. And, as I have previously said, the ignorant examiner, looking only at the *results*, and considering only market values, immediately misunderstands the entire system. Thus newspapers have unthinkingly compared the results of the work done by little children who had had, many of them, only a dozen lessons, or at most twenty, and that once a week, with that effected by grown-up young women who had been for years employed all day, and every day, in higher art schools. Yet even these children showed, in proportion to their age and opportunities, superiority in every respect to all rivals.

F. W. Moody has, in his "Lectures and Lessons on Art," spoken wisely of the current vulgar opinion that everybody who can produce a work of art is something quite out of the kind of ordinary mortals. "That the study of art *does* produce that extraordinary compound of self-sufficiency and ignorance *called* a genius, is an undoubted fact. . . . There are, at the present moment, in schools of art, probably more —so-called—*geniuses* than in all the universities of Europe." And he might have added that there will never be any true *art* until it is popularly understood that it is as open to anybody as the "genius," and to understand true art should be as easy for one man as another, and that it by no means requires that a man should be born with a certain extremely rare spiritual insight or æsthetic illumination.

PRACTICAL WORK.

In an ordinary experimental school we first need a room. The upper story of a city school, when not in use, is perfectly adapted to the purpose It should of course be well lighted. Tables made of two-inch plank, placed on very strong, firm trestles, are requisite, particularly if wood-carving and brass-work are contemplated. Such tables do not *rock*. There must be abundant shelving for many purposes. The pupils will every one require a place whereon to put

half finished work.   There must of course be chairs and
a blackboard.   An adjacent small store-room or large
closet will be a great convenience.   If this be wanting,
a large plain wooden cabinet must be provided.

It may happen that the director or principal of an
experimental school is capable of teaching not only
drawing but modelling   In like manner the lady
teacher of embroidery may be qualified to teach something else   In the smaller schools of course one
teacher must supervise everything   In the smallest
it will soon be found necessary to convert the most
advanced pupils into assistants.   Economies of teaching may be carried out in many ways.   But where
it can be done the director should have no direct
teaching.   There should be one instructor for every
branch   There should consequently be teachers for
drawing, carving, and modelling in clay   But in
different localities and in large schools well supported
many branches may be taught.   I could easily
enumerate fifty, large and small, all worth learning,
and all very easy to learn if the pupil can design.
Thus *leather work* may be divided into several branches,
all elegant and profitable.   There is sewn leather, in
which fragments of bookbinders' and shoemakers'
waste are cut into shape and sewed together, as well
as the two great divisions of sheet leather stamped
and leather moulded into shapes.   In Russia, Turkey,
and Persia there are whole villages or large communes
devoted to sewn leather work, and if really artistic
patterns were supplied there would be many thousands
of people in England and America doing the same.

With regard to what seems to be the only great
and real difficulty in popularising art and industrial

art education, something may here be most appropriately said. This difficulty is that of getting patterns
to guide taste. I long since suggested in published
lectures that this might be met by either private
charity or municipal or government aid. Sheets
of patterns for every branch of the minor arts, costing
not more than two cents a sheet, would be of incal-
culable value to every industry in which taste is
required. From art works already published, from
our museums and from those abroad, inexhaustible
material could be taken. It should all be drawn
from specimens illustrating and expressing some
marked era of art. Very little should be made or
drawn to order for these sheets, not even by the best
artists What is wanted is instruction and inspiration
for artists, not from men, but from eras of culture.
When the demand makes itself felt our Government
will doubtless supply it. It has been met in England
in an inadequate way by publishing illustrated pamphlet
summaries of the works in the South Kensington
Museum. But what is wanted is simply large sheets
with large outline designs of different kinds of art
industry work Let me illustrate this by a single
instance. In many parts of America, boards, even
of oak, walnut, or more valuable woods, are cheap
enough, and men who can manage saws and planes
are not wanting. These people are often without
furniture, and pay extravagant prices for the flimsy,
worthless, ugly, glued together, and varnished trash
of the factories. Now there is a type and style
of very elegant solid furniture, such as was made in
South Germany for centuries, which would cost no
more than the glued and veneered trash. It is made

by simply sawing, boring, and pinning or bolting planks or boards together. Any man of ordinary intelligence having the design for a table or chair of this kind before him can take the measurements and make it. A series of such designs at a low price would be very welcome and very useful all through the West of America and in the Colonies

Nobody need hesitate to begin a school Get a few simple patterns and begin to learn with your pupils to draw and teach together. In England the Home Arts Association will supply you with designs, manuals, and practical directions, and help you on

There are several useful industries which would soon be practised in thousands of families were cheap illustrations devoted to them disseminated everywhere. Such pictures would form a very important aid to industry in schools I have done what I could to help in this respect by giving in the series of Art Manuals, which were written for education, large working patterns, those in any one of the works being adaptable to another. Thus a design for sheet brass may also be used for flat carving It is to be regretted that in works of art half the engravings are executed not with a view to making them practically useful to workmen, but to give a general picturesque effect. There is a great deal of expensive shading, but the details are scumbled. This is the case even in many of the illustrations of the South Kensington works.

An almost indispensable element in art-work is inventiveness The popular mind instinctively settles to certain branches as embracing all there is to learn, while the fact is that when design is once mastered the applications of it are infinite. A small wooden platter sawed from board one-third of an inch in thickness in the shape of a boar's head, a tortoise, owl, or other animal, touched with carving, inlaid with eyes of ivory and bone, and finished with ebonising varnish, is a trifling object. It cannot constitute a staple of industry But many thousands of such platters are made in Vienna and sold. An ingenious person can invent, revive, or discover such a small manufacture every day. It is one of the great causes of poverty and suffering in the world that the so-called practical men reject with scorn all branches of industry which are not regular and "staple" The idea of providing for the poorer classes in Ireland by means of small industries has been treated by writers as petty and ridiculous. When I published my "Minor Arts," a London review, ignoring all I had said as to establishing village and industrial schools, made its main point by making me appear only as a teacher of fools' work, because there was in the book instructions for making certain children's toys. Now the entire population of Ireland might be employed in the minor arts without glutting the market, while the fact is that only a fourth or fifth of it need relief, and very large fortunes have been made in America within a few years by the manufacture of some single toy. It would be an excellent idea for the teacher of every art school to request of pupils and their friends suggestions as to what may be made.

TO BEGIN A SCHOOL.

Many hundreds of persons have written to me saying that they would like to establish an art school, or a club, but do not know how to go about it. And when I reflect on the time and practice which it has cost me to learn how to fit out classes, it does not seem strange. I would therefore suggest that to begin, the interest of a number of persons in the undertaking should be awakened. As an aid to this a perusal of the pamphlet on "Industrial Work in Education," which forms the basis of this chapter, may be commended By sending a list of names and addresses to the *Commissioner of Education, Bureau of Education, Washington,* with a note stating the object of the writer, the Circular No 4 will be forwarded to all thus indicated, *gratis and post-paid* This circular has been the direct cause of thus establishing hundreds of small art schools and societies I commend this because, by so doing, in a great many towns interest sufficient to organise a school or classes, or a club, has been awakened Few people know the power latent in the simple phrase "calling attention to a thing and exciting an interest in it"

It is well not to begin by attempting too much Even for a large school, design alone will be sufficient for several weeks, and for six months nothing need be added to this except modelling and embroidery. For these little money is needed. I have found that there is a mania with many to buy all kinds of articles which may possibly be needed.

I will here recapitulate the possible or probable requirements of an experimental school on a large scale for a city :—

A large room, *well lighted*
From thirty to fifty feet of common pine shelving.　More if possible.
One gas burner to six pupils.
Water, soap, and towels.

One closet or cabinet (pine)
One waterproof barrel or large box for clay.
Clay, from 30 to 100 pounds.
Modelling tools, one set.
Carpenter's compasses
Chest of carpenter's tools.
Drawing boards
Drawing paper
Pencils
Fine sand paper
Cups or small tumblers
Indiarubber
Tiles for colours.
Foot-rules
Compasses
Water-colours.
Paint brushes
Blackboard
Wood-carving tools for each pupil.
Wood, half inch to inch, at from 4 to 10 cents a foot
One set of Art Work Manuals or other handbooks, $3 (12s.)
Whetstones or hones
Broken china and cement
A china-cracker, 2s 6d (or about 63 cents)
One grindstone
One bucket or pail
One fret-sawing apparatus
Material for needlework for each pupil
Leather, from 25 cents to $1 a skin, besides waste
Tools for leather work, each pupil, $2 (8s)
Stencil cutting, each pupil, $1 (4s)
Brass work, each pupil, tools, $1 ; brass, $1 (8s.)
Flour paste or dextrine
Plaster for moulds
Coarse towels to clean the tables of dust
A hand-bell.

It will be seen that it is very difficult to adjust the prices for such a list. For a small school or club on the humblest scale, drawing materials, two or three carving tools to each pupil, boards or wood (such as can be generally had for a trifle), waste newspapers, and common paste and clay for papier-maché, with a little paint, bits of marble or stone of different kinds, and a hammer and iron bar for mosaic making, with rags for artistic rag-carpet work, and manuals, will not, with management, cost in all more than from $20 (£4) to $30 (£6). A clever teacher with clever pupils could almost undertake to begin work on $10 (£2), and increase the stock of implements by sales. If the teacher can only design, all the rest will or may follow of itself. A good quality of wrapping or cartridge paper costs less than drawing paper, and answers quite as well for beginners. Many decorative designers use nothing else. If a majority of the patrons or pupils approve of it, elementary carpenters' work may form one of the primary branches. Every boy and man should know how to handle carpenters' tools. But let it be distinctly understood that *design* should precede all the minor arts, if there is to be any system of practical instruction

HOW TO SELECT WORK FOR PRACTICE.

It is extremely difficult to determine, beyond design-drawing, modelling, embroidery, and wood-carving, exactly what may or may not be taken up. There are places about factories where the material for rag carpeting is very cheap; in others it is dear. In others mosaic stones or marble may be had for the taking, while in certain places such material is not to be had. It is true that the prices of materials and implements for industrial art work are very variable; but there is no place in which some of them are not within the reach of the poorest. Sculpturing or moulding brick is a beautiful and profitable art, not difficult to learn, and bricks or clay are to be had almost everywhere.

There is one rule by which all such schools may be safely guided. Making money immediately should not be the main object of any branch of education, but where schools are very poor a sufficient income to pay for tools and materials may be confidently relied on. Let the teacher, or those who are interested in the pupils, after they can design patterns, and not till then, consider what industries in their neighbourhood will pay. In the first place, a stencilled wall is really, if well executed, better than a papered one. Elegant stencilling costs little more than that which is ugly. It should be found in every house in the country. Just at present it seems to be confined to the most expensive mansions. If brass or sheet-metal work is taken up, fronts for fireplaces are easily made, and can be sold, as also finger-plates for doors, sconces, and frames. Leather work will supply baskets, chair-seats, and coverings for the backs of chairs, table-covers, and albums. Of sewn leather, cushions or pillows are extensively made in Turkey, Russia, and Persia. These can be made from bookbinders' waste. Elegant coverings for furniture, rugs, and slippers are also made of this now wasted material, which may be used for a great variety of purposes. Let it always be remembered that if the teacher and pupils set themselves resolutely to make certain objects well, according to what authority recommends as good patterns, they can always find some agency in every town where their work can be sold. But if they only produce average charity fair work of the common flower plaque and dog's head school, it will not sell. The writer is in the constant receipt of letters from people in the country asking him where their small art work can be sold, or even requesting him to kindly exert himself to sell it for them. Now there is always a market for anything worth having, but the only way to sell it is to find out by inquiry some honest agent or merchant in a city or town who will deal in art work, and trust to him. The ladies' decorative art associations in American cities all sell such work, with a discount in their favour of about 10 per cent It is to be advised that, in all cases where the pupils produce work of substantial merit, specimens adapted to house decoration —such as brass fronts and tiles for fireplaces, leather chair-covers, and carved panels with squares of mosaic —be exhibited, not for sale, but as samples of work which will be executed to order.

APPLICABILITY AND VALUE OF ART TRAINING.

It is a curious matter to reflect what may be done for an ordinary country house by a family who will devote their evenings to its improvement, with a few tools and cheap materials. In the first place, good planed plank or boards can, by pattern and measurement, be converted by most men or boys into solid and even elegant furniture. It will cost less when finished than is usually paid for machine-made varnished and veneered rubbish. I have before me, as I write, two chairs, each 250 years old, as good as new. The chair back fits by a socket into the seat, and is bolted beneath; the legs are simply stuck through holes, as in a three-legged stool, into the seat. The backs are carved, and the result is a very beautiful yet convenient piece of furniture They could be as well made by the boys in the school. Tables, settees, and all kinds of furniture may be made on this plan. The floor of the cottage may be set in mosaic, at the expense of time, an iron bar, a hammer, and stone of different colours; or it may be inlaid in wood and covered with rag carpets in Etruscan or Greek pattern —all home made The walls may be covered with stencilled designs, or ornamented with carved panels at intervals, or strips or panels of stamped leather in old Spanish patterns, touched with gold The doors may be hung with rag carpet portières, or cheap materials, such as crash towelling, dye painted and outlined with embroidery. The ceiling may be stencilled or adorned with papier maché mouldings.

There are many people who say, as many have said to me, " What is the use or sense of inducing a backwoods dweller in a log cabin or shanty to adorn his house in a manner which he can neither understand nor enjoy ? " There are others who continually cry that educating girls up to æsthetic tastes unfits them for "mechanics' wives." This has been the old cry in one form or another in all ages. It was heard everywhere a century ago, as it may still be heard occasionally from a few, that reading and writing are the ruin of the "lower orders." There is a gentleman in Philadelphia who has always maintained that our civil war, which he regarded simply as a needless nuisance because it inconvenienced him, " all came from educating the common people so that they could read the newspapers." Industrial art is rapidly becoming, in education and in life, as essential as reading or writing Thousands who are absorbed in politics, whisky, or business, are as yet ignorant of this, even some editors seem to ignore it, but the women, the clergy, and the teachers are already generally aware of it. But all the people in America do not live in backwoods shanties, and where they do they are not on that account to be universally set down as incapable of appreciating homes made beautiful. There are millions of people in America, as in England, not so badly off, whose homes, in which much money has been spent, are not really creditable, good-looking, nor comfortable. They would all have tasteful or artistic and cheap adornment if they could get it. The money which they pay for their present ornamentations represents just so much labour Now, this labour would be better bestowed on making for themselves what they want, or, in other words, in keeping the profits which at present simply go to enrich the manufacturers of machinery made, and very trashy and ugly objects. The problem of political economy lies in the greatest possible distribution of wealth and industry, and machinery does not distribute, but places capital in a few hands.

The majority of men in America speak and think of "art" in any form or phase as something that may very well be dispensed with It is to them "fancy." Yet these men are all engaged in making money, and when the spending it comes, they are ignorant, and make fools of themselves. Deny it as we may, there is a standard of taste, known to those who have been educated in design and its applications, and according to this standard, the ignoramus in America is continually making himself ridiculous. "We are a new people," they say; "ours is a *new* country. Wait till the time comes—say in a century or two, when all the West shall be populated—and then———"[1] And then—we should have reverted to barbarism in our zeal for multiplying and "improving" property. We have, as it is, over sixty millions of people—quite enough to begin a few small experiments in culture when we consider that Athens in its palmy days had only twenty-five or thirty thousand free citizens.

There is another argument in favour of industrial art education to which I have already referred, but which cannot be too earnestly or too frequently repeated It is the enormous and rapidly growing demand for hand-made objects As education and culture progress, people begin to find out that in jewellery as in pictures, or even in fire-irons, a thing to be truly artistic must be hand-made It is not as yet generally understood that machinery, though it may manufacture pretty things, cannot make anything *artistic*. There are no such things as artistic works made in any way except by hand. Only the vulgar and ignorant confuse or confound that which is beautiful with what is artistic. The merchant is guilty of an illiterate blunder who advertises as "artistic" goods turned out by the million from moulds. It is more correct to speak of a pair of well-made and handsome trousers as artistic than of a

---

[1] This is effectively what was said by a newspaper in commenting on my efforts to encourage industrial art. The English reader will bear it in mind that this work is intended for both divisions of Anglo-Saxony

chromo-lithograph as such. This demand for hand-made art will ere long give employment to that very large class whom it is at present difficult to fit to anything The day is not distant when the public will be so well educated as to distinguish clearly between hand-made and machinery-made in every-thing pertaining to ornament When that time comes, we shall be a nation not only of artists, but of mutual purchasers of art work. Meanwhile let it be dis-tinctly understood that art does not consist entirely in prettiness. Its best characteristic is the impression of individual character. This disappears in the machine. In fact, the more perfect machine work is the less is it artistic. The faultlessly finished piece of silver work, such as no mere smith could ever rival, shows indeed the result of ingenuity, but not of art. A Soudan bracelet made with a stone and a nail is far more artistic than a Connecticut mill-manufactured dollar bangle, yet the latter is infinitely the more " finished " of the two.

As for the argument that girls are unfitted for becoming mechanics' wives by a knowledge of art, it is like the hackneyed cry against the piano and against all kinds of education or culture for the poor. The best arbiters in this question would be the young mechanics themselves, especially those who have been at art schools. Much as has been said against the piano, the mechanic himself is generally the first to make his wife a present of one, and I doubt if he would object to arts which are practised at home and which bring money in. There is much cheap ridicule of dados and what is misrepresented as being the staple of all decorative art work, but the truth is—

and it is to be desired that all newspaper wits would admit it—that the fancy work of the last generation is gradually assuming a substantial and valuable form. The "china craze," as it is called, was at any rate better than potichomania or wax-fruit work. The arts of which I have spoken deal with something more "practical" than plaques And here something may be said of the very generally disseminated opinion that the present popular desire to collect works of art, and antiques, and archæological "curiosities," and to ornament houses, is all an "æsthetic craze" or fleeting fancy, which will soon pass away Be it observed that such "crazes" have always manifested themselves in every country and in every age, beginning with every era of true culture and intelligence, and have only ended with it The Medici family had such a "craze" for six generations. Whenever people begin to know anything beyond eating, drinking, and the vulgar display of money and "family," they begin to read—that is to say, to take an interest in history and humanity as it has been; and this leads at once to an interest in the past, and to intelligent collection and preservation. This "craze" begun again during the eighteenth century in England—with WALPOLE and Bishop PERCY—it had never ceased on the Continent since the Renaissance among the better educated, and it has been gradually progressing ever since While the absurdities of old spinning-wheels, with other merely *odd* and crazy antiques in drawing-rooms, must cease, it is quite as certain that the value of any old work impressed with the true *cachet* or seal of art will never diminish until a new revival of taste shall have culminated and decayed.

F

ART INSTRUCTION IN ITS RELATIONS TO THE TRADES.

I cannot set forth too strongly the fact that decorative art is to be taught to children and girls, simply because it is better adapted to their age or nature than a trade or mechanical pursuits, and that whenever it is possible the pupils should be put into practical work. Thus when boys or even girls manifest an aptness or a fitness for it, they may be taught simple carpentry or joining, turning, or any of the trades, if there be an opportunity to do so, and they can learn. It requires many thousands of dollars or pounds sterling to establish an industrial school, but industrial art may be taught from the infants' school upward   Let it, however, be borne in mind that industrial art, especially as regards boys, is really only a training for a trade, and that far from giving them a distaste for useful work, it only whets the appetite.

I was one of the first, if not the first, to point out, many years ago, in a lecture, a fact which has since been clearly proved, that the decay of the apprentice system must very soon lead to industrial education in schools.   Machinery is making men into machines at such a rate that humanity is becoming seriously alarmed at the inevitable result.   The old apprentice had a chance to rise, since he learned a whole trade; the modern workman, who is kept at making the sixtieth part of a shoe, and at nothing else, by a master whom he never sees, is becoming a mere serf to capital. Even the industrial school with its "practical" work can do nothing against this onward and terrible march, of utilitaria.   It is in the teaching of art, and of the superiority of hand-work in all that constitutes taste, that the remedy will be found. By and by, when culture shall have advanced—as it will—there will be an adjustment of interests. Machinery will supply mere physical comforts. Man, and not machinery, will minister to taste and refinement. Machinery promised to supply food for all. There are more people at present with virtually nothing to do, than there ever were in the days of hand labour. They do not starve, and they are not in rags, but they are paupers. They walk about in decent clothes, but they are dependents on parents, rich relations, or on somebody. If they had any calling, industry, or art, however small, they would not be paupers. And it is for industrial art in schools to save them.

I have been assured by practical-impractical men, that industries not "staple" are not worthy of being recognised by a government. But these people mean by "staple" certain settled, old-fashioned industries, and they assume that there can never be any new ones. Now when I, as I am credited for it by high authority, revived repoussé in brass, and its sister art of stamped leather, or *cuir bouilli*, as manual employment for amateurs, I gave an impulse to an industry which has set thousands of people at work. But I am told "this is a fancy-work craze." Well, when the same craze first sprung up it lasted more than a thousand years, and it will do so again. The great reason why Germany is taking the lead in the world's markets is, because she teaches *art* and *letters* to her apprentices.

THE PHILADELPHIA SCHOOL.

This now (1887) consists of about five hundred pupils, boys and girls, all studying in the Public Grammar Schools. Most of them before coming to it have already learned to hold a pencil and draw a little, but this is less of a qualification than would be supposed, since none can then produce a design, a practical working drawing fit to be " put in hand." In fact it is almost a matter of total indifference to me whether a child can draw or not. Those who can, and who have been taught by the old method, continue to rest all their weight, or press on the right hand or arm, and require a long training to draw *light* lines, while there are few indeed who would not make a bough smallest next to the trunk, or who have a single ornament by heart. It is needless to say that a pupil who knows nothing at all of drawing is preferable for decorative design to one whose ideas are limited to heavy lines, stumping, shading, and picture-making. The pupil on arriving is set at copying some very simple design in outline only, and is then told to double it, or else to draw a leaf so as to compose a wreath by repeating it. There are two classes—one attending on Tuesday afternoons from three to five; the other on Thursdays at the same hours. These lessons are freely open to the public. Those on Saturday afternoons, at which brass and leather work are practised, are strictly private, as the noise causes a confusion which is greatly heightened by visitors walking about.

I have known one or two very clever girls who had previously learned to draw properly succeed in making a good original design even at a third lesson. But this is very unusual indeed. I remember that once a young lady of Boston who could draw, *ι e*, copy very well, argued with me for a long time to prove that I could never teach *her* to design, for she had no originality. I finally said—"You have talked for half an hour to convince me that you are incapable of doing what I have never failed to teach to any public-school child of twelve. Will you now devote half an hour to learning to design" The result of the lesson was that next morning at breakfast she showed me a really beautiful original pattern, fit to be worked. But as a rule children require from twenty to thirty or even fifty lessons to produce good designs This is partly due to the fact that I have often from fifty to sixty to teach at once, and that other avocations prevent me from devoting my time to making or preparing "copies," that is to say, *motives* for the pupils to work on. I am positive that with abundance of good models or designs, and with more time, or smaller classes, I could teach a pupil to design a pattern in much less time than is now required. It is a great disadvantage that in my school the *majority* of the pupils are withdrawn when they have not had more than fifteen or twenty lessons, or before they have had time to fairly learn to design and model This is caused by my receiving chiefly the eldest, or those who are about to leave. Despite all these and many other drawbacks I have fully succeeded in proving what this chapter was written to demonstrate, that children may be taught while attending school to make a living, or, if this term be equivocal, I would say to be so taught as to become preferred workmen and workwomen, or learners in many kinds of factories and callings. Thus a boy or girl who can design at all is very desirable as an assistant or junior designer in a carpet-factory. To get such a junior the manufacturer now goes to an art school to receive a youth who has been trained for years solely towards picture-making. The boy can copy blocks and shade them, and draw landscapes in perspective, and has been over-educated in rules and precepts, but as for making patterns such as the manufacturer needs, he rarely knows much about it Many of my pupils have produced designs which have been sold, and work which has a value.   But I have not as yet deemed it advisable to lay much stress on the school-work as suited to either exhibition or sale.

The school was originally established chiefly by the kind aid of Mr EDWARD T. STEEL, the President of the Philadelphia Board of Public Education, but it was entirely carried out and kept in operation by WILLIAM GULAGER, JOHN SHEDDEN, ISAAC A. SHEPPARD, WILLIAM M. SMITH, and JAMES J. COOPER, of the Committee on Industrial Art Education.   These gentlemen aided me through much local opposition, and if the school succeeded fully in proving what it was designed to establish, it was due to their constant help and encouragement.   Since this was written I have left the direction of the school   It has, however, been greatly enlarged, and is successfully advancing.

GENERAL OBSERVATIONS.

EQUALITY OF THE SEXES IN ARTISTIC CAPACITY.

IT may interest the reader to know that in design-drawing there is no difference as regards merit or capacity between the sexes In *brass-work* boys excel, not because it requires more strength, for it does not, and the gentlest worker who makes least exertion does best, but because women and girls will not take so much pains to learn to run a line well with a tracer on brass before proceeding to make what they are confident will be saleable and beautiful productions In wood-carving the sexes are more nearly equal, with an advantage, however, in favour of the male In modelling the equality is almost re-established Teachers who have had much experience in Europe all declare that American girls or grown women, while clever, are the most difficult to teach, owing to their impatience. As a rule, when not under restraint, they have not the patience to learn to design, but are eager to take up at once one or several arts, hoping to beg, buy, or borrow patterns, as luck may provide Those who do proceed by the right road of drawing learn rapidly and do well. While it is continually urged that women who are all players of the piano never produced a great composer, or indeed a very great artist of any kind, it is at least consoling to know that in the minor decorative arts, which produce great eras of art, there is but little difference as regards results, and if from small beginnings we date our winnings, it may be that from this training something may arise surpassing aught in the past.

MISAPPREHENSION OF "ART" AN OBSTACLE TO INDUSTRIAL EDUCATION

The most serious obstacle with which industrial art has to contend is the extravagant and inflated ideas which are popularly attached to the word *art*. It has been so long identified with pictures and statues, that in every newspaper, under the heading of "The Fine Arts," nothing but news of pictures and statues is expected. Now, as not one person in scores can accurately distinguish a good picture from a bad one, and as the kind of art knowledge which is current sets itself forth in a vast vocabulary of cant, it is not remarkable that "art" has become a terror. There are men in high places who profess to be authorities, who declare that "art" is something for only the very few to rightly understand, and that it requires a special inspiration and much education to appreciate it. When every one, rich or poor, shall know what design is, though it be only simply decorative, and has become familiar with a tastefully ornamented house, however humble, then art in its highest, purest, and noblest sense will have no mystery for any one. It is most unfortunately true that, while taste, learning, and culture are spreading rapidly, there has been so far no

rational or common-sensible effort to really teach
the poor and ignorant anything of the kind.   There is
a great deal of writing about the ennobling tendencies
of art, but there have been as yet very few efforts to
really go down to the basis and make a proper beginning   The dilettanti and cognoscenti, and of late
years the æsthetes, have all preached in their time
and way the glory of RAPHAEL or MICHAEL ANGELO,
and how desirable it would be to bring a knowledge of
them down to the people   But they have never tried
bringing the people up to RAPHAEL.   Now, RAPHAEL
and MICHAEL ANGELO sprung from the people in an age
when every object was made with decorative art   They
were results more than causes.   And when this shall
be the case with us, we shall have RAPHAELS again, and
not till then.   There never was a real art in the world
that did not spring from the people, that was not fully
shared in by the people, and that did not belong to the
people   If there were to-day as much knowledge of
and fondness for design as there seems to have been
among the prehistoric savages of Europe, we should
in a few years raise our manufactures of every kind to
pre-eminence, and with them improve ourselves personally, morally, and socially.[1]

---

[1] Mr WILLIAM MORRIS, the eminent poet and artist, speaks to the
same effect in an address at the opening of a Fine Art and Industrial
Exhibition at Manchester, England —

"In truth, these decorative arts, when they are genuine, real from
the root up, have one claim to be considered serious matters which even
the greater works do in a way lack, and this claim is that they are the
direct expression of the thoughts and aspirations of the mass of the
people ; and I assert that the higher class of artist, the individual
artist—he whose work is, as it were, a work in itself—cannot live
healthily and happily without the lower kind of art—if we must call it
lower—the kind which we may think of as co-operative art, and which,

There is a great coming revival of culture and of art, but it will not be with us until we teach its principles to every child in every school There is an instinct in mankind for decoration, for colour, for manifestations of what is beautiful. It has been starved out temporarily by the practical developments of science or by the useful. This was well, but while comfort should be paramount, there is no need of suppressing taste. Those who talk about the sunflower mania and "art craze" as something temporary, and who mistake the æsthetes for the main army yet to come, are like the ambassadors sent by an African king to visit London, and who at the first small Arab village thought themselves at the end of their journey. As yet the *people* have not moved A writer in a Cincinnati journal, I know not who, has wisely said that " because some people have blue jugs, and one gentleman an art gallery, therefore we are a great artistic people. But where are the works of our united citizens ? What have the masses of our people done ? ".

What the masses of our people can do will be first shown when every one of them shall have been taught, first, decorative design, and then one or more minor arts This design will be simple, and deal merely with outline and mere ornament at first. This is the only easy and proper preparation for more advanced drawing, be it practical or technological, or for prospective picture-making. Hitherto all elementary drawing has been misdirected either in copying shaded pictures, or, what is little better, in stiff and formal

when it is genuine, gives your great man, be he never so great, the peaceful and beautiful surroundings and the sympathetic audience which he justly thinks he has a right to "

"systems." When all can design, and all know something about decorative art, the mystery will depart,
and the world feel less awed before old masters and
modern Gothic churches; neither will it believe that a
pile of building is necessarily beautiful because it cost
fifteen million dollars.

MORAL EFFECTS OF ART INSTRUCTION.

I cannot urge too earnestly or too often on clergymen, as on parents, the fact that an interesting industry
is conducive to moral culture. Boys who are really
absorbed in some kind of industrious amusement are
kept out of much mischief. The world, unfortunately,
while it observes those who are always in mischief,
takes no note of those who are kept out of it. How
much the more, therefore, is art industry in school to
be commended, since it not only keeps children busy
as an amusement, but aids them practically as to
future callings Year by year sees the old bugbear
fading away, the demon of our childhood, which taught'
that as all medicines to be effective must needs be
nauseous, so all school study must needs be wearisome
and painful. I am sure that industrial art will go
far to make children love school In England rural
clergymen and many ladies soon saw into this, and
Mrs. JEBB, of Ellesmere, was the first to establish
village art schools. But if it be advisable from moral
grounds to teach children some way to employ their
leisure pleasantly, what shall we say of the terrible
number of the older grown who rush into vice, im-
pelled by the sheer ennui of idleness? Here is an
immense number of girls knowing nothing but a little

plain sewing, or, in the higher grades, a little piano playing They cannot all get places in shops or factories, and if they do, many of them break down. When a rainy day comes there is suffering indeed. At such a time almost any fancy work, however trifling, often intervenes to save them from ruin There are now many thousands of young women in America who owe the real comfort, or what constitutes the enjoyment, of life to the teaching or making what is in itself almost worthless, to feeble cards and washy plaques and wretched drawing and daubing; yet it saves them. How much better would it be if they understood design and the decorative arts, which are not more difficult, and which are far more certain to command a market ?

There is another class of young people, mostly female, who, having taken the first step in vice, linger awhile before the second, and then are rapidly and utterly degraded. If we look through the ranks of the uneducated, half educated, or even so-called educated young women, how many are there who have any resources to fill up their leisure ? Is it a wonder that they gossip, and thereby develop the sociable evil, who makes even more mischief than her humbler sister, the social evil ? I do not think that among the best educated there is one in ten who has any hand-work or resource, artistic or literary, in which she really delights. It is the same with the men. Hence politics, gossip, and the most frivolous waste of time. The clergy know this, and they would welcome any remedy for it. When I recently published in *The Messenger* an appeal to them to aid in introducing art into schools on moral grounds, I began at once to receive, as I still do, letters from clergymen all over the country in reference to the subject. It is a fact that when a girl once masters an art she generally remains true to it and makes the most of it. Its practice gives a certain sense of superiority and of self-reliance which goes far to strengthen morals in the truest sense of the word.

INDUSTRIAL ART AS AN ECONOMIC FACTOR

There is not one person living, having the usual command of brain and hands, who cannot learn to design well in simply decorative drawing in a few weeks, or, in extremest cases, in a few months, if he or she will try to acquire it. There is not one person who can execute simple design who cannot also master one or more minor arts. And finally there is no youth of either sex who understands one minor art who cannot make a living by it or by teaching it By mastering an art I do not mean the ability to feebly copy a wreath of flowers on a china plate, or to indifferently hammer on a brass plaque a borrowed pattern. As it is within the power of all to learn design, so it is quite as easy to perfect themselves in these arts without a master. All that they require is will and industrious application. This is not mere theory. It has been proved in millions of instances. The history of whole countries, nations, and eras has proved it. I will give the examples.

In the East from remote times, during the days of Greece and Rome, and through the European Middle Ages, the conditions of life were such that but for hand-made minor art the number of paupers would have been literally overpowering Nothing produces idlers and beggars so much as aristocracy or an extravagant and wealthy court and nobility, and society was then entirely aristocratic. Yet there were fewer paupers then than there are now, if by paupers we mean the entirely dependent. To-day in the United States they wear good clothes and seem well off, but they depend on somebody. There have been states of society in which the producer was more cruelly taxed, but none in which he supported so many. It is very creditable to the average mechanic of the United States that he spends twice or thrice as much on his family as does his British brother, but it is very discreditable to his family that they take so much. Now, if there were such a demand for hand-made decoration in this country as there was, let us say, in Europe five hundred years ago—if every home, however small, were properly adorned—all in the country who are willing to work would find employment. It is a curious reflection that even in the time of Elizabeth the "sitting room" of Anne Hathaway's cottage was far more beautiful than most of our drawing-rooms, for it was entirely lined with old carved oak. This was the home of people who were then called poor. The demand for hand-made decoration is coming very rapidly. When it comes—when people learn the truth that a thing is not artistic *because* it is beautiful— there will be a vast field thrown open not only to the poor, but to the poor who are neither very clever nor strong. In any case, it is always worth while to have some art which one can always teach for money, or by which one can live. How many poor young people, with spare time, spending all they earn for living,

would be really happy when holidays approach if
they had a few dollars more ? And how certainly
they could depend on earning them if they could
embroider, model, and ornament, or colour and glaze
vases, carve panels, work in leather, or, in fine, decorate
homes in every way. It is hardly possible to suppose
that any one who could do all this need be very poor
Yet all these arts, and many more, are actually within
the reach of all who choose to master them

I have shown that the expenses of designing and
modelling amount to so little that they may be introduced to the poorest country school.   I find that
embroidery is often made to cost moie than it should.
The wool for crewel, at five cents (2½d) a skein, crash,
or common stuff of several kinds costs very little.
Scraps of velvet, cloth, and ribbon, for appliqué work,
are expensive or the contrary, as people are careful in
collecting   A class may be well-taught in design,
chiefly with the blackboard alone; beyond this, good
wrapping or shop paper and lead pencils are not hard
to obtain   No rule can be laid down as to selling
work.   The pupil should not try to sell anything
until it is really well made.   Unfortunately the
delight of the amateur at his own work is always
such that his first or at least second or third attempt
always seems to him to be very valuable, and there
are always ignorant friends who are of the same
opinion.   What has degraded china painting is the
enormous production of it by women who knew
nothing of design, and who were accordingly destitute
of the energy and character which spring from originality, and which is acquired by designing.   And this
is applicable to all the feeble art work, or rather art

degraded to fancy work, which is turned out in such incredible quantities from unions, schools, and clubs into depositories and agricultural or charity fairs. This will be the case so long as women or men are satisfied with easily producing rubbish which is admired by the ignorant, and which can be sold "somehow" at some price To sit in rows painting flowers, dogs' heads, and cupids, or even copying chromo lithographs *en grand*, without the least knowledge of drawing, is not art, and it is not amazing that small wits find in the results much food for ridicule.

OBJECTIONS CONSIDERED.

I have found that a great deal of the opposition or indifference to art industry in schools comes from men who, because they are themselves ignorant, do not like to have the whole world trained to what they are too idle or stupid to master. Others argue that as their children are not intended for pursuits into which art knowledge enters, therefore no children need or ought to learn anything of the kind In the face of these and many other equally wise objections, such as are generally urged at meetings where the subject is discussed, the facts remain that art industry can be taught without infringing on other branches of education, that children while at school can learn to design and model so well in a few months with one weekly lesson as to readily obtain a place as under-designers in factories; and that, thirdly, they can even produce wares which will sell. They can, at the same time, acquire more culture and intelligence than the objectors to the system can appreciate, but which is appreciated by all persons who are themselves really well informed or intelligent. On this point I speak with knowledge from experience I have observed that my pupils, from the time they ceased to be mere copyists, began to observe many things to which they were previously indifferent, and manifested the awakening of a much higher intelligence.

But there is a final argument which cannot be resisted: it is that there is a tremendous demand among the manufacturers of Europe and of this country for decorative artists and artisans. It was thought in England that the great art schools of South Kensington and Manchester and such places would afford a supply, but it has been as a drop in the bucket. The industrial schools have been as inadequate. For it is not only a supply of artistic goods that is needed, but also a *taste* for them—a manufactory and a market as well as a greater demand; and to meet this double want there must be extensive radical art education among the people. The highest statesmen in Europe know this, and the saying of the Prince of Wales, cited in a late article in the *Nineteenth Century*, that learning and earning should go together, indicates the solution of a great problem by a brief rhyme. True, there are millions who do not see this. The year before gas was introduced into Philadelphia all her most influential citizens signed a protest against lighting the city in any such abominable way. The light which gas casts is trifling compared to the enlightenment which would result from the reform in education of which I speak, yet there are still many in that city as in others who ridicule the very idea of industrial art in schools.

G

From time to time the world comes to a period when it discovers all at once, like a hungry somnambulist awaking in a room full of smoking charcoal, that it is both starving and strangling It cries now that in education we are starving for fresh knowledge, and are being stifled with old methods. People are beginning to think there must be some shorter and more practical cut to drawing than all the old road, with its blocks, perspective, diagrams, and geometry, ever indicated. These are all good in their way, but there is no practical easy introduction to the art. There is a growing belief that all study may be made easier. There may be no "royal road" to mathematics, but that is no reason why the way to everything should be over corduroy planks and break-neck rocks. There must be work to win art or learning, but even hard work need not be offensive

There is a final plea to be offered for the introduction of industrial art into all schools It is that by making *hand-work* a part of every child's education we shall destroy the vulgar prejudice against work as being itself vulgar. This we greatly need, for there is no country in the world where manual work is practically in so little respect, or where there are so many trying to get above it, as in the American republic We have had those by millions who proclaimed that "work is only fit for negroes or mudsills." As it is, the native-born citizen all too eagerly flies to any occupation in which, by wearing a black coat all day and keeping his hands soft, he makes one move nearer to being "a gentleman." It is only in my native land that I ever heard a man (a tavern-keeper), gravely boast, as a proof of his social superiority, that he had never done "a

day's work" in his life. While there are a few
superior to this snobbishness, there are still millions
who are practically enslaved by it   It arises from the
fact that work—hand-work—is not as yet sufficiently
identified with education and culture.   Now, industrial
art in schools, based on design, and associated with
studies, will go very far to make manual labour "re-
spectable" in the eyes of those professing democrats
who pant *in petto* for aristocracy as the hart for the
water brooks

Perhaps half the real *suffering* in Europe and
America is the result of the effort to appear "genteel"
by those who cannot afford it, or to seem richer than
they are.   The small tailor sends his sons to college-
where they learn words and nothing more, he dies
leaving nothing, and the boys must earn a living in
some way for which their school, or, perhaps, college
training is worse than worthless.   There is a novel by
GAUTIER, called "Raoul," in which the author endeavours
to show the terrible results of this mistaken aiming at
a mistaken ideal.   The hero is the son of a poor
gentleman artist who has sent his son to college, where
he has learned Latin and Greek, and nothing more.
And with this slender equipment he must fight the
battle of life.   So he teaches languages at a franc a
lesson—"just what one gives to a street-corner porter
for running a five-minute errand"—and so he goes
from misery to suicide.   His friend, who is like him in
education, becomes a swindler   Now, the world says
of such men that they *ought* to have had more sense,
more energy, and have got more out of Latin and
Greek.   And so one man in five or ten can or does.
But the others ?   Suppose, however, that it is only the

alternate *one*?   So these must make a failure of life because they are not "sharp."

"Raoul," with a knowledge of a few arts, could not have really sunk to the mud of poverty.   The father who sprung from poverty, who had all the strength and roughness and obtuseness, with the natural fangs and claws of the "practical," vulgar, ignorant man, succeeds in life.   He trains a boy so that he may lose all this—draws his teeth and claws, tames him, and then expects him to do better than himself, because, forsooth, he has given him an "education"—such an education as I myself received at college, the only marvel in relation to it being that any of its graduates ever rose above being members of American Southern Legislatures   In fact the last number which I read of its monthly magazine distinctly declared that if any of these unfortunates ever had risen to literary distinction, it was not by the aid, but *in spite of* the education they had received.   Truly the boast of the number of great men who have graduated of old from certain American colleges sounds like a BRINVILLIERS or BORGIA pointing to her escaped victims as a proof of her humanity.

It is not by carving panels, or modelling owls, or such work, that I propose to rescue society from the fate of "Raoul," but I *do* earnestly believe that an universal familiarity with practical hand-work will go far to train people to take up trades or callings which they would now never think of   There is no universal panacea for snobbery or poverty, but this cure will go far to help many a weak brother to work   As regards women, who claim a thousand times more pity and sympathy, I am confident that if they will take decorative art up in earnest and study it properly, not as fancy work, but as *art*, or as rational and practical industry, it will do more for them than all the learned professions. There are more women than men in the world, and for a long time men will take the lead in those higher callings, so that really not one woman in many can hope to do well as a doctor or lawyer But in manual minor arts she has as good a chance as anybody. Now I wish to call attention to this fact. I have seen an advertisement in a newspaper in which a lady familiar with four languages and their literature, with first-class certificates as to proficiency in drawing, music, mathematics, &c , sought a situation as governess for four shillings a week and her meals And I should not wonder if her employers got her for less Well, both in England and in America at present any lady who can teach design and two or three minor arts can easily get employment as a teacher. With some knowledge of drawing she can in six months be qualified to teach. I had in Philadelphia a class of twenty-five ladies who did this in one session, and who all became paid teachers Be it observed that they were taught *gratis*, and that great pains were taken to make it known that anybody might be taught for nothing; but it was not a very easy matter to get such pupils It is possible that the classes would have been larger had there been a charge, so deeply rooted is the feeling that what can be had for nothing is worth nothing The result, however, was that those who came, being superior to such vulgar prejudice, showed themselves superior in intelligence. This was several years ago, but even now it does not seem to be understood that the application which would qualify a girl to teach the piano and Mangnall would enable her to do far better in the minor arts

The standard of taste in art or decoration is the result of the study of what is generally admired as best in what man has produced in all ages, and what is most beautiful in nature.   It is not true, as the vulgar believe, that there is " no disputing about taste "   Now it must be admitted that the general standard of popular taste is very low in Europe or in America.   Among a hundred carpets, such as would sell most readily, it is unusual to find more than two or three of a merely passably decent pattern.   There are three grades of carpets made in Philadelphia for different parts of the United States, and those of the third class are almost without exception to the last degree abominable in outline, and, if possible, worse as regards colour.   This is just what I was told by a carpet manufacturer who was perfectly aware of the ugliness of his wares, who laughed at it, and regretted that it was a necessity.   He illustrated it by showing me the kinds of carpets and rugs which " sold like hot cakes "   It was pitiful, for no Red Indian and no savage negro would ever have designed aught so repulsive.   Savage art is never half so savage as that produced by the most enlightened nation on the face of the earth, and English carpets are little better.   A lady who had studied art conscientiously writes to me to say that her designs were rejected by manufacturers as being " too artistic "   I once had an experience which illustrates the popular conception of a work of art.   A manufacturer of " artistic furniture " in a far-western city was shown a cabinet designed, carved, and inlaid with bone in our school.

The design was Spanish-Moorish, the inlaying was made simply with three dozen counters or " chips," on each of which was etched with a graver a mediæval head, or *Allah* in Arabic letters The visitor, on being asked what such a work would cost, replied promptly, seven dollars (28s.) "That is to say," he continued, "I would imitate the carved panels by sawing the pattern out with a jig-saw and gluing it on—it would look just as well, and nobody would know the difference; and the pieces of bone would cost only two cents a piece. There would be no need of engraving a different design on every one, and most of my customers would prefer them plain." To which I answered, "You could not execute such a piece of work for less than fifty dollars (£10). I do not ask what a glued-together *imitation* would cost, but what would be the expense of an original work? You have not probably in your State a man who could give you such a design, and I am sure that any professional designer in the East would charge you twenty-five dollars for one, if you could get it for that. Neither have you anybody who could even select from books, and copy the etchings, and execute them by hand. If you had they would cost ten dollars (£2) more. Now at our school there would be a new design made for every cabinet executed. The making-up of that cabinet cost twelve dollars, and it is much below the usual rate." The visitor, on examination, agreed that the cabinet-work had been cheaply done, and that an original work would cost fifty dollars. Now I would remark that this gentleman was very far from being an ignorant or narrow-minded man. He had enlarged and intelligent views as to education, and was active in endeavouring to have industrial art introduced to the schools of his city. He simply reflected the universal popular idea, that the patterns may come from anywhere, that all work is to be in thousands of duplicates, and that an imitation at half price which is glued and varnished up so as to pass muster with the ignorant is "just as good as anything." His conception of original designs was *theft*.

It is a fact that machinery-work does not give any objects so cheaply but that hand-made art can rival them even in price. What with expensive advertisements and the enormous profits required by every agent through whose hands it passes, the trashy duplicates cost in the end as much to the consumer as he would have to pay for original hand-work [1] It was pointed out to me by KARL KRALL, of the firm of BARKENTIN & KRALL, London, that the credit system has had much to do with producing a low standard of art in decorations. A workman would gladly produce, let us say, a set of fire-irons by hand-work. They would be elegant and original. But he needs, as all workmen do, money down on the completion of the job. Now a very great many rich people in Europe and America cannot and will not bring themselves to pay cash for anything if they can help it. If a debt brought them in compound interest ten times over, they could not be more desirous of letting it run on than they are. Every good has its evil: one of the evils of the vast develop-

---

[1] I have seen in a shop window hundreds of times a brass coal-scuttle, machine-made, for forty shillings, or some other object of the kind. A *better* one, hand-made, can be had *for the same price* (cash) at the Home Arts and Industries Schools.

ment of the credit system has been this antipathy to pay ready money. The result of it is that the workman must wait six months, and perhaps twelve, and "call again" The result is that he charges for time and interest. The same happens to the maker of the machinery-made and glued-together rubbish: he too must give long credits And the result is a deterioration in taste.

A very direct tax on education and taste is to be found in the barbarous and ridiculous American law by which Customs-duties are laid on objects of art, antiques, old books, engravings, and in fact on almost everything which could be of use in teaching decorative art. I once imported two barrels of small stones or cubes for mosaic work for the use of pupils in the public school. Although the law declares explicitly that material for the use of schools is duty-free, the Custom House officials declared that we must pay 55 per cent on the value. They knew very well that this was not legal, but possibly thought that to avoid trouble the demand would be paid There is a great deal of such work in all Custom Houses. Fortunately we had friends who set the matter right. There is in plain terms an almost prohibitory duty in the United States on all objects which are of the greatest importance in teaching decorative art. As these objects are not and cannot now be made in the country, the absurdity of such revenue laws is the more apparent. And as they are generally imported in small quantities, even when they are intended for schools, the officials have it in their power to "squeeze," or attempt to squeeze the duty, à la Chinois. Many persons will pay a few dollars rather than undergo delay. Whether these squeezes are handed over to the government, I do not know. If they are, so much more shame to the general government It will be seen from what I have written that if the American people were desirous of *directly discouraging* art and manufactures and culture, they could not do it more effectively than by taxing the articles which above all others tend to develop the higher branches of industry.

The last consideration connected with familiarity with the minor arts is of great importance. Few persons have reflected on their connection with the intimate history or inner life of every age. They are closely allied to intellectual culture. He who reads history as it was taught in my youth is like a guest at a cheap hotel table where all the dishes have the same gravy The great conquerors or orators of an age all appeared to us as very much of the same sort: the people were all very much alike. I remember being told in my infancy, by my old quadroon nurse, ' that at the time of the Deluge the people were taken all aback by it. They never expected such a thing. "Some were out a-shoppin' and some out a-gunnin' when the rain fell. They hadn't even trust enough in NOAH to take their umbrellas." There is more of this ignorance and cant among us than we are aware of. Decorative art gives us the colour of an age. He who has read DANTE once has read him, he who knows the Cathedral of Florence has read him twice, he who knows the pictures and decorative art-work of his age has read him many times The minor arts are as much associated as the fine arts with all that pertains to the very cream of culture. To know them at all is to know in time the names and works of BENVENUTO CELLINI, ALBRECHT DÜRER, in a word, of all the great men whose names and works cast the highest splendour on splendid ages. The boy or girl who has gone even but a little way into industrial art, visits the great museums and collections of this country or of Europe with a hundred times more real knowledge and appreciation of their magnificence than can the amateur who has only *read*, though it be "never so wisely." No boy or girl learns to design, model, and carve, inlay, and embroider, without in time reading with keenest interest OWEN JONES, LABARTHE, FERGUSSON, WHEWELL, HULME, COLLING, DE RACINET, and DRESSER, with many more such writers. And with such practical knowledge and reading, every object of taste and almost every book reveal beauties and awaken associations such as the many envy and the few possess; for the one who has worked in industrial art understands and feels decoration and beauty as no mere reader can. I once read through all that I could get on wood engraving, but two days' work at a block taught me more than a library on the subject could have done. For of all learning since books were invented there was never aught like experience, and of all experience there is none like one's own.

It should be remembered that industrial art may not only be taught in schools, but also form the subject or principle of a club, a society, or a private class, or be practised by a family or an individual. There should be indeed a Ladies' Industrial Art Association in every village. It will promote culture; it will or should lead to much reading of history and its social developments; and it will be a source of pecuniary profit.

It is to be supposed that in most instances these private societies will aid the local schools by teaching and by joint sales. Where even two or three unite for such a purpose they will find that mutual aid and consultation are quite equivalent to a teacher. Last, not least, I can assure them that the work is fascinating or agreeable to a degree which none can realise who has not attempted it. When asked what was most remarkable in the Ladies' Art Club of which I am president, I replied, "The love of the students for their work."

There are certain facts which may well be borne in mind as regards the School of Industrial Art in Philadelphia. Firstly, It was a conscientious *experiment*, based on much observation and study, to ascertain of what work children are capable. The result was a conviction that under fourteen years of age what they can mainly master is what may be called minor art-work, but that this is an admirable preparation for all trades, because it makes them familiar with designs and proportions, and gives them that use of the fingers and familiarity with tools which renders all manual labour easy.

Secondly, The development of constructiveness, or the learning to make things, also enlarges or stimulates the intellect. It was found by inquiry made of the teachers in the grammar-schools that the children who attended the industrial art school manifested more intelligence than those who did not. They stood high in their other studies. They were interested in subjects which the others did not understand.

This will not seem remarkable when I say that there were several girls of thirteen and fourteen who could design very beautiful, or really faultless, Moresco patterns on a large scale, and work them out so well in stamped leather as to be able to earn a pound in two lessons,[1] while others could produce equally good work in repoussé, wood-carving, and barbotine, or clay-modelling   This, and the familiarity with patterns, and living amid such work, manifestly awoke an interest in literary culture and in general information.

Thirdly, It was found by strict inquiry that the art-work, far from being an extra burden or task added to the ordinary school course, was really a relaxation, and that it greatly aided other studies   I call special attention to this, because I find that a great many object to it as an additional load laid on the already overtasked pupil, while others, in spite of every argument, see nothing in it but an extra holiday or afternoon devoted to play, which must be made up by extra hard work.   I never knew an instance in which the children, in order to have the precious privilege of working in the art school, did not cheerfully make up their " averages " of study in some way.   It is not sufficiently borne in mind that when children enjoy study there is seldom much injury resulting from cramming, and that play is rest.

Fourthly, It would have been difficult in any place to

---

[1] When I speak of children earning such sums, it must be understood that the work in every case went directly to the "consumer" for cash, without any intermediate brokerage or commission   I have been told many times publicly that a skilled workman in brass—sometimes a very able artist—can only earn thirty shillings a week   The only conclusion from this is—is it necessary that the one who buys work of him to sell again should earn perhaps thrice as much.

have had pupils so perfectly adapted to give one an idea of the average capacity of the young. Philadelphia contains a million inhabitants, and there were 115,000 scholars in her public schools alone (1884) It was from these that my scholars were taken Consequently I had them from every class, rich or poor. There were a few blacks, mulattoes, quadroons, the children of Germans and of German Jews, and those of other kinds of foreign parentage Some of them were very poor, but these were rare, as there is perhaps no city of the same size as Philadelphia in the world in which there is so little poverty or so few very rich people. The general behaviour of the children was incredibly good. Only once during four years did I have occasion to severely reprimand and dismiss three pupils (girls) for impertinence I allowed them to converse with one another on the condition that they should only talk about their work in subdued tones When I observed that a pupil was disposed to talk overmuch, and be idle or restless, I. had him or her (it was generally a boy) changed at the next lesson to another seat. I carefully studied the children, and adapted my teaching to every individual. I am no believer in *systems* by which a school can be taught as an army is drilled, by platoons and masses The feebler and the more incompetent a teacher, the greater the desire will be to teach by system and rule. Hence the popularity of progressive courses, of drawing books, and other methods of machinery teaching As for me, I loved my pupils one and all, and worked with every one as if I had but one to teach.

I am often obliged to hear in England, when I

speak of the success with which I taught—" Ah, but your American children are all so clever, you know" I do not know anything of the kind, nor do I believe there is anything to choose among any children as regards a capacity for industrial art-work. As I never had occasion to find fault with more than three or four out of more than a thousand during four years, for bad behaviour, and as all the rest invariably acted like little ladies and gentlemen, and as I am assured that this would not be the case in a school of mixed classes in London, I conclude that republicanism conduces to more refinement and good manners among the poor than any other form of government. And as docility and gentleness are certainly conducive to art studies, I must certainly admit that American children have in this respect a very great advantage over others. When it was proposed to me in England to teach art industry in a school in the East of London, I was cautioned by my adviser, a well-known English writer who had been in America, that I would find my pupils much more coarse and unruly than those whom I had taught at home. I speak of this difference simply as a philosopher. It is possible that in the future it may give America an immense advantage in her manufactures.

I am not aware that any writer has called attention to a fact which I observed from an early period of my experiment, and which I studied very closely, taking great pains to test it by inquiry and observation. It is this, that industrial art-work pursued during one or two years is infinitely better adapted to qualify children for the varied possibilities and contingencies of life than if they had been taught a single "trade" or only one practical mechanical calling For an industrial art (I do not say a fine art) training makes it very easy for boy or girl to take up any calling whatever, though it were cookery or shop-tending or tailoring, because other and more practical faculties than those involved in "the three R's" have been awakened. I had ample opportunity to ascertain that my female pupils did positively make better shop-girls in consequence of having had their quickness of practical perception and constructiveness developed. No *single* trade-teaching can effect this. Now to learn industrial art-work, design is necessary, and the pupils thus acquire intelligence of the great fact that there is *a system* in all works, and in life. Those may call this too theoretical and ideal who will. It will be more fully tested in the future. The greatest difficulty with which I had to contend was that of making the public understand that my system was a general preparation of the young for any occupation, and not a special training for certain kinds of works. I do not know how many scores of "sensible, practical" people, after looking at and admiring the children's work, have said : "It is all very fine, to be sure, but don't you think the children would do better if they were learning the beginnings of trades by which they could make a living ? " Now I have never doubted that it is better to teach boys turning and metal-work and carpentering than nothing. But I contend that for all children, *i e.*, of both sexes, of tender years between the infant school and fourteen years, or let us say from eight to twelve, the *minor arts* are the best which can be taught, and that they form the one proper preparation for trades.

When I first made my system known to the public in London by a lecture before the Society of Arts, it was objected by one newspaper that teachers could not be found to manage art classes in every school. To this I reply that no difficulty has so far been found either in America or England in this respect. By this system the teacher is partly self-taught, while those who need advice, elementary designs, easy practical manuals, and aid of many kinds, can obtain them by simply addressing the Secretary of the Home Arts and Industries Association. This society have now in course of instruction a class of teachers who will go from school to school. The whole rests upon a knowledge of the fact that there are minor or easy arts which any child or labourer can learn. This I have heard denied in face of the fact that millions of mediæval Europeans and modern Arabs or other Orientals with less brain than an average English school-child have produced exquisite decoration. The truth is that beyond what is very easy in such work the world generally produces only confused and corrupt design. As for mere hand finish, it is a matter of time and industry.

There is something in reference to all that I have said as to art in schools which I feel obliged to mention, though it is done most unwillingly. Since I have returned to England, the classes which I established in Philadelphia have been very much enlarged, and new branches added. One newspaper commented on this "practical common-sense reform" in a manner which would lead a stranger to the conclusion that my leaving the school was really a good

H

riddance of bad rubbish, and that the only misfortune it ever had was my having anything to do with it. This was at least the opinion of a friend who sent it to me. Now it is a fact that I had for years earnestly desired to introduce these very "reforms" or additions, and was only kept from doing so by want of money. Immediately after I left, the appropriation for the school was greatly enlarged, and the number of pupils doubled. It does not seem to have occurred to the editors and private individuals who spoke of a branch more or less (not introduced on account of simple poverty), as if that constituted the whole system, that the main object was the making hand-work a branch of instruction in public schools on a large scale. Nor did they consider the wearisome exhausting labour of years in trying to find out by experiment what children *could do*, and how to do it, or what it was to inaugurate a great and radical reform which had never before been successfully attempted anywhere. For it was in studying such work, and fitting it practically into a course of public school studies, that the real system consisted. Industrial or technical schools with large endowments had existed many years before, and it was because I did not teach what they did that my school attracted so much unjust criticism. I was continually asked why I did not introduce branches, which would have required far more money than I had at command, and that too when it required all the ability of the School Board, inspired by the utmost goodwill to me, and the highest intelligence on their part, to secure for me the allowance which they had done their best to get. On one occasion the City Council, wishing to

put an end to my classes, passed a law that my appropriation should be divided among the six or seven other
art and technical schools in the city. It was only by
the resolute action of the School Board that this was
evaded.

DECORATIVE ART IN PRISONS, LUNATIC ASYLUMS, RE-
FORMATORIES, AND SIMILAR INSTITUTIONS.

While conducting the Industrial Art Schools in
Philadelphia, I often reflected on the similarity in
certain respects between children, criminals, and
lunatics. The first have minds not as yet developed;
the others are simply intellectually defective, owing to
organic faults or moral weakness, whatever that may
be Genius itself is too often allied to these in having
certain faculties developed at the expense of others.
Now these exceptions to those whose faculties are well
balanced, have almost uniformly a fondness for artistic,
or easy work involving taste they will labour indus-
triously at it, when a "solid industry" repels them.
Reflecting on this, it seemed to me to be a great pity
that prisoners and paupers should be put on tread-
mills, or kept at picking oakum, or at any such work,
if it were possible to find for them some more congenial employment, by which habits of industry and
application might be formed, so as to prepare them for
more serious or practical labour. Picking oakum or
even shoemaking very rarely leads criminals to like
their work, but wood-carving does decidedly.

My first inquiries were in Moyamensing Prison,
Philadelphia. I was, thanks to Mr EDWARD ROBINS, an
inspector, enabled to converse freely with the prisoners.

The first was a Frenchman, a very clever artist and engineer, but a man who, owing to a want of will, or moral feebleness, could not keep himself from petty larceny, &c. By casually, as it were inadvertently, using *argôt*, or French thief-slang, in my conversation, I little by little drew from him the fact that he had been an old jail-bird in France. He had while in prison invented a method of nickel-plating, and showed me, drawn on W C. paper with a stump of a pencil which he had concealed, all the different batteries of Siemens and others with the one of his own invention. He had nearly lost his mind at one time for want of work. Being set at shoemaking, he learned in an incredibly short time to make very good, even admirable shoes, and having as a favour been allowed a few paints and brushes, with paper, became almost happy. He disliked shoemaking, and said to me that he could earn for the prison £5 a week if he could only have architectural draughting given him. This was quite true, for his work was far above the average. My great familiarity with gypsies, and all kinds of such loose fish, and my talking with him as if he were only "unlucky," enabled me to win his confidence and interest. He thought, according to his experience of prisons, that one-third of all the criminals would eagerly take to decorative art-work, and that the rest would fall in with it. If I had had this man all to myself to employ as I pleased, I could have "kept him straight," for what he needed was some one to "boss" or rule him. After I ceased to visit the prison he often asked after me, manifesting great attachment. Before he was discharged he sent me a beautifully executed model of a working steam-engine made of cardboard as a parting souvenir.   In the same prison was a German fresco-painter   as I spoke German, I won his confidence. This man seemed to be suffering from want of congenial employment.   He was, like the Frenchman, very sure that art-work would be welcome to the prisoners, and "keep the devil out of their heads" I did not think it worth while to examine any Yankee prisoners, for I knew without asking that they would, if supplied with tools and materials, invent and manufacture champion apple-parers and patent mouse-traps forever.

As for the women prisoners, they take to congenial, i.e, to art-work, more eagerly than men.   At one time a few ladies in Philadelphia were accustomed to go once a week to the prison to teach the women confined there embroidery.   This lesson was the great event, the great treat of the week, and it had a sensible influence in refining the poor creatures and making them patient.   After a time one teacher went to Europe, another was married, and the classes were discontinued.   The matron of the prison regretted very much that there was not such agreeable work constantly taught.

I assembled all the officers of the prison, including the physician, and laid before them my experiences and my theory.   They understood the whole affair far better than I did, and they expressed the opinion that if work of a congenial and agreeable character could be introduced, the discipline of the prison would be diminished one-third.

There is in America a very large and influential Prison Reform Association, which holds annual congresses. I was invited to attend the last and set forth my views. I could not do so, being in England, but I am happy to learn from the Secretary, W. F. ROUND, that an Industrial Art School on my system has been introduced to the Elmira (N. Y.) Reformatory, and is a pronounced success. "I have," he writes, "at this moment plaques and sconces (repoussé brass) from your designs by one of the pupils who had only ten weeks' training in the reformatory. A sconce made by a coloured pupil (black) after a design of his own is full of vigour and grace. Before his training by Professor WELLS it was not even suspected that he had any talent in this direction Now that he is out of the Reformatory, I hope to get him into one of our schools of technical design. It was after reading your pamphlet on 'Industrial Art in Schools' that Mr BROCKAWAY of the Elmira Reformatory established, at my suggestion, the training school of industrial arts, Professor WELLS being employed as teacher, and it was a great success. The experiment will soon be tried on a larger scale there, and I hope in some of our prisons. I will let you know the result."

There is near Philadelphia a very large reformatory school. Into this my assistant, Mr J. LIBERTY TADD, introduced the industrial art system, and formed classes with great success I had, however, great difficulty, with many very excellent and zealous friends of education in Philadelphia, in making them understand that there is a *great* difference between teaching strong boys a *practical trade* at once, and *preparing* all boys and girls for practical trades or for all work by early training adapted to their faculties. It was too generally assumed that I simply taught *æsthetic* and fancy work, such as wasted time and disqualified children for doing anything "useful."

The industrial art-work of our school was also taught by Mr. TADD in KIRKBRIDE'S Lunatic Asylum, one of the largest and best institutions of the kind in the world. It is to be remarked that the boys in the reformatory school surpassed those in the public city schools in cleverness, while the lunatics excelled —in ornamented pottery.

I could add more to this, for I could give scores of interesting instances of such work being introduced with happy results into asylums, schools, classes, and families What I have said will, I trust, induce all who are in any way interested in prisons, reformatories, and lunatic asylums, to consider the subject of agreeable industrial art-work. I am certain that there are no institutions where the inmates form, as it were, a family or community, in which such work would not exert a good moral influence.

I am quite aware of what has been tried in English prisons as regards teaching trades as a reward for the well-conducted, &c, but I still doubt whether the moral possibilities of attractive work, especially on a certain very large class, are as yet understood. Certain branches taught are not the same as the principle of all, that is, design, developed into all conceivable branches. And, again, it makes a great difference as to what kind of design we teach.

Part II.

—×—

ON DEVELOPING MEMORY.

"What man has done, man may do"

IT is not too general or too sweeping an assertion to declare that there are for all subjects which are discussed two parties; the one, generally in the majority, which is cautious and conservative, and the other, inventive and progressive   The world has recognised this by declaring in a popular saying that "there are always two sides to a question"   Those who are on the progressive side give us the new ideas which in due time are adopted; their first advisers being generally as soon forgotten as the pioneer who clears out the bush is forgotten by the farmer who succeeds him.

There is at present a question very much discussed by all who are interested in education.   Now as education is, if rightly considered, the most important social question in existence, it follows that one which involves its whole nature and progress must also be discussed from a conservative as well as radical point of view.   This question is—What shall be taught in schools, and how much?   How many hours can the average pupil study? How many branches of study can he take up? Are reading, writing, and arithmetic sufficient on this side the university—or the grave?—or is it a fact that the enormous latent capacity of the schoolboy has never yet been developed, and that he is like the monkeys which are supposed in Africa to be able to talk, or do anything which man can do, but refuse to display their talents for fear of being set to work? When one reflects on the vast number of things which journalists and orators tell us every schoolboy knows, it would indeed seem as if knowledge is supposed to be poured by the pedagogue into the brain with a funnel, as the Nuremberg people of old suggested it might be done.

Now it cannot be denied that this age, especially in England and America, exacts much more as regards knowledge than any preceding it ever did. We are proud of our intelligence, we wish our citizens to be generally "well informed." "Well informed" means the knowledge of a great deal, in fact almost as much as there is in the British or American Cyclopædia. It was for a long time popularly believed that all that pertains to true culture and useful knowledge could be "picked up" from newspapers and lectures. During that period of easy, happy faith, the universities were ridiculed; even high schools were looked at with suspicion. That was the golden age of Penny Magazines and Treasuries of Knowledge, and as yet an army of enterprising book-pedlars are living on its remains. But its glory has departed. Even the ideal "smart Yankee" who could get himself a fair classical and general education in three weeks, from the shop signs and placards of a city, has been compelled to reluctantly admit that the average human being who is his own schoolmaster generally has an ignoramus for a pupil.   It is not true that all the cleverness and "smartness," and picking up and self-educating in the world, and reading at odd hours, and studying in odd ways, will ever fully *educate* anybody.   ABRAHAM LINCOLN is a wonderful example of what perseverance under difficulties may effect   ABRAHAM LINCOLN was a man of a million, and yet to the end of his days he was always painfully conscious that he was an *uneducated* man, as every clever but uneducated man must be, unless vanity has fairly carried him away.   He had not brought himself into identity or easy relation with the world's culture, he could not understand or feel without an effort the things which a really educated mind takes in or recalls naturally.   My authority for saying all this, which is so repugnant to popular opinion, is that of one of the most distinguished men of science whom America ever brought forth.   He was a college professor, entirely self-educated, and so far as the results of study are concerned he was far beyond ABRAHAM LINCOLN, yet he often said, "There is not a day of my life in which I do not regret the want of a regular education."

The basis of this popular error, this trust in the efficacy of Penny Magazines and the superiority of irregular haphazard self-culture, is the false belief so very generally current that education, in the main, means only the acquisition of knowledge   Even those who disavow it really believe it and act up to it.   They are like idolaters, who in every climate glibly declare that their idols are only symbols of an invisible God, yet who do really adore the wooden or painted image itself, as is shown by their belief in its miraculous powers The more ignorant and vulgar a man is, the more he thinks that knowledge alone is power, and that the school must give a certain equivalent in tangible acquisition for a certain sum of money. During the Middle Ages it was popularly believed that the mere knowledge of Latin in itself conferred strange and mystical power. We find this superstition perpetuated at the present day, for instance, in the exaggerated importance attached to the mere knowledge of many languages. It is like confining our admiration of a painter's works to his palette and brushes, and the apparatus of the studio To many children these constitute the marvel and mystery of art. The small boy is always under the impression that if he only possessed the paints and brushes, he could work wonders. The world is much like that boy, as regards education, which is in reality much more than knowledge.

We hear it continually admitted that education, as derived from *educere,* to draw forth, means the development of all the powers of the mind, and yet there is no practical manifestation of the faith If there were, we should hear nothing of too many studies being introduced, of pupils being crammed and overworked, or of a battle between the three R's and the three hundred requisites for culture. On the one hand, the age and increasing culture call for much and varied knowledge in the well-informed man ; on the other, the overtasked teacher and overworked pupil declare that it is quite impossible. And this is what we are to consider.

As regards the cry of " cramming," I am reminded

of the fairy tale of the girl who was required to put all the milk of a herd of cows into a pail. She did it by miraculous aid. At present science would do the same without any miracle, by condensing it into a solid powder. It was an axiom that a pint cup filled to the brim with water would hold no more, until some philosopher discovered that added little by little you could also put into it almost another pint of salt Few will deny that if school-children had better memories or quicker powers of apprehension they could learn more. We can add the salt of industrial art. And yet, knowing this, we go on, assuming the memory to be a constant quantity, and trying to find out how much we can cram or force into it, instead of improving its absorptive powers or concentrating that which it is to absorb. The great problem is whether, in addition to filling the memory, we cannot also first develop or *create* it.

Now it would seem that the first thing a child should learn is the art of learning And this is not taught at all We hear mothers boast of Miss, that she is learning French, and drawing, and German, and geometry, and history, and science, and has lessons in a dozen branches, and we know that it is all like Mr. Blimber's Academy, "ve-ry ex-pen-sive," and very genteel. But we do not know whether the young girl is being taught what is worth all of this, and more than twenty times more than all this—*the ability to master anything*. And yet there is no miracle or mystery in it, and there have been teachers who understood it, acted on it, and taught it. It consists simply in making the pupil learn everything *perfectly* from the beginning.

If a child were never allowed to "scamp" a lesson or learn it imperfectly, it would soon develop a stronger memory. It is really of little consequence what is at first learned, compared to the *manner* in which it is mastered. Whether the lesson be short or long, whether an hour or a week be allowed for that lesson, the pupil should never come into the class until it is learned, as the school-boy saying is, "up the middle and down the sides, inside and out" Be it spelling, arithmetic, grammar, or geometry, it should be so perfectly acquired that the recitation shall be simply *perfect*. And it should be so often reviewed as to put the least forgetfulness out of the question. We have an illustration of this in the so-called OLLENDORFF method of learning languages By mastering every lesson quite perfectly the pupil can always attain perfection through this method, but if a single stitch be dropped, the work is spoiled. Even in studying by OLLENDORFF, a pure pronunciation should precede the use of the book; otherwise the pupil will be impeded by the effort to learn two things at once. In one form or another there is a great deal of this dual difficulty tolerated in education.

There are certainly difficulties in thus developing memory and intelligence. Children often cheat their teachers as well as themselves in recitation. Who is not familiar with the wonderful girl who learns her lesson in ten minutes and forgets it all in five? Who does not know a boy who can conjugate a Latin verb *in due order*, so as to deceive the very elect of teachers, yet who, when called on to give the Latin for "*you might be*," is "all at sea?" There are the perplexing creatures, too, gifted with visual memory,

who, by shrewdly observing on what corner of the
book the teacher's eye is fixed, can recall the text?
There are those whose memory spasmodically, yet
obstinately, rejects certain words or subjects, and who
are more blamed for it than they should be.[1]   To
train memory or the power of acquiring and understanding in this way, requires not only unusual
patience, but great study of the pupil's peculiarities.
Therefore it is not attended to.   When I was young
I went to several so-called first-class private schools,
but there was not among them one in which the
pupils were made to feel that the power to learn a
lesson was at first of far greater importance than the
lesson itself.   Yet, on looking back, and living again
in that life, I can feel to the depths of conviction that
it could have been done

The multitude are perhaps not to blame for ignorance as to all this   They know that knowledge is
useful, they believe it is a power in itself, and they
think it must in some way be whipped or forced in,
no matter how.   "You can't drive that horse fifty
miles to-day," said a stable-keeper, aghast, to five
Cockneys.   "Vy not?" was the reply, " ve've all got
vips."   Now it is a principle of humanity that under
no circumstances should there be the immoderate use
of even a single whip.   There are few, even among
thinking and reasoning people, who like to change
their views, any more than they do their homes.
The prisoner feels a pang at leaving his cell.   Were
there not some of this principle implanted in us we
should have no stability, perhaps no principle what-

---

[1] I myself am one of these   If my "recording spirit" or memory
once realises that it *must* retain anything, it utterly refuses to do so

ever. But very good principles must yield to better when the hour comes It is painful, I admit, for a man born of a line of conservative ancestors, and in whose brain certain great grandfathers are still literally and automatically thinking by transmitted cerebration, when newer minds force upon him new ideas They tell him to discontinue the whip, or ask him for other arguments against a reform. And then you find out what he is, and whether his will and reason or his transmitted qualities and abilities are the strongest. If he is weak, he takes to special pleading, side issues, and hearsay evidence Thus in England the majority of people who plead for the use of the whip in prisons or in punishment tell you that since garroters have been whipped there is no more garroting. It is not true, since in fact garroting has increased, just as all kinds of brutality have increased since government has set the example of corporal punishment.[1] Men in all ages have shown a great disposition to model their family discipline upon that used by the authorities Many argue that we have all just so much memory allowed us, and that nobody can increase it. A wiser type of conservative admits your principle, but points out the difficulties in the way, and asks how they are to be broken. Such an objection is this: "What will you do if, in a class of ten, five pupils advance rapidly in acquiring memory or developing intelligence, while the other five are so slow as to seriously impede the clever ones?" Well, it is something gained if we admit that five could be made cleverer than they would otherwise have been, but I grant that this is really

---

[1] Harriet Martineau understood this. Carlyle did not.

a great difficulty, and the larger a class must be the greater the difficulty becomes   There are children who are prompt to avail themselves of unlimited kindness and indulgence, and who, like *Punch's* little boy, call at once for plum-cake when they hear that moral suasion is to be adopted.   They are capable of coming up every day for a month with the same and the easiest lesson always half-learned.   Yet strong as this objection is, it is not insuperable   A very clever teacher would not be troubled with it, for there are men who drive and direct the will of even the meanest boys as they please.   It would yield in many instances to the stimulus of rivalry   But the true resolvent of the objection lies in this—that if there is anything at all in the theory, and if the memory or power of perception can be at all stimulated beyond what it would have been under the old system, or if *any* beginning can be made at all, the pupil will inevitably gain on himself.   We all know that water when it once begins to run soon washes itself clean

Everybody admits that bad habits are soon formed. It is a pity that popular pessimism pays no attention to the fact that there are also many very good ones which may be quite as easily adopted   Now it is a very good habit for a boy in the beginning of his education to learn *how to learn* his lessons, and I believe this could be done by making him feel at first that the manner in which he gets his lesson, and the perfection of it, is the end aimed at.   As it is he thinks naturally enough that to *understand* the lesson in hand is all he has to do.   To get through it with the teacher is, as he believes, sufficient.   Now if he knew that to commit it perfectly as well as to understand it is *inevitable*, I believe that the dullest boy would soon take a different view of it. If he knew that it would come rolling back on him again and again until it was mastered, and yet again at any unforeseen hour as a review, he would take a new view of the situation. He should learn it so as to dispense with prompting—so as to take it up where the last boy left off, and to do this he should not in the beginning be impeded with many lessons or long ones In the end he would be able to grapple with twice as many tasks as he is now ever expected to study. For knowing that he had simply one thing to do, to get a lesson by heart and nothing more, and that this was exactly graded to his capacity, and that further he would not be perplexed by exerting his intelligence, he would attempt his task with more hope and less unwillingness than is the case with complex lessons.

In my youth I was at several schools and a college, and I am firmly convinced that there was in all an average waste or loss of time and work of at least fifty per cent., owing to the needless difficulty of the tasks allotted   I never once had a lesson that was not really harder than it should have been.   In a class of twenty the lessons are such as are easily learned by the two or three cleverest ones, and this is the standard for all.   It is a false one   It is exactly as if because a horse can occasionally do his mile in two minutes, he should be expected to keep that pace up all day.   A boy should never have a lesson which he cannot learn with ease, and it should be adapted to his intelligence and power of memory.   And therefore I would oppose with all my heart the principle of com-

I

petition in education where the object is not to teach
all as much as possible, but to reward a very few for
being cleverer than the rest, and so induce the majority
to neglect work.   We are told that there is no royal
road to learning.   If this be so, it is time we made
one
Very few people know what the average human
capacity or latent power of memory really is when
it is properly trained.   We have discovered that every
boy can learn to draw and design, despite the vulgar
error that it requires an innate talent.   A very few
years ago this was a general belief.   Now we have
learned that it was absurd.   But we have not learned,
as we shall, that the same time which a boy takes
to learn arithmetic might, if properly expended, render
his memory and power of quick perception almost
miraculous.   Yet it would in fact be no invention,
but only a re-discovery.   It is certain that for centuries in ancient India stupendous works, such as
few Europeans have now patience to read, were kept
in existence by memory before writing was known,
or at least before it was used for anything except
inscriptions.   We think it a great thing when a
scholar can repeat all the odes of HORACE, but what
must memory have been when thousands knew the
whole of that three hundred thousand-legged lyric, the
Mahabarata ?   The great grammar of the greatest of
grammarians, PANINI, was taught verbally and transmitted orally with a mass of commentaries by other
authors for three hundred and fifty years.   So were
the works of HOMER.   Among the disciples of PYTHA-
GORAS as among the ancient Druids and many other
schools of antiquity, memories were the sole or chief

libraries   I have been intimate with a learned Chinese who had passed the great examination of Pekin, and I am confident that, though quite a young man, his memory contained ten times as much as any European I ever met.   There are Jews living who can repeat by heart from any given word the whole of the Talmud, which is almost a library in itself   I am indebted to Mr. T. C. HORSFORD of Manchester for a well authenticated instance of memory in a Hindoo, which shows in a striking manner the degree to which memory by ear may be cultivated.   This man, who did not understand English at all, having had fifty lines of " Paradise Lost " read to him, repeated it accurately, and then rehearsed it backwards   It is very remarkable that in all European education children are set at hard intellectual tasks, on the theory that memory already exists, instead of giving them the proper training to create it.   It is just as if children should be set at physical labour far beyond their power, on the theory that strength will come at once.

There are a few old people yet living in the Highlands of Scotland who can repeat thousands of verses of Gaelic poetry.   I myself, in collecting the legends of the Algonquin Indians, have been amazed at the incredible masses of tradition which these Indians had retained, word by word, sometimes for sixty or seventy years.   Among the ancestors of the Scotch, as among the early Scandinavians and Teutons, not only were long epics and thousands of ballads preserved by the bards, but with them all the legends, history, and business affairs of their tribes.   There were among the Icelanders very learned lawyers, as I gather from the *Saga of the Burnt Njall.*   Their courts and legal proceedings very much resembled our own, but these jurists all carried their libraries under their hair. Now we know that these wonderful results were in all cases obtained by training the mind in boyhood with a view to developing the memory. Truly the first thing which should be taught is simple memory.

Before printing had been a century in use people found out that "the art preservative of arts" was destroying the art of memory. In *The Schyppe of Fooles*, a pedantic book-collector declares that all his learning is in his "bookes," though not in his head This widely spread and rapidly increasing habit of referring to books for much which had better be in the brain, is having its result intellectually in the increasing rarity in literature of very great and original men. Science, it is true, leads the clever men who follow it to great discoveries. But science is systematic, art is accidental. It seems wonderful indeed that the world still has great scholars and thinkers in the face of this great decay of memory. Fortunately many make exertions in after-life and recover something But they do not owe anything to early education for this. Education set them lessons, not to improve memory, but that lessons might be learned, and a certain amount of knowledge crammed into the mind. I never once heard, and I never dreamed during all my school-days, that perfection in the manner of learning my lessons was an *absolute* object I believed that I was taught arithmetic that it might help me in business affairs in future life, and geography that I might know about the world, and Latin that I might get into college; and as regarded the last I had suspicions that it was really of no use at all, but only a venerable heirloom

or custom. I know better now. I know that Latin
is one of the most valuable of mental disciplines, that
for a majority of students it is more valuable than
mathematics, and that any study properly conducted
should give us far more than mere knowledge. Is
it any wonder that we hear continual attacks on Greek
and Latin in education, when the only plea put forward in their favour by their professors is the value
of a knowledge of the classics? The ordinary man of
the world will always maintain, and rightly, that as
regards mere utility, and even mere accomplishment,
a knowledge of French and German is worth more
than that of "the classical tongues" But as regards
what should be the primary object of education, he is
wrong, for Latin and Greek, when thoroughly and properly taught, are unrivalled as a means of developing
memory and judgment. Discipline of the mind should
precede "knowledge."

I have heard the objection raised to such a thorough
method of teaching memory that it would have the
effect of making the pupil learn his lessons probably
very perfectly and rapidly, but possibly in an unin-
telligent way, so that he would catch like a magpie
and recite like a parrot, but understand no better
than an owl. It is, in fact, assumed that a *very*
excellent memory detracts from intellect, and in some
manner injures judgment or reflection. This is as if
it should be believed that a great knowledge of languages would prevent a man from fully appreciating
the literature which they contain, when in fact great
poets are mostly good linguists. The main point to
my purpose at present is that it shall be granted that
by training by a particular method, and with no other

end in view than to perfect the memory, it can be thus perfected How any memory, no matter how powerful it may be, can be prevented from becoming dominant over more valuable faculties, I propose to set forth in another chapter.

The world abounds in theories untried and untested, but the assertion that the memory of the average scholar may be improved indefinitely has been tested and tried to perfection. It was perfectly proved in the early ages, when there were no books, and when scholars were self-dependent. And with this the fact was proved during the Middle Ages that not merely the minority of men may have what would now be regarded as marvellous memories, but all who pretend to study at all. In the thirteenth and fourteenth centuries students flocked to universities by tens of thousands. Books were then very dear, and the ancient custom of committing whole works by heart still prevailed. What we read of the scholastic disputations of the Middle Ages, and what we observe of the colossal erudition then current, has often drawn forth the remark that there were giants in the land in those days. It is great scholarship at present to even know how to find out in books what we want to know

It is very currently and very incorrectly believed that this vast development of the memory kills off more active and more valuable powers, and that it makes the mind "a charnel-house for dead thoughts." In proof of this, instances are alleged of men who could master books at a single reading, or remember whole sermons and repeat the entire Bible, who were nevertheless not remarkably clever. All of these instances may be true, but one might as well argue that all clever arithmeticians are idiots because the most remarkable ready reckoner I ever met could do nothing but reckon. These one-sided minds are all very rare and exceptional cases. Where there is some incredible feat of memory in a feeble mind, it very often happens that the mind not having been gradually trained to retain, was stretched and exhausted by its effort. GEORGE BORROW tells us of a common Spaniard who thus destroyed his intellect by forcing his mind to retain a long poem in a language which he imperfectly understood. Young men at college sometimes improve their memories at the expense of their judgments or imaginations. These instances of minds ruined by overcharged memories only prove that they were not strengthened and trained beforehand to carry so much.

I have read a remarkable and a probably authentic case of a man who, owing to an accident or injury to his brain, became, after his health was recovered, feeble-minded, with the exception of his memory, which developed to a prodigious extent, so that he could repeat whole volumes after a single reading. But to argue from this against developing the memory would be entirely illogical. I have known an instance in which a young girl had been so trained by unprincipled and vulgar parents to exert only self-will and cleverness, that everything like truth, morality, or humanity had almost entirely disappeared. I have known another whose legs being crippled, all their muscular strength had gone to the arms. But neither of these cases would prove that young people should not be taught self-reliance, or that the arms need not be developed by exercise. For after all the fact remains, that in a vast majority of instances the man of letters, the thinker of the age, the poet and the scholar, are identical, and that all greatly require very good memories. For a language at least three thousand words must be learned, and all who search deeply into literature or science should know three or four languages.

There are some very interesting facts connected with the study of languages which go very far to verify what I have said as to the possibility of cultivating memory, and with it observation. To talk a language with aught like ease requires, as I have said, a knowledge of about three thousand words. As many of these come from the same roots, or are correlated, we may say that twenty-five hundred, or even two thousand, will barely suffice. Now I have found by inquiry and experiment that the average intellect can acquire about thirty words of a strange tongue in a day, and that it invariably diminishes the number to twenty-five, and then to twenty. This includes fixing the words in the memory by exercises or conversation, and constant reviewing. I remember when I was in Egypt that Prince HASSAN, son of the late Khedive, said he began the study of English by learning fifty words a day, but soon found himself obliged to reduce the number to thirty. Now at the rate of thirty words a day any one can learn three thousand words in one hundred days, and with them during the same time acquire considerable facility in using them. For such high pressure work as this I will suppose that from three to six hours are taken daily. But then I also assume that the language shall be a very strange one, such as colloquial Arabic, Hindustani, or Persian, in which the grammar is easy, but the words are quite foreign to the English speaker. Teutonic or Latin languages will be found easier. Now it is established that young pupils who are thus exercised in memorising vocabularies, and at the same time in working the words up as fast as they come in, soon acquire a remarkable facility in learning in this direction. It was essentially in this manner that Latin was taught to children till within two centuries; that is to say, during the days of great memories I have in my possession two works, probably the first ever published, for the purpose of teaching little boys Latin One, of the fifteenth century, by MURMELLIUS, in black letter, is in German, the other in English. The latter gives a great number of woodcuts illustrating all the trades and professions, in which every object is numbered. Thus over a blacksmith is *one*, over his hammer *two*, over the anvil *three*. Under the picture and in type we find, *one, faber ferrarius*, a blacksmith; *two*, a hammer, *malleus; three*, an anvil, *incus*. Beneath the vocabulary are exercises; giving the inflections, conjugations, &c, in conversation This simple method would be laughed at now in these days of philosophic grammars and systems, but after all there were a hundred boys then in the fifteenth century who could not only read and write, but even *talk* Latin, where there is one now. There was an immense advantage in thus teaching Latin familiarly and colloquially, that the students were soon interested in "the classics" As it is, with the very great majority, Latin or Greek is one dry and wearisome grind from the beginning to the end.

Latin is no longer taught as a living tongue, nor

memory as a *means* of learning anything. Step by step tuition has shrunk from the vital and practical in these, as in many other matters, to the formal, timid, and difficult. We would like to have great scholars, great results, and great general information, and we employ the pettiest means to pursue them. We are like the Indian who believed that the earth rested on a tortoise, but what the tortoise rested on he did not know. We are aware that knowledge is based on study, but that study itself could have a foundation is not dreamed of in our philosophy.

This training children to very great thoroughness in the beginning, or to absolute exactness and perfection in the acquisition of lessons, with no regard at first as to acquiring mere knowledge, would be a little more difficult for the teacher at the beginning, and a great deal easier for him long before the end It seems to me that to make a pupil try to acquire the art of memory and knowledge at the same time with it is very much like the current error of making a student learn to pronounce a language, acquire its form, and learn a new handwriting to put it in all at once Dr. SCHLIEMANN, the archæologist and discoverer, who is at the same time a remarkable linguist, says that the only way to acquire a language rapidly and perfectly is to learn the pronunciation perfectly before attempting anything else. I never knew of but one person who acquired French "like a native" after twenty-five years of age In this case it was effected by studying the pronunciation and nothing else for many weeks at the beginning. *One thing at a time, and that thing perfectly,* is the golden rule of learning.

Most people will be ready to admit that children should from the beginning be obliged to learn their lessons perfectly. But as a matter of fact is it ever done? Did anybody ever witness or experience such instruction? I never did in any country. I mean apart from the subject-matter of the lesson, adhering to a single text-book, caring nothing for *what* the pupil is learning, but everything as to how he learns it, until the growing grasp shows that the strength thus acquired may be set to useful, more intelligent work.

Now it is well known to everybody who is practically familiar with manual arts, that a man may carve in wood, or work in plastic material, separately without knowing how to draw; but if he can draw, though but a little, all these arts, and many others with them, become much easier, because all modelling and relief-working are only applied drawing. So it is with memory, which is to all learning whatever what drawing is to the fine arts. And by proper tuition it is as easy to acquire the one as the other. The mistake which we make lies in believing that memory is entirely an innate force, of which some have more and some less, not to be materially varied by culture, while we all practically act in the faith that if it can be increased, it is to be done while acquiring knowledge, simultaneously with it. Now it is a fact that while beyond a certain point of proficiency one branch of study or one art strengthens and assists another, *within* that point, if it does not positively hinder, it certainly does not help. That is to say, that after a man has learned several languages thoroughly, or several arts, or several branches of study of any kind, the studying several at once will be advantageous, but, until memory has been greatly improved, it will not. Therefore it seems that in the beginning there should be as few varieties of study as possible, that there may be more in the end. The strength of the trunk must be in proportion to the weight and number of the branches.

It is difficult to imagine on what grounds any opposition could be made to such a system of education as this which I propose. The sternest opponent of novelties and of reforms can hardly object to the proposition that pupils should be obliged to learn their lessons perfectly. Now to learn *perfectly* involves at first only one or two subjects studied with great care Learning perfectly, let me say, also involves the exercise of intelligence as well as memory These are mutual aids As it is, in most schools, the object is to get the pupils over as many lessons as possible in a certain time, instead of making them as clever as possible in that time The text that the letter killeth, but the spirit giveth life, is as applicable in education as to religion. As the Germans would say, we make our education objective when it should be subjective It certainly cannot be said that this method of educating memory is an untried novelty, when we reflect that it was in successful operation for thousands of years, during which time the greatest triumphs of intellect were achieved. It is not a mere conjecture of mine that in order to remember whole libraries perfectly, the memories of the students of ancient India were systematically trained beforehand and strengthened "As far back as we know anything of India," says MAX MÜLLER, "we find that the years which we spend at school and at the university were spent by the sons of the three higher classes in learning from the mouth of a teacher their sacred literature. This was a sacred duty, the neglect of which entailed social degradation, and the most minute rules were laid down as to the mnemonic system that had to be followed. Before the invention of writing there was no other way of preserving literature, whether sacred or profane, and, in consequence, every precaution was taken against accidents. Stranger still is the fact that those Brahmans who may be considered the especial guardians of the sacred traditions of India in our own day do not employ either the written or the printed texts in learning and transmitting their holy lore." "They learn it, as their ancestors learned it thousands of years ago, from the mouth of a teacher, so that the Vedic succession should never be broken," and so well do they perform the duty and so accurately do they transmit the text, that " there is hardly a various reading in the proper sense of the word, or even an uncertain accent in the whole of the *Rig-Veda*, which consists of more than a thousand hymns, averaging ten verses, and contains more than one hundred and fifty thousand words."

Educated as we are, we think with impatience, or else with unreasoning admiration, of these stupendous feats of memory. We say, what is the use of it all? or else wonder at the superior patience and memory of the Hindoo. Now the Hindoo has, by nature, no better memory than the Englishman, as is shown by the many young Indians at the English universities. As for calling such perfect study a waste of time, I would like to ask if the average university graduate is, on leaving college, any better off than the Hindoo? The Greek and Latin which he has acquired is half learned, his memory has not been one quarter trained He has experienced the refining influences of culture and of scholarly association, but his mental strength has not been awakened. Now be it observed—and this is a very strong point—that despite all our libraries, lectures, newspapers, and progress we of the nineteenth century have no more surpassed or even equalled the Sanskrit-writing Hindoos in literature or thought than we have the Greeks in art. Our scholars are beginning to recognise Buddhism as the most stupendous and brilliant *system* ever invented by man; no dramatist of our age has equalled KALIDASA. I regard the story of Vikram and the Vampire as the most perfect work of humour ever written,[1] while PANINI has never been equalled as a grammarian The fact that the early ages when memory was so much cultivated also brought forth correspondingly great works of intellect deserves to be seriously studied. SCHLIEMANN, in his *Ilios*, tells us that his memory was *bad* originally, but that he so perfected it by an indomitable *will* and hard work, that he at last learned a new language every six months, so as to write and speak it perfectly. As he was all the time engaged in business, in which he eventually made a large fortune, as a wholesale grocer, we may see that even at the present day there are practical men who appreciate the virtue of thoroughness

Let me give a last illustration of the possibility of creating a powerful memory in the young by means of

---

[1] Not so humorous as the works of RABELAIS, it makes a far higher application of humour.

practice. Japanese children, like Chinese, must pass at least two years in studying mere letters or signs before the process of reading may be said to begin. The study is intensely hard, much harder than anything known in our schools, and involves the exercise of memory only. The result is, that among the literary men of Japan we meet with wonderful instances of learning There is a work entitled the *Koshi Seibun*, which is a great compilation of all the myths and early legends of Japan, made in the year 1812 by the learned HIRATA ATSUTANE. "It is said," according to SATOW, "that he composed the three volumes of the text and several volumes of the introduction without opening one of the books from which his materials were drawn." In fact he had been many years employed in what we may call writing it on his brain Every sentence of it was in his mind before he touched a pen, and his authorities were, so to speak, hung up before his eyes, and not stowed away in places whence they might or might not be recalled when wanted.

"What man has done man may do." What was done of old by our Aryan ancestors or their sons can be done by us. The art of printing should have been our staff; we have made of it a crutch, and used it till we cannot walk without it. There is no reason why man in gaining so much from science should not also regain all his own strength which has been lost.

I have intimated that the radical defect of our present system of elementary education lies in our teaching the pupil too much at once. Thus a boy of let us say eight years, set at the Latin grammar, is expected to train or develop his memory, his pronunciation, and his understanding conjointly, or at one and the same time. A man can learn to play on six instruments at once, but no great performer was ever made by such training. The education of the future, like chemistry, will owe its improvement, first of all, to *analysis*. We shall teach memory separately from what is now supposed to be the main object of every lesson. Common sense will tell every thinker that this cannot be in every case mere memory. The mind of the dullest scholar—or even of the quickest, who are generally the most heedless and likely to forget—will always take in so much of the sense of the text as will serve for mortar to the bricks thus made. But in the beginning the lesson should be solely for memorising. Such epithets as "parrot-like" will not be spared as regards this system, but it is not intended that the training shall cease with the acquisition of memory

To put the system of developing memory into practice is not difficult. The parent or teacher should begin by giving the pupil *very easy lessons* in an English text-book. Proverbs or texts from Scripture are to be commended, since they are almost invariably in pure, simple, easy English. One thing only is to be insisted on, that the lesson for the day be learned *perfectly*, and that no effort be made to explain the text, as this will introduce a new and entirely foreign element. Therefore it will be well to select lessons which the pupils already understand. One half of every lesson, after the first one, should consist of reviewing the previous lessons. It will hardly be believed by old-fashioned teachers, but it is true, that most children take pleasure in thus memorising when the lessons are not too long. It was the great fault of all my teachers in my youth, that from the infant-school to the university there was not one who did not require lessons which were far too long for the majority of the class to acquire perfectly. Those who were slow or not clever were shamed by the example of the more gifted; but while it sometimes made them work harder and out of due proportion to their abilities, it did not change their natures or encourage them. The simple development of memory alone, if "parrot-like," is both easy and agreeable, especially if the teacher, instead of regarding the aim of the lesson to be a set task to be equally mastered by strong and weak, looks upon the development of each mind to be the main object

Under the present current system the chief intention is that the pupil shall simply learn a lesson. By memorising with absolute accuracy—this only being required—the dullest pupils soon perceive that they are working, not to master a fact, but a faculty. The only reason why we have not more clever scholars is because great account is made of facts and very little of faculties A prize-fighter in training knows that the object of all his daily sparring and exercise is to become strong, but we teach children as if the exercise in itself was to be the end of all.

When children can recite and recall at will several scores or hundreds of texts, proverbs, short poems, or similar sentences with *perfect* accuracy, it will be found that the faculty of memorising has begun to manifest itself. At this stage the teacher or parent may at any time begin to give out, without book, phrases to be learned. Very great care should be taken not to

K

do this prematurely. This will be found to be a very critical stage of education. It should not be attempted until the child invariably masters the printed text This will not require nearly so much time as would be supposed. In about three months pupils of ten years of age will begin to manifest a remarkable increase of power in memorising It should not be carried on or confused with any other lessons at first After from four to six months' practice, the exercises in quickness of perception, described elsewhere in this book, may be begun. These greatly aid memorising In time they will form one with it, both in due order uniting with hand-work or constructiveness to make a whole.

When the pupil can learn and repeat from reviewing many proverbs or sentences, and has been found capable of grasping and retaining phrases given verbally, his or her mind will be invariably in a very interesting condition A new and really wonderful *power* then begins to manifest itself. The force of this power, which makes it marble to retain, as well as wax to receive, lies entirely in frequent reviewing. It is a very curious fact that the more vigorously and frequently the reviewing or reviving lessons is exercised, the quicker the memory or "mind" is to receive first lessons. Such is the theory or method of the Oriental sages, who have achieved miracles of mental grasp. From this critical point memorising has two forms—one that of printed matter, the other that of spoken sentences. To such an extent can both be carried that it will become perfectly possible for a youth to recall, not vaguely and by association, but directly, every word heard during an entire day

It is perfectly possible to train any average mind t recall with absolute accuracy every word of an acte play, of a sermon, or of a conversation. And thi can be done without weakening the mind in any manner. On the contrary, such exertions of memory when carried on under the influence of a correlative training in quickness of perception, greatly strengthei all its powers.

From this time poems and literary extracts, whicl should be always so easy to comprehend as to require no explanation, may be learned At the same time the exercises in committing verbal tasks may take a wider range. If the pupil manifests decided or superior power of memorising after four or five months of practice, the lessons in quickness of perception should begin. It will generally be found that after six months the ability to simply commit lessons will have increased so rapidly that more time should be devoted to reviewing than to memorising. After â year the latter will become the chief exercise, in due time it will constitute the only one. With earnest work, in twelve months most pupils of ten or twelve years will have acquired what would now be called a wonderful memory Younger pupils will learn easily, but the reviewing will be for them more difficult. Those who are older will learn easily if they *will*, but they will be far more apt to confuse the meaning of the text with mere memorising.

Any teacher or parent who has taught successfully for six months will know how to adapt the lessons to the pupil's progress and capacity. As the learner's memory improves, of course longer sentences from more advanced works must be given. If the ear has been well trained, sentences in languages unknown to the scholar may be at times tried. It is needless to say that at this stage exercises in reading, pronunciation, or elocution will not interfere with memorising, but that on the contrary they will materially aid it. This forms a second critical period, to be closely watched, since lessons may now be studied with more regard to meaning. No rules can exactly determine when the pupil shall cease to merely memorise; it must depend chiefly on the discretion of the teacher

As it is the first notes of the bird which determine his future song, so the first teaching of the boy or girl goes far to determine the accuracy and quickness with which sentences can be grasped and retained. It may here be observed that both in memorising and in acquiring quickness of perception the beginning is almost mechanical. This is more than remarkable, it is encouraging, since it induces the belief that sluggish and stupid children may be rendered quick and clever by being led through mere practical adroitness to thought How often we find in a boor a certain shrewdness or activity of mind induced by experience The Germans have a word *dummklug*, or "stupid-cunning," which exactly expresses this condition. It is too generally assumed by most people that whatever is is immutable, be it for good or bad, be it an usage of society or the mental condition of a child If my practical experiments in education have conducted me to any belief or conclusion, it is that every child not actually idiotic or mentally diseased is capable of infinite intellectual development, if a proper method of education or of development be applied for the purpose. And for the rudimentary stages certain merely mechanical or very simple processes, as yet but little used, are of great value.

The pupil must be taught from the first to use the will, and to understand what this means Thus I may see an object for hours, or every day, without my taking much notice of it, or without its being impressed on my memory. But if I look at it intently, and try with closed eyes to repeat the image, in a word, if I WILL to do so, and if I repeat this a few times at intervals, I shall perhaps remember it always. By repeating the process very frequently with other objects I shall soon acquire the power of easily recalling objects visibly Now there are children who can in a listless way con over a lesson scores of times without learning it, just as we may see objects every day without remembering them, all because they do not use the will or make decided efforts to retain it If these children had been trained in memorising alone, they would not relapse into such apathy. For it is much easier to excite the action of the will on a single simple subject than on a difficult and complex one In most primary education, at present, the *will* is discouraged or enfeebled by having tasks set it which are too confusing and too difficult.

Every musician knows to what an extraordinary degree the memory of sounds may be developed. If these sounds thus retained iepresented words and thoughts, none of the instances which I have given of Oriental scholarship would seem remarkable. The musician is trained to remember sound alone: if children were in like manner exercised on words alone, they would call into being a power which would in time enable them to recall words, sounds, sights, and *thoughts ad libitum*

It is not unusual to see men devote many months or years to learning shorthand   In the majority of attempts years are required before the student becomes absolutely proficient.   If the same time were devoted to memorising, it would be found that note-books are needless, and that the reporter need only listen to the speech or play which he expects to write out at home or in "the office."   Every one is aware that there have been exceptional cases of people who could remember anything from a single hearing or reading. The day is not far distant when it will be as generally admitted that by a simple process of early training every child may acquire the same power

Part III

ON CREATING QUICKNESS OF PERCEPTION.

"Blood goes far, but breeding farther"
—Old Icelandic Proverb

IT would be as interesting as important to be able to determine "how much, how far, what way, and by what means" the average mind may be developed or changed by education and circumstance from what it is? CARLYLE has wisely assured us that no culture will develop a cabbage into an oak, though he benevolently admits that training may determine whether the cabbage shall be a good or a bad one. The comparison is too limited, and unjust. Man is no more a vegetable than he is a mineral. Had Mr. CARLYLE risen to the animal kingdom, his simile would have been better   Let us say that a lion cannot become a dog, since no two types of mankind differ more than the extremes of these animals. Yet, by training, the dog was developed by the Assyrians of old into a beast so monstrous and ferocious that it could grapple with the lion, while the king of beasts in captivity is often degraded into a very currish creature. Most of the people whom we meet declare that we are clever or the contrary, according to our "gifts" or natural endowments, although they generally assume full credit for all the talents they possess. What they *have* they tell you they got by exercise of will and hard work; what they have not, cruel Nature, they say, denied them. There are very few people who have been too lazy to study languages or to draw who do not declare that they have "no faculty" or talent for such acquisitions, there are quite as few who have learned something of either who do not take full credit for having done so by cleverness. From which we may learn that vanity is often the popular measure of human capacity

I believe that observation and experiment would very much enlarge the sphere now assigned to this human capacity Let us suppose that four English infants, of average English brain, are removed to, and grow up in, four foreign countries The one is educated in the Frenchiest of French circles in a provincial town, among shrewd and lively but very narrow-minded people, with whom a certain quickness of observation in all small matters is greatly admired, by whom no pettiness of mind is reprehended, so that it be kept from openly offending, and to whom the theatrical in life is the real standard of morality. Another child grows up in an old-fashioned German circle, equally excluded from all foreign influences, but among well-educated people who assume, as a matter of course, that culture in every form of literature and art must be absorbed by whatever is a rational human being. They are extremely strict in certain points of morality and etiquette, in others they are tolerant to looseness. The third child may be brought up in the most reckless and independent circle of the Western United States, and the fourth in an aristocratic or royal family of Inner India, Siam, or Burmah   Now can any one doubt that when grown up these children, who would have been in all probability very much alike had they developed in England, will be entirely different from one another, and manifest talents and abilities of such varied quality that most men meeting them would not hesitate to declare that their natures were "radically different."   However much their ancestry might manifest itself from time to time in force of will or talent, training would tell to the extent of developing new talents and tastes. In one of the four at least some inherited ability or characteristic which would have fallen on stony ground in England would spring forth in rank luxuriance, in another case something would be repressed. I may remark, in this connection, that I have observed that young Americans in England Anglicise' very slowly, while English youth in America, and even English grown men, Americanise unconsciously with startling rapidity, and lose very slowly the characteristics thus acquired   Young Americans and Englishmen Germanise rapidly, but they acquire French characteristics very slowly after mere boyhood.   In the East even grown-up European gentlemen who have lived many years entirely among the natives often develop to a striking degree all the external polish, all the shallow deceitfulness, all the transparent reserve and suspicion which intuitively repel intimacy, and which are so characteristic of the higher class Oriental.   I knew one of this kind who could not apparently do the simplest thing without involving in it some reserved "dodge" or wily hidden device, which could be plainly seen through, just as one sees through the deeply laid devices of an artful child He had lived at an Oriental court for many years, seeing very little of Europeans, until his English nature had become entirely Eastern, and full of "tricks that were vain."

Now, making every allowance for any manifestations of the original English nature, no one who had studied such cases as these would deny that they would in fact radically refute much of the popular presumption that the mind is incapable of any great deviation from what it has shown itself to be. Of the greatest interest and value would be the knowledge not only how much children can change according to their culture, but what are the leading and latent faculties which may be brought out to greatest advantage I incline to think that of all these the one which would exercise the most influence on the character is the faculty of immediate or quick perception This and memory, I believe, are susceptible of artificial culture to a degree which is little dreamed of, and from these great intellectual results may be derived.

It is to be observed that as parents or others decide that a child is "naturally quick" or "naturally slow," they cast its horoscope for life. Now it would be more than merely "interesting," it would be a matter of immense importance, to know whether we could not in our schools at home bring to bear influences which would have as great an effect on the young as a foreign education. A boy brought up among French boys will be much more observant of all that is droll, *gauche*, or "characteristic," than if he had been educated in Germany; and in whatever country he might have been trained he will develop in it a certain kind of quickness or power peculiar to the nation. If he is brought up at sea he will start from the soundest sleep at hearing an alarmed whisper, although the whisperer himself can hardly hear his own voice in the tumult of the storm. If trained on the American prairies he will be as readily roused by the imitated sound of an owl's cry or a wolf's howl, although he will not mind the original. Could we conceive a boy as brought up from infancy as a girl, and kept in innocent ignorance of his own sex, like MADEMOISELLE DE CHOISY, who will doubt that he would acquire all the usual feminine quickness of perception as to the details of dress? In every kind of calling we can see, if we will, wonderful instances of development, of readiness and tact when necessity has been the master. Whether quick or slow by nature, the boy of European or American birth will, as boys go, develop, according to his education, such a variety of quickness of perception, in so many degrees, as to fairly justify us in concluding that if we had only duly mastered the subject, the means exist of enabling us to make any child observant. A man may judge very wisely of a thing when he sees it, and yet be slow to observe; another may see everything, and form no judgment whatever   But judgment was never any the worse for quick perception, nay, it often springs from it. Those who *see* readily think rapidly.

I have elsewhere spoken of the manner in which thieves train dull boys to become observant, and how by merely practising with the eyes in watching objects in motion these children in time are able to take in at a glance and remember all that is in a room.[1] Children who play at games requiring cleverness are generally "brighter" in many or most respects than those who do not. The degree to which whist-playing improves the perceptive faculties and the memory is well known.

There is an American artist, EDWARD A. SPRING, who, while teacher in a military academy, tested with best results the possibility of creating quickness of perception in its primary stages. He would write a word, in letters three inches long, on a card or on a revolving blackboard. This was rapidly conveyed or turned from the right hand to the left, giving the class opportunity for a mere glance at it   At first no one could distinguish the letters, in time the young eyes caught everything   Then the letters were diminished in size and multiplied in number. At last, instead of presenting, for example, the word BAT, there were on the card only the parts of the letters separated, *e g*, $|\ \mathrel{\mathrm{3}} \ /\!\backslash - |\ ^-$ This was still more difficult; but in time even this by no means easy eye-conundrum was promptly solved, as were others of a similar nature.   At the time of which I speak, all the rocks and walls were covered with the well-known ST. C 1860-X advertisement.   Mr. SPRING one day prepared a card with the letters SP C. 1861-Z   Of course the entire class on being asked what it was replied ST. C. 1860-X   This led to deceptive tests, but the boys, forewarned, became still more observant In fine, the principle was fully tested, and I am happy to say that Mr. SPRING fully agrees with me in

[1] *Vide* Eye Memory.

believing that by beginning with merely mechanical experiments which simply awaken quickness of sight, we can step on imperceptibly to those which make the pupil quick to observe not only with the eyes but with the mind The result of this is an increased tendency to contrast and compare, to perceive antitheses and affinities of colour and of form in the visual world, and eventually to do the same as to ideas in intellectual action. This is the true golden chain of culture.

I believe that every teacher of a Kindergarten can prove that quickness of perception is not merely drawn out of children, but that it is actually *created* in them by the exercises which are practised under FROEBEL'S system I remember to have heard that a lady at some wayside resting-place or hotel was very desirous to know of what kind of strange children a certain party might be which burst one summer day into the reception-room. They observed the dimensions of the furniture, they compared the colours, they noted the design of the carpet, and all things in the room or pertaining to it; for they were pupils of a Kindergarten, and had been trained to perceive, and that promptly, by a clever teacher. But for their education, doubtless the faculty of quick perception would have remained dormant in many, and with it other talents would have slumbered

There are still many people who, after reading all this, will say it merely amounts to what everybody knows—that a good education develops our faculties, and that they may lie dormant without it. But I mean more than this. I mean that as in acquiring knowledge by study the development of the memory should precede everything, so in regard to all culture or conduct the mind should be trained to quick perception, and with a determined view to draw it out and balance the memory. We know enough when a man is to have a prize-fight or a foot-race, or take part in a rowing-match, to train his muscles beforehand, but as regards the memory or quick perception we wait till the match comes off in the struggle for life, and bid the pupil become strong or train while fighting for the prize An examination of all that has been drawn out of the mind, or to what it has been raised in different ages and in different lands, cannot fail to convince us that education has not kept pace with science in its advance. The professor has distanced the schoolmaster.

It must be admitted that while quickness of perception or mental activity is closely allied to and forms a part of the highest intellectual action, and even seems to be a stimulus to the *will* itself, the methods which I have commended for awakening it are quite objective or physical, if not purely mechanical There are few boys so dull that they cannot be made bright by the process followed by the London thieves, so far as mere observation is concerned. But what an immense advance is it towards thought when a boy has cleared the space between eyes and no-eyes, between noticing and not noticing! Now it is no novelty that bodily quickness and litheness are in many respects allied to and productive of corresponding mental qualities. It was not without reason that the writers of the last century really believed that fencing had a great effect in forming character. "Any one," says the old general in "Claude Melnotte," "who has carte and tierce at his finger-ends, is a gentleman." "The rhetorician," says a writer in the London *Globe*, "was recommended to engage in it so as to acquire ease of gesture," while WRIGHT, the author of the "School Orator," declares that "it diffuses elegance and ease all over the body, and even characterises the look and gesture with an appearance of intellectual vigour."

It would be not only interesting but important to decide whether the extraordinary difference as to observation of certain things which exists between men and women is not quite as much due to the difference between the games and physical culture of boys and girls as to any innate difference. While they are far more observant than men as to each others' clothes, or of objects in shops, or indeed of anything which is of *personal* concern, women pay little attention to anything of *general* interest. They do not notice placards on walls, while caricatures and comic pictures in shop windows are only looked at by men or boys. Once when I was an editor I was very much annoyed by visitors knocking at the door So I wrote in very legible large red and black letters three inches long, COME IN WITHOUT KNOCKING, and put it on the door. I soon had occasion to observe after this, whenever I heard a knock, that it was made either by a negro or a lady The negroes could not read, and the ladies did not. This does not in my opinion prove that there is a radical mental difference between the sexes, but that a great difference has been caused by early education and habits. This may indeed have become hereditary and a source of unconscious cerebration, but it would be removed in time

All the sports of boys tend to produce quickness, self-confidence, and universality of perception; those of girls bear on themselves only. The nursing by a girl of a doll, which is the replica of herself, is entirely conducive to self-concentration, and teaching her that she herself is born to be petted. There are great advantages in it, and yet it would be better if girls were trained more to physical culture, more to vigorous exercise, and less to tenderness and dainty egotism. The fear lest they should be "unfeminine" is misplaced when it makes them effeminate even a tomboy is much likelier to take good and proper care of herself in life than a mere "pet" I know what the prejudices of society are, and what sentimentalism has to say on this subject, but the most plausible of its assertions would be ludicrous and laughable did' they not entail so much wrong to women and such disaster. The assumption in America that a whisky-sodden foreign peasant, who cannot read, is fitter to decide by vote as to public officers in the United States than the average American woman is charmingly grotesque.

Boys are more generally observant than girls, principally because being naturally of the belief that they are of the stronger sex they cultivate sports and practices to be continued through life, which develop quickness and observation different from that developed by the other sex. They create will out of faith. I believe that this difference will, in a great measure, disappear with culture. I do not believe that woman can become mentally stronger than man, or ever equal him physically. But I believe that as man progresses woman will also advance, and that many points of difference which are now a source of injustice and of suffering must disappear. But there is a very important matter which has been as yet quite left out of sight in considering woman's place in politics. It is this, that as no household is well managed without her influence, and no education *truly humane* into which it has not entered, so there can be no government and no policy truly perfect without it. In the most brutal and barbarous states of society woman is the least respected; those who would keep her back are those who at heart retain most of the savage.

In recommending such very radical methods in education as beginning it by developing memory and quickness of perception before proceeding to the actual acquisition of knowledge, I recommend a fundamental thoroughness which I am aware is most distasteful to what is called "the American mind." This "mind" represents a clever crude youthfulness which is inordinately vain of its genius and its successes, which loves short-cuts, chances, and lucky hits, and which is most impatient of plodding hard work and of discipline. The result of this is, according to the researches of American statists, that in no country is there such a waste of labour and capital in speculation, or in endeavours to get rich in a hurry, and most assuredly none in which so many youths leave college knowing so little, or with minds so feebly trained. We are "a wonderful people," and we certainly can show for a wonder the greatest number of graduates with a mere smattering of Greek, the fewest lines of Latin, and the least knowledge of their own literature "of any civilised nation on earth's face." This also is a waste of the best capital—time.

When HOBBES the philosopher was six years of age, he was, like GOETHE, and many others who have become great, already at Greek. "How often does it happen," says Professor GEORGE S. MORRIS in his "British Thought and Thinkers," "or does it *ever* happen, in free America, that youth are thus early directed into the way of genuinely humane culture? How many of us, who repute ourselves liberally educated, have not been painfully conscious, that, at the age of twenty-five or thirty, or even later, we were still painfully limping over ways in which, not simply the enthusiasts of learning in an earlier time, but the men who, in Europe, as thinkers and statesmen, now lead our civilisation . . . while not only they, but thousands of their less distinguished but classically educated contemporaries, were already in youth vigorous runners. We have yet to learn as a nation not to waste our time in disputing about the value of different styles of education, but to go on and educate ourselves by early, persistent, thorough, and never-ceasing training We may claim that our national temperament is such that early and persevering mental application is dangerous for us. But patient thought and study are not half so perilous for our nerves and brains as the passionate fret and worry incident to the strife for the possession of the thousand, now alleged, necessaries of decent existence—comforts, luxuries, knick-knacks, places of honour, means of showing-off, the not desiring which we are accustomed to regard as denoting lack of honourable ambition, or ignorance of that which makes life worth living. Genuinely patient thought and study are as much a sedative as an excitant, for they bring the repose of strength."

I cannot understand what objection can be raised to the principle which I advance, that quickness of perception should be cultivated in children as a means of awakening observation, and as conducive to taking an interest in all things within the scope of a child's mind. This is already done to a certain extent in the Kindergarten. When the Kindergarten becomes the care of the State, and shall be incorporated into the regular system of public education, then it is probable that this—which with memory forms the most important factor of mind—will be duly developed with scientific care by the ablest intellects. For a day is coming when education, and not petty politics and the personal interests of mere ignorant demagogues, will claim the active care of the people

Games and sports are of great importance in developing quickness of perception in childhood, and for this reason the subject deserves great study, that those may be encouraged which are most conducive to cleverness. I believe that amusements may be made as helpful to mental ability as to bodily strength and health. In the great English schools six hours a day must be devoted to play, and six to study. Seen from a higher point of view all this play is really study, as serious in the results as any book-learning. When I was a boy, play with the most indulgent parents was barely tolerated, in too many cases it was directly discouraged. Hearty games were supposed to be attributes of street-boys At the colleges and universities there was then the same dislike of amusement. Students who were known to play at ten-pins or billiards were ignominiously dismissed. At my own Alma Mater in America, there was literally no notice taken by anybody of the recreation or health of the students, beyond enforcing rules prejudicial to them.

I am speaking entirely of the olden time, long ago, when such ignorance did manifest itself not infrequently. But still, strange as it may seem, considering the perfection to which schools are believed to have been brought, something still remains to be done as regards recreation and health. Much could be suggested, much discovered, much applied, with happy results, even in such trifling matters as amusements. For it is a fact that there are games which are positively superior to any book-work whatever in awakening that quickness of perception which, once awakened, goes forth into all the faculties, arousing new life, even as light goes into all the worlds. No one will deny that the street-boy who is obliged to make his living as he can about town, develops, of a kind, far greater cleverness, shrewdness, and observation than the pet of the nursery. This cleverness is perverted to low aims, but it might just as well have been developed in study, in personal politeness, or in anything good. If a hundredth part of the genius which has been given to scientifically difficult Latin grammars and astonishingly useless algebras had been devoted to sports for developing quickness of mind, the world would have been the better for it.

A very great objection often urged as to stimulating memory and quickness of perception in childhood, is that they would awaken a precocity which would probably be followed by premature mental decay, or the development of certain faculties at the expense of others. I call especial attention to this, for it is an objection as plausible as it is false. Every one who has ever known a feeble-minded boy crammed to idiocy—and who has not?—will perhaps be prompt or prone to declare against any new invention to force undue cleverness into youth. And many, too, who have come across a child with one special natural inherited talent, which has been carefully developed at the expense of every other faculty, will declare that it was the result of overdoing the youthful capacity Now, it is very true that it is not advisable to draw all the mind into one talent, any more than it would be to sacrifice the growing strength of the legs to feed that of the arms. But I utterly deny that any amount whatever of development of the memory in childhood would have any injurious effect, if it should be properly counterbalanced by an equal development of quickness of perception. And an examination into examples proves not only this, but that an astonishing proportion of great men have been precocious, and that this precocity was due to early education by teachers who had hit upon methods analogous to those which I now urge Much is also due, of course, in many cases to hereditary endowment, but of this transmitted excellence, while I believe in it, I would remark that it is like wit and stories of witchcraft, wherein the lucky hits and strange coincidences stick, and the misses are never counted There are, after all, a great many clever people who do not have clever children, owing to something falling short in tissue or cells, caused by neglect of health or the cropping out of some feeble-minded ancestor, and there are not a few geniuses who owe more to education than to any other influence.

I cannot dwell too earnestly on the fact that the

development of quick perception by culture will be found on inquiry to have been going on to a far greater extent in the playground than we are aware of. We do not know to what degree this or that boy has become quick and observant, but if you had taken him from infancy, and kept him from play, or only at feeble sports, you would assuredly have found him slower in many respects. Nature has implanted the instinct to play in children for a wise purpose, and to deeper intent than most parents suppose. Savage children all have stupid games As romping and frolicking and hallooing are conducive to bodily health and development, so the games which follow them in due time are adapted to ripen the intellectual forces which then begin to manifest themselves. Now this fact should be recognised and turned to proper account in education It has been partially so in the Kindergarten, wherein some of the most valuable truths and discoveries of the age have originated. But it may be studied and applied to great advantage when the pupil shall have passed beyond the Kindergarten into higher schools. At present it is allowed to take care of itself, just as boys were left in a great measure when I was young to amuse themselves in their own wilful ways. But it is better for the boys when they are supplied with suitable means of sport: the gymnasium is better than the street, and draughts more commendable than pitch-penny, albeit the latter is no mean sharpener of the wits, as most gambling games are—"more's the pity."

Nature has indicated to man the proper course to follow in education, more than this, she has indicated the means. The romping, bounding, and screaming of infancy are, as I have said, instinctive efforts to expand the muscles and develop the purely physical powers. As the mind begins to show itself, the young take to games, which are also the result of an instinct to expand the budding mental powers. Observe that the instinct is not *as yet* to acquire knowledge or do anything conducive to the practical business or duties of life. It tends simply to develop the powers which in time will enable the youth to fulfil his higher task. Now while sensible parents know enough to aid Nature as regards health in infancy, and while there are libraries of books on the subject, there has been very little attention paid by anybody to the processes by which the intellect really develops and prepares itself for thought. You may think that this is done in the schoolroom and by lessons, but it is not there that the sword is sharpened. Far from it. The majority of boys do not like their lessons, and it is a law that these early developments shall be instinctive, that is, agreeable. You may keep a man alive and perhaps fatten him on food which is disagreeable to his taste, but Nature does not approve of such compulsion. When I was a boy it was quite a general rule in Presbyterian New England that children should be *made* to eat whatever they specially disliked, and that it was a great virtue in them to do so. It was a great mistake.

There are many processes by which quickness of perception may be awakened. The most rudimentary is that described by JACOB ABBOTT in " Rollo," by which an infant's attention is drawn to an orange rolling in the sunshine. I have elsewhere mentioned in the chapter on Eye Memory the method pursued by thieves of tossing up a handful of mixed objects, which the boys must observe at a glance and name. The same may be done in a better and a different way when the teacher is on one side of a screen and tosses the articles up in the air. It is also a good exercise when a number of round objects, all alike, such as apples or balls, are rolled from one side of a door so as to disappear on the other, in one room, while the observers on the other are obliged to count them while rolling. Better still is the game of Morra, which may be best learned of any Italian, but which consists of two throwing out any number of fingers simultaneously, each player crying out as rapidly as he can the number cast by the other. These are simply elementary exercises, but they are of great avail to awaken simple quickness of observation; of such efficacy indeed that by their means the dullest and most sluggish boys may be made in certain directions and to certain degrees wideawake as foxes, or as the thieves call it "fly." These exercises are simply optical, and excite at first only visual observation. This however is a great deal. A dull child who has been made clever, though ever so little, in any way, has made a beginning which can with deliberate care be increased to a remarkable extent. A step beyond this is the measuring distances by eye, which I learned when I was in an artillery company during the Emancipation or Rebellion. A stake is planted at a certain distance from a given point, and all the company are required to guess the number of yards or feet from one to the other. In a short time young men develop extraordinary proficiency in thus ascertaining distances, and it is of advantage in many ways. The eye thus trained has taken an important step towards art. This is an advance on mere observation; by means of it a higher faculty, that of comparison, has been awakened. Now a very important element in practising these "games" is this, that while the boys shall regard them as games, to be enjoyed with free will, they shall be exercised regularly, frequently, and to a *greater degree* than is usual. Games are generally wild weeds: I would cultivate them. No boy is unwilling to have his sports improved: the *Boys' Own Book*, and all such publications, so dear to youth, prove this. It is very important that these exercises, however repeated and elevated, should *not* assume too much the character of drill and discipline, and become monotonous. Should they cease to please, they will lose half their value.[1]

As there are a great many women who continue children through life in their devotion to dress and gossip, so there are men who do the same by giving their souls up to "sport" in its different forms. It is difficult to conceive of any boy so stupid that he could not by practice attain some kind of position in the sporting fraternity; the fact that such multitudes of young men who are utterly without intellect or true culture of any kind become such good judges of horses, such expert gamblers, such knowing and "leary coves" in the muddy mysteries of the town, sufficiently proves this. These men all show that quickness of observation alone may be developed by the means of which I have spoken, and that the faculty is really almost universal. Their defect is that while quickness of mind has been developed, it has been misapplied.

[1] This is a frequent fault in the Kindergarten.

The mere "sport," like the savage, is simply an over-grown child, a poor creature not of arrested growth, but of arrested moral development. Understand me, reader, that I do not here confuse the athletic sports or exercises conducive to health with any lack of brains   I am speaking not of them, or of games, but of the lower orders of humanity—of all ranks of society —who never get beyond games or gambling, and for whom life is all a playground without a school.   On the contrary, I am advocating the extended use and application through life of all games and sports.   But the study of these overgrown children is interesting and profitable, as is that of their congeners, the savages, because we learn from them that a certain kind of shrewdness and quickness may be developed in all men. Not only are all gypsy boys extremely clever and artful in many ways, but also any other boys brought up with them.   In fact there is not one child in a hundred who, under the pressure of necessity as a gypsy or street arab, would not develop a quickness of observation in certain directions which would seem miraculous in a well-bred nursery child.

Now I find that many admit that there are marvellous powers of memory latent in every mind, which may be drawn out by education   But they apprehend that the development of a great memory will crush the finer powers of intellect.   Memory, they think, grown to a certain size, will, like the cat in the old German tale, become lord of all the house, or nothing.   On the contrary, others believe that develop-ing quick observation and insight will lead to clever superficiality, and neutralise memory and solid study. I, however, believe that in due measure, fairly balanced, they will aid, support, and increase one another. It would be an easy matter to fill a book proving this from examples. No one will deny that an undue premature expansion of one portion of the mind or of the body will destroy the balance. But a judicious development of all the organs at once, *pari passu*, will give the happiest results.

Education has for a long time been tending towards this higher and joint development of memory first and higher lessons afterward, combined with quickness of perception developed by physical aids. It is growing up in the Kindergarten, it is found in the rapidly increasing conviction that the whole modern system of teaching languages, with its complicated array of hindrances in the shape of grammars, and its opposition to the use of translations, is a weariness and vexation of spirit. The final objection is indeed the hardest to overcome, and it is this: "Where are you to get teachers clever enough to understand and apply all your principles?" Even to this there may come with time a solution While it is true that the man who can do nothing better turns teacher, while teaching is only a bridge by which ambitious youth crosses over the gulf of poverty to a profession, while the tutor costs no more than the coachman, and the whole education of the family less than the dinner parties; while the father really understands less about the training of his children than he does about his horses, while bouquets outbalance books in the annual expenditure, and ball-dresses brains, teaching will *not* be the profession which it should. In Japan that man is believed to be damned eternally who leaves behind him no son to celebrate his funeral rites. Perhaps a wiser age than this will decide that the man ought to be damned who treats the education of his children as if it were of less importance than amusements, society, and display.

It is remarkable when we reflect how much our current education consists of merely cramming into the memory, or even into setting other faculties at work for a temporary purpose, equivalent to cramming, and how little is done to awaken that quickness of perception or ready apprehension which may be developed to almost any extent, and that into forms and phases of wonderful variety, reaching up into the highest powers of the intellect. Let those who think this is Utopian study the most recent writers on physiology, and judge by facts as I have done. I find on inquiry that boys who are put into places requiring great promptness of thought and action in all kinds of business and manufacturing can do things which seem miraculous to even grown-up ordinary people, and yet where is the school which develops this wonderful power at the same time with memory? How the two might mutually stimulate and aid each other is beyond belief. And it can be done.

There is a great desire at present, as there is good reason, to have all office-holders in the United States qualified by Civil Service or Competitive Examinations. The popular objection to this as a test is thus set forth by an extract from an editorial article in the Philadelphia *Evening Bulletin* of February 7, 1881:—

" Some of the newspapers which are not very strongly in favour of Civil Service reform are busy just now urging that the system of competitive examination among candidates for office is not always likely to procure the best men. One of the authorities quoted in behalf of this theory is Sir ARTHUR HELPS, who in 1872 wrote of the system as it now exists in England. 'In my judgment, although the system has long been adopted in China, it is a most inadequate one for its purpose. It detects qualifications which are little needed, while it fails inevitably to discover those which are most needed' And another Englishman, a writer in a late number of a London magazine, says of the system: 'The man who succeeds in examinations has quickness in acquiring, memory for retaining, and readiness in producing knowledge; but he may be altogether deficient in reflection, in grasp of mind, in judgment, in weight of character. It appears to me that the examination system tends to select minds acute rather than deep, active rather than powerful; and the worst is that the heavier metal, being generally more slow in development, is apt to be left in the background.' Without doubt there is a good deal of solid truth in these propositions. The man who can obtain the highest averages for his responses to certain fixed questions in arithmetic and geography may, of course, have really less practical and general acquaintance with those things than one whose responses are not so good; and he may have much smaller fitness for the performance of certain official duties. We are not aware that anybody holds opinions different from these. The most ardent advocate of the competitive examination plan has not insisted that the certain result of that plan is to produce the best men.

"The plan is urged because it is about the only conceivable method which can be substituted for the present method. It is absolutely impossible for the

President of the United States to pick out the best men for the offices from his own knowledge If he is forced to choose at random from the crowd, he must permit other men to designate the lucky men, and that duty of designation naturally and almost inevitably devolves upon members of Congress, who are supposed to be acquainted with the people in their districts"

That is to say, that the world has gone on perfectly satisfied with examinations as a test for its lawyers, physicians, clergymen, college graduates, and many other kinds of qualified persons, but the instant it is proposed to apply this method to Civil Service candidates, its opponents at once rake out the radical error which underlies all European or American education! There is not a single word in all that Sir ARTHUR HELPS or any one else has said against it which would not be more strikingly applicable to the qualification of men for any of the learned professions. Why candidates for consulates in France should not be examined in French as well as International Law and other necessary qualifications it is difficult to conceive. To which the unprogressive says, "You don't want merely a French scholar or a lawyer for a consul." "Well, what do we want?" "Why, you should have a gentleman, and a *live* man—one who is wideawake, and quick to his business."[1] And I quite agree with

[1] Since this was written I have read in one of the most widely circulated and influential newspapers in the West of America an editorial article in which it was boldly asserted that a knowledge of French and a generally good education was a positive disqualification for office abroad, with the old cry that what was wanted was a "live" man, a practical person, &c It may be remarked that, with occasional exceptions, these illiterate "live" men are dead failures when misplaced in positions for which they have not been educated.

this. As society is constituted, the surest way to obtain a *gentleman*, as I understand such an ideal, would be to select men who have never been in " politics," especially in its dirty or primary work, there being nothing so belittling or enfeebling to the intellects or antagonistic to refinement as such employment, and a " live " man should know enough to learn French or at least one living language properly

The ultimate result of quickness of perception is to induce " reflection, grasp of mind, judgment, and weight of character." Observe how naturally in this citation "grasp of mind " is associated with reflection. To catch readily at and apprehend single objects, statements, or ideas, is only the first step in this branch. After the pupil shall have been exercised for a time in this, comparison and association will come of themselves. The popular tendency is to sever quickness of perception from reflection, but the wisest thinker is always keenest to grasp ideas. This is illustrated both in philosophical reading and in jurisprudence: he who is slow in either is useless in their practice.

It is certainly true that quickness of perception is not in itself, any more than memory, reflection or wisdom. But the two mutually aid and develop one another into higher qualities. The world is so well satisfied of this that it has gone on for a long time taking even memory alone as a satisfactory test of cleverness. Few and far between have they been who objected like Sir ARTHUR HELPS. As Uncle Toby would have it that the mother must be in some way related to her child, so these good people have insisted that in default of a better way, a young man who could repeat the wisdom which he had learned from books was about the nearest approach to being book-learned which they could conceive of. If the world is willing to trust so much to memory alone, what will it not trust to it when allied to a faculty which quickly associates and compares all that memory brings ?

I trust, however, that no reader will think that the training of the mind to quick perception and prompt action is to be limited to the casting up of divers objects, to measuring distances by the eye, or even by games up to chess and whist. It is true that the study of games except as mere amusement has not much occupied mankind. In RABELAIS' splendid scheme for educating a perfect gentleman there is included every game at cards or aught else then known. But from games upward there is a series of developments of the faculty of readiness which gradually approach and blend, or are identified with much higher powers. A very remarkable mental exercise, but little practised, consists in reading to a class propositions more or less difficult to grasp, either in mental or moral philosophy, mathematics, or any branch of science, the object—as in mental arithmetic—being for them to understand as promptly as possible what was given. When minds have been *properly prepared* for this, they exhibit results which would startle most people. But they seldom are properly prepared by being gradually led up to it. I have seen something like this in a school, but the object of the teacher manifestly was not to strengthen or develop the capacities of the pupils, but to strain them—to puzzle and overload them. And there is a great deal too much of this in all our current education. *Non multa sed multum*, "not many but much,"

should be the motto for every school. I suppose—
that is to say, I lay it down for consideration—that
this exercise of requiring pupils to promptly appreciate
or catch the sense of what is read to them is capable
of great development, and of exerting a great influence
in expanding the intellect. We know from COUTURE's
method of teaching drawing, that the great majority of
artists can not only learn in time to sketch with great
accuracy people as they walk past us, but that those
who draw in this manner do so more accurately
and with greater power and better expression. Now
ordinary lectures do much to make students quick to
catch difficult points. But the student who should be
exercised in difficult points alone would have a vast
advantage at the lecture. The process is precisely
parallel with COUTURE's glance-sketching.

It would be of little use to attempt to teach memory
or quickness of perception unless they be taught
properly; that is, very gradually. My own recollec-
tions of all education are that of being loaded to the
last ounce I could bear, of being required to do more
than I could do thoroughly, of "staggering" at all
seasons, and of always having been under fear that I
could not accomplish my duty. To this day I am
tormented in dreams by the fear of my American
college examinations, the old torture and anxiety rises
as from the grave, till I wish in my soul, on awaking,
that I had never seen my miserably mismanaged Alma
Mater. Let me observe that these torturing dreams
are drawn only from the American part of my student
career. Of Heidelberg, Munich, and Paris, where I
studied to infinitely more profit for three years, I
never dream at all.

M

I have in fact no recollection whatever of having been at any time taught *how* to study rationally or in any way by anybody. I can remember that as a rule I had a multiplicity of long lessons which I could by *very* hard work just contrive to learn by heart, with little understanding and less interest, to be succeeded the next day by an equally confusing swarm. And I can see now that if my mind had been properly prepared to study before being set to learn by rote such quantities, that I could have been trying to understand and perhaps enjoying my texts. As for students appreciating the " beauties " of Horace, the golden glow of Ovid, the grand glory as of sunlit seas of Homer, the mystery to me is that one in his soul ever sees any difference in interest between the text and the dictionary. That a few do, in spite of the way in which they are taught, is a proof of the wonderful recuperative powers possessed by the human intellect.

The application of the principle of mental arithmetic to all branches of thought, but very gradually and cautiously, is perhaps the greatest problem in education. The world has been " getting on after a fashion " in most of its education with little more than memory, which the pupil was obliged to pick up for himself as he went on. I have shown, as I trust, that memory may be greatly improved upon certain principles, and that the pupil thus provided and strengthened will then begin to study with a clearer mind, not being obliged to do two things at once—that is, to learn to remember as well as to learn the lesson. Secondly, the memory will be even more aided and developed by exercises in quickness of perception, and it is in the mutual action of these on each other that the highest results may be anticipated If we examine the history of education, and especially that of great and wise men, we find that in many forms these principles have shown their truth and vitality. Memory was of old systematically developed to a degree now unknown, and that among millions of men. Quickness of perception has been brought out in manifold ways by the needs of life and by amusements, and we know it can be created, but to take it from its wild flower stage into the garden of culture, and scientifically utilise it in education in connection with memory and as a corrective or aid, lies in the future

SUMMARY.

To recapitulate, and to set forth clearly what I have written, I would say, firstly, that memory can be developed in all children to a greater extent than is usual by the simple method of making a child learn easy lessons perfectly, taking great care not to exercise it on more than one or two subjects, until the art of learning is acquired. Secondly, that the memory must be counterbalanced by increasing quickness of perception. This is brought out at first by processes which train the eye only to rapid perception, but which, as they are changed, awaken intellectual observation and rapid action of the mind. When a person has been thus trained we may expect that he will be observant of resemblances, contrasts, and probably readily perceptive of humour and the principles of poetry. Exercising quickness of perception is extremely conducive to detecting or perceiving contrasts, and real or apparent resemblances or points of identity. This leads to "a sense of humour," a ready comprehension of simile and metaphor, and by proper training to an appreciating of poetry in every form and phase.

The stages of training may be set down as follows:—

Training the eye to perceive objects at a glance, as, for instance, when a handful of coins, beads, keys, &c, are thrown up and caught. Counting as they roll by a number of balls or marbles. Doing the same with balls of different colours and sizes, and then with different objects. Passing cards with inscriptions from the right hand to the left. The art of juggling or legerdemain abounds in exercises well qualified to render a pupil quick to perceive. Solitaire with cards illustrates this.

Measuring and estimating distances by eye, as marked out. Conjecturing the proportions of houses, rooms, and all objects. Mental perspective. Comparing and classifying faces, heads, and figures of men and animals, with observations of proportions as characteristic of species.

Mental arithmetic. Applications of its principles to all other studies—that is, it may be succeeded by verbal instruction in geography, composition, languages, &c., with examinations. It is a fact that a wide-awake, quick-minded boy or girl can learn, understand, and remember a lesson better when thus communicated than from a book. And the process induces quickness.

Problems in mental geometry, physics, moral philosophy, physiology, and æsthetics, given to the pupils with a view to their rapid appreciation. This is not proposed as a method of study, but simply as an aid to such study.

I assume that the scholars thus trained have also been continued in improving their memory, and in hand-work. This supposes that they will be apt to remember, and that their memories are in fact supplied with certain material. By increased quickness of perception they will gather rapidly, and by memory they will retain it all. Now as quickness of perception improves and leavens memory, so hand-work or constructiveness acts on the two, or their resultant, inspiring a certain practical and common-sense quality into education, which cannot be too much esteemed or encouraged.

The world has long recognised the truth of these principles, particularly as to quickness of perception. But while it has smiled at them approvingly, as curious and pretty when seen in infant schools, it has never thought of developing them into serious and higher branches any more than it has of making art or hand-work an integral part of all education. Now I would keep not only the schoolboy but also the university undergraduate busy, among other things, with exercising his mind to quickness, as he should his body. For I assume gymnastics to be accepted as a part of all education. Improving the memory, and with it rapidity of thought, should not cease with the rudimentary exercises of childhood. Like rolling snowballs they should be kept going, in order to increase in growth.

Singleness of purpose is a great power. Until the pupil has positively acquired the ability to memorise at will, until he can grasp and retain almost whatever he pleases, he should not be confused with other studies or exercises But when this power begins to really manifest itself, then the exercises in quickness of perception may begin. It will be found that the two greatly aid one another. To see rapidly is a faculty which perishes with the realisation, unless it be aided promptly by memory, while memory grows rapidly when exercised by her rapid partner.

We will suppose that a child has been so long trained in memorising alone as to readily retain any sentence, or to a certain degree a sequence of sentences. At this stage the exercises in training the eye to perceive may be begun. For the very young the throwing up a handful of different small objects is the best beginning, to be accompanied by rolling different coloured balls across a doorway. Pictures of all kinds may next be shown, and the class required to describe them from a minute's observation. It is also well to train the pupil to observe as rapidly as possible the dress and appearance of a certain given number of people, so as to describe them *accurately*. Very few grown people can do this well, but any child may be trained to do it very well in a few words. It is a valuable art, which will be of great use through life. To perceive accurately is in fact almost the same thing as to describe accurately; at least it will be found that those who observe closely always describe well. This is another illustration of the great truth that simple elementary, almost mechanical beginnings, with ordinary minds can be made to lead directly to far higher intellectual powers.

At this stage the pupil may also be shown sentences distinctly written in large characters, which he may just have time to read, and then be required to repeat. This is not unknown to the Kindergarten teachers, but its importance is as yet far from being understood. There are very few grown-up men who would not acquire a really marvellous mental power if they were to practise it The adult who enjoys in all its fulness quickness of perception has acquired a power which will aid him in every profession or calling Priest, lawyer, doctor, shopman, or artisan succeed in most cases more by being readily observant than by any other faculty. That this may be acquired in its every form or phase admits of no doubt I knew a man of whom it was said that he never knew how anybody was dressed. This came to his ears, and from that time he could describe the garments of all his acquaintances.

As memory after certain exercise acts in accordance with quick perception, so the two, especially the latter, give and take to and from eye-memory The showing a written sentence on a board, only so long that it may be read, will recall the method by which COUTURE advised beginners to learn to sketch passers-by. All of these experiments have been made with success, as curiosities; unfortunately they have not been persevered in, or made constant influences in education. Another stage, that of games, has rarely been regarded save as mere amusement. It might be a curious subject of inquiry to ascertain what humanity would be if it had never known any games of skill? Can any one imagine a childhood *entirely* devoid of such exercises, and what the probable results would be on the subsequent adult minds? Many of my readers can well appreciate how practice in games would be aided by a greatly improved memory. Add to this mental arithmetic, let us say to two hours of memorising daily let there be one of the latter branch and one or two of games of different kinds, all conducted with a view to make the pupil observe and remember.

Memory and quickness of perception unite and can be perfected in the development of the constructive faculty which is allied to both and calls for both. The two are one in art. How this should be studied is shown in the chapter on Industrial Art in Schools.

If there are any readers who ask when, where, and how in this system the ordinary branches of education come in—the reading, writing, geography, and arithmetic—I reply, what the more intelligent reader has probably surmised by himself, that if the teacher have any intelligence at all he will begin to introduce such branches as require thought at his own discretion very gradually, as he perceives that the memory and quickness of perception of the pupil are becoming so strong that the grasp is easy. Two points he must bear in mind. Firstly, not to abandon at any time the training of memory and quick perception ; and secondly, to beware of overcrowding or forcing the ordinary subjects of learning The harder he works in the morning the easier will it be in the afternoon.

Part IV

EYE MEMORY.[1]

THERE are few people who have ever reflected on the fact that every one has within him a faculty which, if properly developed, would completely change our system of education, by increasing to an incredible degree our power of mental acquisition. This faculty I term Eye-memory. It has already been recognised by writers as Visual Representation, Imaginary Appearance, and Volitionary Pseudopia, each term expressing the subject in a manner characteristic of its inventor. It occupies a ground between memorising and quickness of perception, belonging to one as much as to the other.

We are all in the habit of hearing the utterances of other people during our waking hours, of reading books and catching sounds. But unless we deliberately set ourselves to work to get these utterances, ideas, or sounds *by heart*, we only retain a vague general impression of them Getting by heart, or "memorising," is effected by concentrating or intensifying the attention, and by frequent repetition.

[1] A lecture delivered before the Franklin Institute of Philadelphia, March 29, 1880

When this is extensively practised in youth, the power of memory is thereby greatly strengthened or improved, while the thinking faculties are, by the same process, stimulated and disciplined. This is, in fact, the real aim of most early education Only the vulgar and ignorant believe that the acquisition of knowledge and the learning certain definite quantities of mathematics, languages, or history alone constitute an education A wiser man knows that it is the training of the mental powers which forms the true result of culture.

Now just as the mind may be instructed and disciplined by mere *reading*, that is to say, indirectly taught by symbols called letters, so it may be directly supplied with facts or phenomena by eye-memory. This is the impressing by will on memory things which we have *seen*. Thus, for instance, if you close your eyes and try to recall the exact appearance of any object with which you have been familiar, you will find great difficulty in doing so As a .rule children possess this faculty to a much higher degree than grown people. But if you put the object before you and look at it frequently you will succeed in learning it, so as to be able to read it at will. The longer you study it with a determination to remember it, the more vividly will its colour and general appearance come before you. It is possible, with practice, to develop this faculty so as to produce the most extraordinary results The absent friend may be recalled at will, so that his form appears as clearly defined as in life, and by frequent exercise you may surround yourself with familiar or imagined scenes which appear like nature. This power may be ex-

tended to books.   You have all heard of people who
" cipher " from imagined visual numerals, and of others
who had the power to recall sheet-music, and to play
from the notes thus brought before the eye.   I have
read of a Scotch preacher who said that, while
apparently preaching without notes, he was really
reading from a manuscript which he saw mentally
before him.   He could see even the marks of punctua-
tion.   And this use of the faculty of visual representation occurred whenever he had written a sermon
and read it carefully before going into the pulpit.   I
venture to believe that it would be possible, with
practice, to recall any page of anything which we had
read, or rather seen, and in like manner to get by eye
a gallery of pictures.   As it is, we may appreciate
and thoroughly enjoy works of art.   But unless we
deliberately exert our will, and intentionally impress
them on the memory with much trouble, they will
not recur to us as real things.   They will not come
when we call to them.   Why is it that, after going
through a gallery, we remember a few pictures and
forget others ?   Simply because we have unconsciously,
through *interest*, brought our memory to bear upon
the few.   Had we been trained from childhood to use
this visual memory in the same manner in which
we are trained to exercise mental memory, we could
probably recall at will any object which we had *once*
willed to remember.

    There have been, however, many persons who have
acquired this desirable art.   Thus we are told that
NICOLAS LOIR, an eminent French painter and engraver,
when in Italy, devoted his time to contemplating the
works of the great masters, his eye-memory becoming

so retentive by practice that he was able to sketch the pictures which had pleased him most.

I have met with a coachmaker, also a draughtsman, who, after seeing any vehicle pass by, however rapidly, can draw and colour it in detail to the minutest ornaments, and who can do the same of any object which he saw even forty years ago, if he had taken pains at the time to learn it. I know a lady who, while in Europe, memorised many galleries of pictures and shop windows. FRANCIS GALTON, who has of all men most thoroughly studied this subject, has completely established the fact that there are in England hundreds of accountants who carry out sums in arithmetic entirely by visual representation. This power is popularly admired as a rare gift; in reality it is irrepressible in a few, involuntarily developed in others, and is innate in us all.

The importance of developing this faculty has suggested itself to many artists. Thus COUTURE advised his pupils to let the eye rest for an instant on passers-by in the street, and then attempt to draw them I have seen this put in practice with perfect success, and have heard from others authentic experiences of it. The various stages of the process were extremely curious and interesting. At first only a hat, and perhaps the general appearance of an arm, or a leg, can be caught, but in a few days the expression of the whole figure is seldom missed. No one who had not practiced this, or seen it done, would believe how rapidly the observation and memory are developed by this kind of "flash photograph" drawing, or what an air of vivacity and motion is imparted to the figures. I recommend the practice of it specially to those who intend to draw for the illustrated newspapers. They are often obliged to make notes or hasty sketches of moving masses of men, and they perforce acquire a certain degree of eye-memory. But we need only study the details of most of their pictures of crowds to see that it is not highly developed with them.

While collecting facts on eye-memory, I wrote to Dr. OLIVER WENDELL HOLMES for information, and I need not say that I was not disappointed, as I received from him his work entitled "Mechanism in Thought and Morals," in which I find that the subject of "pictured thought," as a branch of conscious mental action, has not escaped his attention. He has ingeniously illustrated it "by the panorama of their past lives, said by people who have escaped from drowning to have flashed before them." This actually happened to Dr. HOLMES himself, as it did to my brother HENRY PERRY LELAND. I also received from Dr. HOLMES the work on "Visions," by Dr. EDWARD H. CLARKE, edited by himself. In this book that which the author calls "the power of the will to produce objective *pseudopia*," or to see that which is not before the eyes, is treated almost exhaustively, as regards the physical explanation of the faculty. "Sight," says Dr. CLARKE, "is not a function of the eyes, but of the brain. There is a way by which volition plays with its utmost energy upon the angular gyrus, or some other centre, and drives its machinery into action. If this can be accomplished, vision is accomplished. When we consider that there is no part of the body which cannot be affected somewhat by volition, it would be singular if the visual ganglia should be the only ones withdrawn from the influence and authority of the will." In illustration of the fact that the will can reproduce what the eye has seen, Dr. CLARKE cites the case of a gentleman who, being fond of statuary, succeeded, after a few trials, in producing visions of statues, and even in imagining new ones This author has, in my judgment, completely established the fact that every object making an impression on the brain, or visual apparatus, leaves an organic trace there, which may be reproduced at an indefinite period afterwards by cerebral action. I find in fact, in the "Visions" of Dr. CLARKE, as in the "Mental Physiology" of Dr. WILLIAM B. CARPENTER, a sound basis for, and a perfect confirmation of, all that I claim as regards eye-memory

GOETHE tells us, in his work *Aus meinem Leben, Wahrheit und Dichtung*, that having one day seen ideally a picture by VAN OSTADE, he cultivated the faculty so as to afterwards produce at any time subjective copies of pictures and works of art. DE QUINCEY recognised and distinctly describes the faculty of recalling or creating visions at will In fact, the illustrations that this power exists are so numerous, and the physiological explanations of it are so copious and satisfactory, that it would be impossible to bring them within the limits of the longest lecture. But I have not been able to ascertain that any writer has ever contemplated the deliberate cultivation of volitional vision as an aid to every branch of intellectual education and of art I do not know that any one has contemplated the possibility of its being introduced into schools and taught in classes. I believe myself that entire books will be thus memorised with little effort, that all which the eye has seen the trained will will revive, and that, far beyond all this, imagination aided by volition, will evoke from the mystic brain cells, where they lie by millions upon millions asleep, all manner of beautiful forms, and create from them at will others more beautiful Would not this be a new life for every man and woman of culture ? Would not, in such a life, much that is mean and much which now degrades us vanish like mists before sunshine ? Yet all this is just as physically possible as that sounds and sights should be transmitted by electricity and preserved *ad infinitum*

But to return to the application of eye-memory to art When I was in St Petersburg, Russia, I found that great attention was there paid, in the School of Design, to free-hand drawing. The happiest results were secured by telling the pupils to study a given object for ten minutes, and then, the object being removed, to draw it Mr. JOHN SARTAIN has told me that, in his youth, his teacher of drawing, the celebrated VARLEY, would place the image or picture to be copied in one room and tell the pupils to work in another, allowing them to go from time to time to look at it. I understand that the Russian method has been practised in some schools in Philadelphia. It cannot be denied that when the model is always directly before the pupil the latter seldom observes anything carefully, nor does he study the relations of the details of form, light, and shade, and colour, as he would when memorising I have come to the conclusion that it requires full half an hour for most people to get by heart or eye the simplest object in the world—that is to say, a billiard ball, with all its lights and shadows. But when the artist is compelled to get the whole object actually by heart, he studies the relations of the different qualities or details, and develops in his mind higher and much more vigorous powers of observation. Thus trained, his eye sees more at the first glance, he becomes self-reliant, he does not depend on the thousand times repeated, half-observant, glance.

We have all heard of BLAKE, the artist, who saw spectral delusions or imaginary phantoms so vividly that he used to copy them. Once, when he was thus painting CHARLES THE FIRST, as he believed, from life, for a friend, he stopped in his work. "Why do you not go on?" asked his friend. "Because WILLIAM THE CONQUEROR has just stepped in the way, and before him," answered BLAKE, very seriously. I will tell you a story upon this story, out of my own experience. Once, in London, after a dinner party, I was in our host's library with a French gentleman, one of the guests. Finding that he was evidently well informed in art matters, and as there were several volumes of BLAKE'S pictures on the table, I showed them to him. He had never seen anything of BLAKE'S before, so I told him what I could remember of that extraordinary man, and how he used to paint from spectral delusions. "But he must have been mad," said the French gentleman. "Not at all," I replied; "he was almost a genius—*enfin, monsieur, c'était un Doré manqué*—he was almost a DORÉ." The point of this remark was not apparent to me till some time afterwards, when I learned, to my astonishment, that it was to Monsieur DORÉ himself that I had addressed it!

Monsieur DORÉ is an artist of wonderful invention and of great fertility, but I know of none in whom the public have perceived so precisely what his limits are.[1]

---

[1] This was written while DORÉ was yet living.

We know what he knows by heart, and what his eye-memory has mastered, and when he is drawing on the old stock figures. Had he cultivated the faculty of visual memory in youth to perfection, he would have avoided such mannerism as we observe. For such culture would fill the mind with facts or objects which would be in the highest degree suggestive and inspiring We have all found in our own experiences that we remember certain scenes with great vividness when certain persons or certain pleasurable associations are connected with them. We remember the brow of the hill, the amber sunset sky, the foliage like dark bronze against it, because some young lady, perhaps, caused us to remember it Our will was unconsciously exerted This association of scenes with persons and events has become part of the stock-in-trade of the modern novelists We all know how a certain scene was indelibly branded in the heroine's memory—how, to the end of her days, the ticking of the clock and the patterns in the carpet all rose up whenever anything recalled "that awful hour." Yet there is a basis for curious or valuable observation in all this We have in it a confirmation of my assertion that there are causes which will strengthen and develop to an unusual degree our memory of objects.

I have said that the power of memory by sight may be increased to a degree of which we have no conception, and also that young people, as DE QUINCEY declares, possess this power more than those advanced in life. To prove this I will read to you a passage from the life of the celebrated French conjurer, ROBERT HOUDIN. It was this passage which first attracted

N

my attention to eye-memory, and caused me to reflect on the indefinite degree to which it may be extended in education, especially in that of artists I must premise that this famous juggler had invented a trick, called Second Sight, which I saw performed by him and his son in Paris in 1848 He found that to effect this it was necessary to cultivate not merely his mental memory to an extraordinary extent, but to remember things as they *appeared.* The trick consisted effectively of getting by heart, or remembering, the exact appearance of every object which might by any possibility be brought by anybody to his exhibition. The son of HOUDIN, a boy, was blindfolded, the father, in another part of the hall, looked at the object, and his son promptly described it. There was, of course, a method of secretly signalling from one to the other; this is sometimes effected by a telegraphic wire in the floor, worked by the foot.

"I resolved," says ROBERT HOUDIN, "on making some experiments with my son EMILE, and in order to make my young assistant understand the nature of the exercise we were going to learn I took a domino, the 4—5 for instance, and laid it before him. Instead of letting him count the points of the two numbers, I requested him to tell me the total at once.

"' Nine,' he said

"Then I added another domino, the 4—3.

"' That makes sixteen,' he said without any hesitation.

"I stopped the first lesson here, the next day we succeeded in counting at a glance four dominoes ; the day after, six, and thus at length we were enabled to give instantaneously the product of a dozen dominoes.

"This result obtained, we applied ourselves to a far more difficult task, over which we spent a month My son and I passed rapidly before a toy-shop, or any other displaying a variety of wares, and cast an attentive glance upon it. A few steps further on we drew paper and pencil from our pockets, and tried which could describe the greatest number of objects seen in passing. I must own that my son far excelled me, for he would often write down forty objects, while I could scarcely recall thirty. Often feeling vexed at this defeat I would return to the shop and verify his statement; but he rarely made a mistake.

"My male readers," continues Monsieur HOUDIN, "will certainly undeistand the possibility of this, but they will recognise the difficulty. As for my lady readers, I am convinced that they will see nothing remarkable in it, for they daily perform far more astounding feats Thus, for instance, I can safely assert that one lady seeing another lady pass at full speed in a carriage, will have had time to analyse her toilette, from her bonnet to her shoes, and be able to describe not only the fashion and quality of the stuffs, but also say if the lace be real, or only machine-made I have known ladies to do this This natural or acquired faculty among ladies, but which my son and I had only gained by constant practice, was of great service in my performances, for, while I was executing my tricks, I could see everything that passed around me, and thus prepare to foil any difficulties presented me."

Having thus cultivated observation and memory, the juggler and his son proceeded to render themselves familiar with an incredible variety of small objects.

Conjecturing, as the result afterwards proved, that they would have many curiosities or antiques, such as old coins, arms, and jewellery, brought to them to describe, they visited many museums. It is very evident, not merely from HOUDIN's own account, but from what was practically shown in his public exhibitions, that in a few months the father and son added incredibly to their stores of knowledge or information, retaining a vivid picture of every object which they deliberately *willed* to remember. Having developed the eye-memory by hard work up to such a point that they could see a thing almost as clearly as if the original object, or indeed whole rows of such objects, were present, they found that the faculty, once well acquired, kept itself in action with ordinary practice. They now learned very readily the characters or letters of many languages, such as Greek, Hebrew, Chinese, Russian, and Turkish, the names of all surgical instruments, and of many other technical objects Walking through a library, they could recollect the appearance of whole rows of books, with the titles on their backs.

There can be no question that ROBERT HOUDIN was an unusually clever man, of great powers of observation and quickness, which had been greatly improved by the practice of juggling. Yet, making every allowance for his remarkable talent, I am all the more convinced that his experiences and discoveries indicate that the faculty of an indefinite development of eye-memory exists in every one, especially in the young, and that it will at some future day enter largely into education, and form its physical basis. Anybody can verify for himself the simple fact that any object may be *eye-memorised* by special study. No

casual observation, unaccompanied by the *will* to remember, will enable us to do so much as can be effected
by determined effort. We may see a face a thousand
times, and yet in most cases we cannot recall it so
accurately for artistic purposes as if we had deliberately *studied* it a dozen times with that object. But
it is especially to art students that I commend the
practice of it. When you are copying an object, it
makes a very great difference indeed whether you
look very carefully at the original, and into its every
condition, or merely *glance* at and set down what you
half observe and *half* imagine For it is a fact that
in the most accurate copying we draw largely upon
our imaginations. We are copying, let us say, a vase
or a book, and, having secured a general conception
of its proportions, we proceed by speculation or fancy
more than we are ourselves aware of. As I have
already said, when the model is *directly before* the
pupil, he does not generally study it carefully as a
whole, nor observe or memorise the proportions of
its different parts. He copies it simply part by part
Now I would urge that the wonderful power of eye-
memory, or of recalling objects exactly as they appear,
should be deliberately cultivated, especially in the
young I think that by practising as ROBERT HOUDIN
practised with his son, and by competing as they com-
peted, very remarkable results would very soon be
obtained The pupils need not be taken about to
shop windows, shelves and tables at home, with
objects arranged on them, would answer the purpose
for primary lessons.

The next step, which goes beyond all that ROBERT
HOUDIN conceived, just as it transcends the ordinary

object-teaching of the Kindergarten, is the photographing some one object, as, for instance, a statue, so indelibly upon the eye and memory by the exercise of close observation, will, and renewal in the memory, that it can even serve as a visible model In children who cannot draw, the faculty may be developed by examining them on maps and the relative boundaries of States   This is often done now, but when I was at school maps were indeed hung before the scholars, and we were required to learn them, yet it never entered into our teacher's head, or into our own, that the whole map might have been learned in less time by visual memory—by looking at and closing our eyes, and recalling at first the different colours of the different States, and then their relative position, and finally their shapes.   The method by which this process of getting, for instance, a map by eye, and even the peculiar processes by which different people will attempt it, are well described by Dr. HASLAM ("Sound Mind"), who in turn is commented on by Dr. A. L. WIGAN in his "Duality of Mind" (pp. 313, 314).

But it would be well if children could all draw, since drawing and memory are great mutual aids.   I quite agree with FROEBEL, the Kindergarten philosopher, that it is highly important that a child should acquire some facility in drawing even before he learns to read and write, since the representation of actual things should precede the representation of signs and words.   In connection with the subject of object-teaching and drawing, EMILY SHIRREFF, the author of the "Intellectual Education of Women," observes that "it would be curious to inquire how much of the loose thinking, the hazy perception of truth, which characterise the majority of even the educated portion of mankind, might be traced back to the absence of any *definite* impressions made in childhood in connection with the instructions given to them Outside the schoolroom they acquire definite impressions, but they are acquired at random, and may be wholly wanting in accuracy "

The writers on the Kindergarten, and on object-teaching in connection with elementary drawing, have hit on a great truth in their endeavour to teach children to form *definite* impressions. But I doubt if any of them, or any one living, knows how indefinite all our memories of objects are compared to what they might be. Object-teaching causes children to learn the appearance, names, and qualities of things "And many persons," says Mrs. HORACE MANN, "object to it because it is playing with things, and the opposite of study." The cultivation of eye-memory must, however, be admitted by the greatest enemy to all new ideas in education to combine all the discipline of intense study with all that is useful in object-teaching. It is the very opposite to anything like loose thinking or vagueness. It calls for the closest observation and the greatest exercise of the memory conceivable. Therefore it is good discipline for the mind, therefore it should be a legitimate branch of education. But be it observed that this practice of the visual memory, while requiring intense application and much practice, is not disagreeable in the sense in which much study is disagreeable. In fact it cannot be pursued with profit an instant after it becomes wearying. As soon

as you tire of it, then, in the words of WESTWOOD,
"the visions flee and the dreams depart." The
memory will only work of her own accord at this,
she will only remain as a willing guest. Force her,
and she flies.

On the other hand, *success* in the practice of visual
memory is so encouraging that after we once realise
our progress the most strenuous effort becomes in fact
a voluntary pleasure. I conceive that for its cultivation classes should be formed, at which maps, pictures,
or any objects being shown for a minute, or for several
minutes, those assembled shall endeavour to impress
what is set forth on the memory. Now the difficulty
at the very outset will be that many of those present,
instead of literally getting the object *by eye*, and
making the exertion necessary in the beginning, will—
perhaps unconsciously—make up their minds at a glance
as to what the object is, and then in their description
or depicting make a clever enough superficial account.
These are the ones who, in drawing from a model,
look at it a thousand times, carelessly, and yet lose
half of what they had gathered in every glance, and
make it up by drawing as they think it ought to be
—not as they have actually *seen* it. Strictly honest
work, and a desire to improve keenness of observation
and accuracy of memory will soon remedy this defect.

I attach great value to bold outline drawings, such
as are used in primary classes, as introductory subjects
for such study These, by their simplicity and the
striking contrast between white and black which they
present, make an impression which is easily retained
by an effort of the will. If this impression be recalled
frequently during a week, and occasionally revived by

study of the original, it will become permanent   Two
things are to be observed in connection with this *first*
study.   Firstly, it is of the greatest importance that
it be accurately and correctly conceived, since every
error of method which you introduce into it will probably be repeated in the second trial, and grow in
strength with every successive effort.   It is the first
notes of the birdling which are almost unchangeable.
Secondly, that the more thoroughly it is effected the
easier will the next experiment be.   It is not advisable that there should be any straining to learn the
object in a hurry.   Your mind may possibly be
involuntarily distracted by some other cause.   Your
physique may be slightly disorganised.   You may be
constitutionally of the disposition which requires many
gentle and gradual repetitions to impress anything on
your memory.   Hasten slowly.

Practice in anything makes perfect.   From outline
drawings you may proceed to objects, from simple
objects to statues and the human figure.   I have
spoken of people who can recall a piece of music,
who can literally see in the mind's eye every note,
and play from it.   I have also mentioned the clergy-
man who learned his sermons by eye   I think that
this might be effected by beginning with a single
line, let us say a text or a proverb, very legibly
written in bold, thick letters, at least an inch in
length, and in learning them perfectly by eye, care
being taken that the imagination shall have no part
in rewriting them on the memory.   The number of
lines may be increased and their size diminished as
the power of acquisition is developed.

We all know that, in some way, this power of

recalling objects vividly is latent in us. We read familiar books in our dreams, we see the departed, we recall past scenes in reveries, we sometimes imagine faces and remember them after waking In fevers and in similar states of nervous excitement we think that we see phantoms mingling with real objects What we thus create involuntarily, in an unhealthy condition, we can also produce healthily, and subject to the laws of reason, by voluntary action. In these dreams, scenes are recalled by association. I have already said that the awaking in our memory of every detail of a scene connected with some startling incident is a fertile theme with novelists. I shall never forget the wonderful, the magnificent sunset which followed the burial of WASHINGTON IRVING The western sky, like a vast sea of golden fire, in which were islands of a deeper crimson glow, as though Heaven had thrown its glorious gates ajar to welcome the ascending soul, will always be impressed on my memory I have doubtless in my time seen sunsets as beautiful in the Far West on the prairies, on the plains of Russia, or in Egypt, but I cannot remember any of them as I do that one on the Hudson.

It may perhaps be thought that as all of this is so generally the result of involuntary action, there is no connection to be established between it and the will. Those who would understand this problem, so far as it has in all probability been solved, may read what CARPENTER has said in his " Mental Physiology " of primarily and secondarily automatic motion. What I assert is that the will can stimulate involuntary or automatic motion Did it never happen to you that you cannot recall a certain tune until you by an exertion remembered the *place* where you heard it, or the person who played it ? Sometimes, in order to remember a certain remark, you must first recall the time of year when you heard it, then the city in which you were, then the house in which you dined, and finally the person who was seated by you who made the remark. All of these preliminary steps are recalled by deliberate, voluntary action. It is not necessary to enter into a metaphysical analysis of theories of free will and causation You will probably admit that we can revive, in a more or less perfect form, when we choose, that which we remember, and that the vividness of these memories can be increased by practice.

The practice of eye-memory stores the mind with beautiful images, and increases our artistic sense It may be developed so as to place at our disposal galleries of pictures and statues, scenes in the opera, landscapes, or picturesque bits, the forms and faces of friends, or, in fact, whatever we have seen. It may be denied by many that such a power exists in us to such a degree, but I venture to assert that, among all who are present, there is probably not one who has done his best to develop it. For there is no mental faculty involving so much which is useful or curious which has received so little attention.

I will now enter upon an abstruse and yet very practical phase of eye-memory, which is also closely analysed by CARPENTER and CLARKE. ROBERT HOUDIN, in his autobiography, carefully explains that whilst performing his Second Sight he always practised a *double consciousness*. That is to say, while performing his trick, he at the same time kept in mind the objects which he had *memorised*   In fact, he lays much greater stress upon this double or simultaneous action of the mind than upon the extraordinary feat of getting thousands of objects by heart.   Every juggler will understand this   Every juggler knows what "working" means   It means, while substituting an object, or effecting "hanky-panky" by *manipulation* (which requires the shrewdest mental action), to divert the attention of the audience at the same time in another direction.   Should he even tell you that at exactly nine o'clock he would pick up a rabbit, with his right hand, from behind a screen, and put it into a hat before the audience you would not see him do it.   Because at that very instant he would raise his left hand and snap his fingers in the air, or point to something.   If there were a thousand persons present, every eye would be caught and drawn away by the left hand, and during that instant the rabbit would be taken out and put in the hat, and nobody present would see it.   To do this, the juggler must exert a double action of the mind.   The simplest form of this is seen in the child's trick of rubbing one hand up and down on the chest, while you pat your head with the other.   ROBERT HOUDIN illustrates this by telling us that while obliged to study law in his youth, he, while reading, used to keep tossing four balls in the air.

Now there is certainly the same double action of the mind while drawing   It requires thought to observe the model or to form the ideal in the mind, and it also requires thought to perform the action of drawing.   You cannot get over this by saying that the drawing becomes merely mechanical.   While I have been writing this lecture I have thought of the formation of every letter while I wrote. There are people who are said to write mechanically, but I cannot. Should I do so my writing would be illegible, even to myself. You would say, perhaps, that to do two things at once must detract something from both. I find invariably that the more I think about something else, the more carefully I write. Ladies say that they can sew best while talking. I have heard of an actress who was never so thrilling in her tones, never so heartrending, as while embracing her rival: she was at the same time pinching her. This was also a double action of mind. There used to be something of the same kind when I was at college, among the young gentlemen who read novels in chapel during sermon-time. Yet, on reflection, I doubt if in this instance the mental action was exactly balanced.

. I have met in my life with two instances of sculptors, both Frenchmen, who required but a single glance at any man to be able to model a perfect likeness of him. One of these artists, M. GARBIELLI, once took an admirable and very expressive portrait of JAMES GORDON BENNETT, whom he had seen only once, as the original went by rapidly in a carriage. A very curious instance of the length of time during which a picture may remain accurately impressed on the memory is shown in a feat performed by Mr. JOHN SARTAIN, well known as one of the ablest advancers of art in Philadelphia. Thirty-five years ago, when the old Academy of Fine Arts in Chesnut Street was burned, there perished in the fire a very valuable picture by MURILLO, entitled "The Roman

Daughter." Very recently Mr. SARTAIN has drawn it from memory. And Dr. ABERCROMBIE tells us that in the Church of St. Peter, in Cologne, the altar-piece is a fine picture by RUBENS. This was carried away by the French in 1805, but a local painter made from memory a copy which seems to be absolutely perfect. The original has been restored, and the copy is preserved along with it, and even when rigidly compared it is impossible to distinguish one from the other.

There is in Philadelphia a gentleman named JOHN RYDER, a JESSUP student at the Academy of Natural Sciences. I am told that he has the power of instantaneous observation, and of subsequently copying, to a degree which far transcends anything I have as yet heard of. Thus, having seen but for an instant any of the rapidly moving animalcules in any medium through a microscope, he will produce a perfect likeness of it, admirably coloured and shaded. I am under obligation to Mr. D. S. HOLMAN, the Actuary of the Franklin Institute, for this curious and valuable illustration of the advantages of eye-memory, And since recording this instance I learn that Dr. JOSEPH LEIDY, of Philadelphia, possesses the same power to as great a degree.

One of the first physicians in Baltimore has informed me that there is in that city, a patient of his, a gentleman who possesses eye-memory to a degree far transcending anything of the kind on record. He can recall, it is said, visually, entire books which he has read years ago, and remembers anything he reads whenever he exerts the determination to do so at the time of perusal.

I know personally a lady, Mrs. ELEANOR MEREDITH,

a teacher in Philadelphia, who at one time, in consequence of illness, lost her mental memory. In order to restore it, she practised getting poetry by heart, beginning with a poem of LONGFELLOW'S of about 300 lines. She could not learn it as she wished, but the result of strenuous effort was its visual acquisition, every line and mark becoming visible at will. After a time the lady's original memory returned. This case is curious, as indicating an absolute difference between "mental" and visual memory. I have also met with another lady teacher in the same city, who was induced to turn her attention to art by finding herself possessed, to a remarkable extent, of eye-memory. A certain landscape, which she could recall at will, delighted her so much that she determined to draw it. It was her first effort, and after many trials she succeeded in producing a tolerably good picture. There is a waiter in New York who is much employed at balls to superintend the *guarda roba*. He can identify the owners of five hundred hats in one evening. He does this by associating the face of the wearer with his hat and recalling it by eye-memory. "I put the face under the hat, and then I know whose hat it is," he says. I know a hotel clerk who remembers with an accuracy which is literally marvellous every trunk which comes to the hotel. There are in America many hotel-keepers who, like the late Mr WILLARD, rival MITHRIDATES in their memory of faces

I learn that in the Art School of Boston the practice of drawing with the model removed, as at St Petersburg, is followed with happy results I think that, after what I have said on this subject, that no one who will carefully examine it can doubt that the application of eye-memory to free-hand drawing can have anything but happy results. It must be remembered, however, that it requires patience. The faculty is, so to speak, not only dulled and blunted in us by never having been used, but is changed by having been vigorously developed in other directions   Therefore I trust those who experiment on it will persevere, and not be discouraged because the experiments of a few days do not yield marvellous results.

There is a faculty so closely allied to eye-memory as to be effectively identical with it.   This is *quick comprehensiveness*, or rapidity of sight with intelligence.   It is the art of seeing and understanding objects completely, even when in motion, in less time than the great majority of people take in so doing. Educationally its practice would form the next step beyond that of eye-memory   It has also to a degree been applied in object teaching.   Eye-memory stores the memory with phenomena ; quick comprehensiveness gives rapidity of perception and of thought   For merely mechanical rapidity of observation, induced by mechanical methods, will awaken mental activity at last, even in very dull minds.   I regret to say that almost the only people who appear to thoroughly cultivate this invaluable accomplishment are thieves and detectives.   It is usual, in training young sneak thieves, for the preceptor, holding a variety of small objects in one hand, to open and close the hand rapidly, and to require his pupils to ascertain at a glance what he holds.   They rapidly attain an amazing cleverness and quickness in such perception.   A boy thus trained is sent out ostensibly to beg.   He obtains admission to a kitchen, he may get a glimpse of a drawing-room, and with that glimpse he takes in everything, remembers everything, and returning reports what he has seen. There are other people, *not* thieves, who develop the same faculty in observing what is none of their business. They pry and peer about here and there, and go home with what they have got to gossip it This power of *unusual* quickness of perception, seldom acquired by honourable practices, is generally transmitted to children It becomes hereditary, and may then be honourably applied. I have had much experience of gypsies, and have observed among them a great development of this faculty. Those petty swindlers who go into shops and practice what is called ringing the changes, or cheating in making change, also develop remarkable quickness of perception Italians are supposed to acquire it by playing *morra*. Civilisation and ordinary education rather repress this faculty than develop it. It is to be regretted that an accomplishment which is capable of contributing so much to our general intelligence, and to the exercise of all our intellectual faculties, should really be deliberately cultivated chiefly by the vicious and the mean [1]

On the other hand, the detectives who hunt these foxes are obliged to become almost as clever. Many years ago Chief Marshal STEVENS, of New York, told

---

[1] There is a class of criminals in Germany called *chalfen,* who steal gold coins while pretending to purchase them They develop powers of quick perception and of adroit rapid fingering which seem miraculous One will literally as quick as a wink convey ten napoleons into the palm of his hand by its fingers, almost under the eye of the shopman, or during the second in which his glance is diverted The power is acquired by practice from childhood (*Die Judischen Gauner in Deutschland, Berlin,* 1848, *von A F Thiele*)

me that he wished to ascertain the character of a man who occupied a certain room which was always kept carefully closed against all intruders. One day he knocked, and the door was opened a few inches for an instant. During that instant his keen eye took in all the contents of the room. He saw that it was hung all round with suits of clothes of a very varied description; he knew at once that they were used for disguise, and observed that some of these disguises were the same as those which had been worn by the man whom he "wanted" One of the most intelligent men whom I have ever known is ROBERT WALKER, Inspector of Police in London. He says that most people, as they walk along a street, look habitually chiefly to the right hand, and that newly enlisted policemen are trained to overcome this habit and look to both sides, so as to become generally observant.

I have spoken of the fact that children receive and retain visual impressions better than grown people. I certainly should not omit to state that Mr FRANCIS GALTON has remarked that women are endowed with this faculty to a much greater degree than men. This great observer has remarked, in *Nature*, that women are not only better gifted than men with what he calls "mental imagery," but that they surpass us in the readiness with which they appreciate the scope and sense of inquiry into it. He says: "I have been astonished to find how superior women usually are to men in the vividness of their mental imagery, and in their powers of introspection. Though I have admirable returns from many men, I have frequently found others, even of the highest general ability, quite unable for some time to take in the meaning of such questions as these: 'Think of some definite object, say your breakfast table, as you sat down to it this morning, and consider carefully the picture that rises before your mind's eye. Is the image dim or fairly clear? Is its brightness comparable to that of the actual scene? Are the objects sharply defined? Are the colours quite distinct and natural?' &c. On the other hand, I find the attention of women, especially women of ability, to be instantly aroused by these inquiries. They eagerly and carefully address themselves to consider their modes of thought, they put pertinent questions, they suggest tests, they express themselves in well-weighed language and with happy turns of expression, and they are evidently masters of the art of introspection. I do not find any particular tendency to exaggeration in this matter either among women or men, the only difference I have observed between them is that the former usually show an unexpected amount of intelligence, while many of the latter are as unexpectedly obtuse The mental difference between the two sexes seems wider in the vividness of their mental imagery and the power of introspecting it than in respect to any other combination of mental faculties of which I can think."

After such a compliment from such a man it would be indeed ungrateful should the ladies who may meet with these remarks neglect the subject.

As summary and conclusion, I would remark that the development of eye-memory, to a greater or less extent, is within the power of almost everybody. No accomplishment affords such lasting pleasure, and it costs nothing. It can be exercised at any odd time without any preparation. In acquiring it stick to one subject until you can recall every detail of its shape and colour. Remember that with young people the development of *quick observation* in a merely mechanical manner leads invariably to widely varied intellectual quickness of perception A quick eye leads to a quick mind, and a quick eye may be developed by training. And I trust that, from what I have said, you will agree with me that eye-memory, though it is as yet little studied, is destined to exert, at no distant day, a great influence on art and on education.

Since the foregoing lecture was written I have collected many additional instances of eye-memory. Its occurrence is so frequent that I venture to say that by proper investigation it may be found to exist in one of every ten or twelve persons. Many exercise it unconsciously It is very common among musicians One lady tells me that she invariably and involuntarily learns her music by eye-memory, which she gradually displaces by a directer and more sympathetic method. Of this I am certain, that the faculty is too common to be regarded as a very exceptional phenomenon The following extract from a lady who is highly gifted both as an artist and scholarly writer illustrates what I have said :—

"BUSORAH, EL BEAR, ALGIERS,
"17th *January* 1881.

"I received your lecture on eye-memory Mrs ——
has set to work to teach her little boy on your plan, and she thinks he is very quick in learning by it. I believe that all artists must have more or less of the faculty of taking stock of objects at a glance I remember going in one season to the private view of twelve studios, and as my friends declared it was quite impossible for me to remember distinctly so many pictures, I made afterwards a pen and

ink drawing of one picture from each studio I hunted up those little sketches when I read your paper, and found that, feeble as they were, they brought the whole vividly before me again. Truly half the world never see anything, and if they could be induced to really use their eyes, their lives would become happier as well as more useful."

I quite agree with my friend that if people could be induced to use their eyes more they would be *happier*. Occupation is the secret of half our happiness, and in the exercise of eye-memory there is a means of curious occupation ever open to every one—without expense. Of its close connection with quickness of perception I need hardly speak, nor how it must draw out and support memory in connection with quickness, or how it would aid art or hand-work. One sense is not more nearly allied to another than are all these elements of education.

In many relations eye-memory belongs as much to quickness of perception as to the creating memory. I have therefore given it a place by itself. In conclusion, I would beg those who are interested in eye-memory, firstly to read what has been written on the subject by FRANCIS GALTON, and again, whenever opportunity occurs, in a society of cultivated people, to introduce it. The chances are nine to ten that nearly all who are present will recall one or more instances of it. This I have tested many times.

Part V.

—+—

ON TAKING AN INTEREST.

WE have all of us met with many men and more
women, who, to explain their ignorance of any branch
of culture, or their indifference to it, declare in the
most innocent manner that they "take no interest in
it." This want of interest, as they intimate and believe,
is a barrier put up by Nature between themselves and
certain fields of knowledge, which barrier it were waste
time to beat down. It cannot be denied that there
are thousands, even among those whose education and
associations should have given them common-sense,
who hold the easy faith that, unless "gifted" with a
genius for art, anybody is excusable for not drawing;
that without a Pentecostal gift of tongues it is needless
to study languages; and finally, that without an "innate
interest" it is sensible and proper enough not to care
for anything except dress, domestic details, dissipation,
and doing as other people do. For it is to be remarked
that these people who are so kind to their own short-
comings are all the more exacting within their own
sphere of knowledge and accomplishment I have
heard of such a person asking a kindred spirit, "Do
you like poetry?" "Yes." "What kind of poetry?"
"Well, most kinds, except blank verse." "Now, I
differ from you. My tastes are more *serious*. I like

blank verse best, and not the sing-song kinds." With people of such minds to like or not like poetry is quite the same as liking or not liking olives or tomatoes. It is a question *de gustibus*, and merely an accidental matter of taste. They have a general impression that blank verse is heavier than lyrical poetry—in fact, more wearisome or disagreeable, and therefore more allied to "goodness" And as every sect has its extremists, so in Anglo-Saxony, especially in the western branch, there are some whose instincts lead them to feel, if not express, the opinion that absolute *interest* in its truest sense in anything is not altogether commendable. For it is allied to *liking*, to pleasure, to the agreeable, and it is well known to them that whatever is nice must be naughty—if not nasty. In all this the saints and sinners of Philistia in fact agree. From learning lessons up to saving souls there are to be neither royal roads nor primrose paths. I once heard a preacher of this principle declare that we *must* "agonise" if we would see God. For there are men who have looked so long upon a cruel past that they give no glance towards a tender future, and have heard *per aspera ad astra* so often that they cannot think it right to get the stars without the stripes

Now if there were but a few people with such proclivities it would be of little law to any one. But in fact they are not few—they are about us by thousands, they influence the press, they control our schools, and are felt in all our popular culture. They may not recognise themselves in the picture which I have drawn, but their works betray them. They may not be bigots, they may be liberal unto unbelief, but they agree in this, that they live in little limits, that they do not regard taking as great an interest as possible in all things as a duty, and that they would stint the whole world if they could to their own range of thought and knowledge

Now there is a great truth beginning to dawn on the world, which is, that the easier and pleasanter education is, the more the pupil will learn and *become*. We have lost out of our language, more's the pity, the Saxon *weordan*, but what a Latin flood has washed away a German wind may blow back again. There is no boy born who may not become all that is becoming and *worth* himself into all that is worthy if he can only be taught betimes to take an interest in what is truly interesting Our whole present system of education bears the traces of bygone barbarism, of asceticism, Pharisaism, and cruelty. SOLOMON may have meant what he said when he declared that to spare the rod would be to spoil the child. It is possible that by such means he kept his stupendous harem in order. At the present day no one would take a Mormon, even though he had written a whole Proverbial Philosophy, as an authority in education It may be remarked by the way that there is no country on earth where the children are more freely thrashed than in Utah, and none where they are so intolerably insolent, vulgar, and ill-bred

If we look into it, we find that there are many teachers and others who no more believe that study can be made attractive than work. They can remember that ADAM was cursed to work; they do not reflect how much worse his lot would have been had he been cursed to be idle. "O Allah!" exclaims the wealthy Pasha in the Oriental story, " would that I had something to do!" "O Allah!" exclaims, it is true, at the same time, an overworked slave, "would that I had *nothing* to do!" We assume too much that all work must needs be overwork, and much that is in our popular education makes it so. Between extremes, work is to a healthy and clever mind an instinctive desire. It is only when it is compulsory that we dislike it. The reader may have heard of the men who found it very hard to dig potatoes all day, but who did not mind playing at digging a cellar by moonlight. It has been observed by some philosopher that a boy can draw two hundred pounds' weight of other boys farther and faster than he can fifty pounds of coal. The merely sporting man who is simply a case of suspended intellect, or a grown-up boy, will play at coachman every day for months, when to be brought down to the road in earnest would crush him. Now work would lose its most repulsive features if we were not really urged by all authority, especially the social, to regard it as a curse ānd as vulgar. And it may be cheerfully conceded that while work was merely mechanical or brainless, and possibly performed, as in Aryan India, solely by subordinate races, *caste* must have arisen. Science and art are little by little identifying all labour with culture, thereby robbing it of the repulsiveness which it was the chief aim of that arch-snob and Philistine Satan to bring about. When this is clearly understood it will also be admitted that education may also be as attractive as it was once terrible. What is common to the reform of both abuses is to teach men and children to take an *interest* in what they do. He who takes a real interest in his work is never weary; the boy who loves his book is always at play.

I must admit that in this question between the curse and the attractiveness of labour, as in that of interest, I have chanced upon a vast problem which I cannot here fully investigate. In both cases it reduces itself to conservatism and progress. Wisdom bids the conservative advance, and the progressionist to take no rash step forward. But I believe I may assume that it is now generally granted by the wisest and most experienced in education, that it is possible to make school attractive, and that the principle of this is to induce the pupils to take an interest in their studies.

FOURIER did great harm to the cause of labour by teaching that it could be based on *la gaîté française*— merriment and monkey-play. Mr. LONGFELLOW and many with him have made still more mischief by making its *animus* a grim and joyless determination to surpass all rivals, even though success should lead to nothing but a miserable solitary death. It is not that the work in itself shall be pleasant or its aims useful, according to the " excelsior " philosophy, but that he who is in it shall *surpass* all rivals or "go ahead." And there are many among the meaner sort, especially in New England, to whom this phase of vanity strongly appeals. I once knew a young man who was greatly admired among his friends as being very enterprising and ambitious, and who was beyond question very conceited   I was talking German with a German in his presence, when he expressed an earnest wish that he could do the same. Whereupon I assured him that with *will* he could easily learn 'it, and that I would gladly tell him how to do so. " Oh! " he replied hastily, as if he feared I thought he meant to pay me a

compliment, "you don't understand me   I wouldn't
give a snap to know German.   It is only that it always
makes me 'mad' to have anybody know anything that
I don't, or to hear one talk what I can't"

Work can never in the world be *mere* amusement or
pastime.   He who works, though he be a child, should
feel that there is a purpose in his work.   When boys
two hundred years ago were made to talk Latin to one
another, they realised at once to what it led.   When
a youth is taught not merely to draw, but to apply that
drawing to industrial art, he feels its practical use.
Still less can work or study be based on the principle
of competition, or that of " excelsior "   This is even more
injurious than the insane idea of making it "amusing."
It induces ten or perhaps twenty per cent in a college
class to study hard, but discourages the rest.   Why
should it not ?   Parents with few exceptions seriously
hope or expect their sons to be among the very first,
but the sons soon find that there are others cleverer and
as resolute as themselves.   There are parents who exact
of boys of very moderate ability that their remaining
at college must depend on being " first honour man," or
near it.   Among the vulgar whose motto is " excelsior,"
and who never think of travelling wisely along life's
road, but simply of racing on it, more or less cleverness
in children goes for nothing.   "They have only to
work a little harder to beat anybody and everybody."
In the little world of school or college the same false
ideas prevail, and the same false standard of study is
adopted.   Caste of a kind is as strong in such communities as in India.   The studies in themselves are
nothing—to excel in them is everything.   Teachers
tell us that whether a youth be " crammed " or not, he

cannot be "first," unless he has thought, but "coaches" and crammers know far better.[1]

It will be long, however, before professors will advocate the abolition of competition. They have gone on so long in the old way that they cannot easily learn a new one And it cannot be denied, and I do not mean to deny, that to carry out the principles of improving the memory, developing quickness of perception, and awakening interest in studies, will require clever and earnest teachers. If half the wisdom which is wasted in America or even in England on petty personal politics were resolved into reform of education, it would be better for us in every way. Since the vast majority of men in the United States have at present actually no more to do with appointing their rulers than have the serfs in Russia, since there are so few voters who have any part in governing beyond paying taxes, why do they not cease to take such an engrossing interest in what their lords and ringmasters or "bosses" only can control, and apply themselves to advancing culture? But as the commonalty in England are absorbed in all the life of the aristocracy, into whose charmed circles they cannot venture, so the American is taken up with the interests of the political aristocracy, of professional office-seekers, whom he admires because, being in a minority, they *rule* him. It is incident to a certain stage of social development to take more real interest in one's

---

[1] Several articles have appeared of late on university cramming; notably one in the *St James's Gazette*, about October 1, 1887, which, if carefully considered, should convince every one of the absurdity of endeavouring to stimulate study by competition. It is not in rewarding youths for passing crammed examinations that education should consist, but in awakening in them a sincere interest in their studies. Where this is not done, either the teacher or the pupil had better be at some other employment.

" betters," or cleverers, or " wealthiers" than in one's own welfare. As yet with most men there is more sympathetic admiration for one who has built himself up at their expense, or even robbed them outright, than for one who has sacrificed life and fortune for them. This indicates the feudal state of society, and it is incident to all men who are at a certain inferior degree of development, whether they live in a republic or a monarchy. Wherever a minority rules by any other than moral superiority, there is serfdom And wherever mere competition, personal ambition, and power are the aims of life, and " excelsior" its motto, there will be a want of morality. You cannot make a government with a name.

Before an apprentice can work well he must have good tools, and be taught how to use them. He cannot work with ease or pleasure until then. This is the first step towards interest. I have elsewhere shown, as I hope, that grounding a good memory and developing quickness of perception make labour lighter. With these the practice of eye-memory or visual representation will go far to bring forth latent intellectual power of every kind. Were all this effected properly with a boy of average intelligence, interest, the greatest stimulant to study, would almost follow of its own accord. But it is not study of books, or mere memory, or erudition, acquired at the expense of more practical qualities, which would be awakened by such education. With all this should come hand-work or art. All of this lies within the scope of a common-school education, if the teacher be but capable The average capacity of youth is little understood, and is generally underrated, because most people set its standard by themselves They know that as they were educated they did their best, more or less, and are sure that others could have done no more. That their radical mental powers, or the very mind itself, could have been re-created, never occurs to them No man likes to think that he might have had a far better memory, far greater quickness of perception, the power of visual representation, or more sense, because he feels that he would not then have been himself. Nor would he have been really what he now is, any more than if he had had a different father or mother. It is bitter to reflect on the better "might have been," and therefore we do not think on it.

Yet it is true beyond all question that there have been teachers who possessed to a wonderful degree the art of developing genius From their schools great men have gone forth by scores, while in the same country and at the same time those who became distinguished under conceited pedants were few and far between. These teachers who made clever scholars were veritable creators of souls Their art consisted in inspiring in their pupils an interest not only in their studies, but in all that interested themselves They awoke ambition, and made it clearer to the scholar what he might do in life, or what become.

As interest in study or in anything depends greatly on the kind of mind possessed by the teacher, I will set forth several types of such men, as I have heard them described or observed them.

One was a man advanced in life, who had all the ungeniality and formal vanity which characterised a certain class of New England country clergymen in the last generation. "Turveydrop" was not more continually self-conscious of his deportment than was this venerable but vain man, who, having been unwisely admired for his affected dignity or good looks when younger, could never forget it. I cannot recall that of the two unhappy years when I was under him I ever saw him smile pleasantly or heard him speak kindly or familiarly to a single boy. Punishment was his only means to secure industry. One boy seemed to be individually as indifferent to him as another; out of school all were of as little interest to him as so many flies. I never shall forget the manner in which he put me down once when I dared to ask him a question not connected with my studies. I had been under another schoolmaster who cheerfully conversed with his boys on any subject. I had been but a day or two with the new teacher, when, in consequence of reading SOUTHEY's poem, I ventured to ask him who was CORNELIUS AGRIPPA. He looked at me as if I had insulted him, and replying in the coldest manner, "a learned man," turned to his papers. With all his pedantry he was a very indifferent teacher, and he certainly possessed to perfection the wretched art of making every association connected with schooling or with himself detestable.

Another teacher had unfortunately certain defects as an instructor of which no man could be more aware than he was. His early education wanted thoroughness, and he did not like the monotony of school life. His after-experiences as editor and business traveller to the tropics suited him much better. He had been induced to take a large school under representations that he would find it a profitable and pleasant occupation, and he had been disappointed. But he was a man who, with but little improvement, would have made a perfect teacher, for he possessed the art of making his scholars take an interest in things without the range of their studies as well as within them. What we did not understand he explained with pleasure. Out of school he was friendly and familiar. I can well remember how, when we met him at an old book-stand—he being, by the way, a great haunter of such places—he initiated our first knowledge of Elzevirs and Alduses. It is remarkable that, though he kept school but a few years, many of his pupils became in after-life noted men—a fact of which he was very proud. He had in fact so many scholars who turned out "characters," that it was probably due in a great measure to his influence.

When a teacher has at one time or another awakened more or less *interest* in fifty subjects in a boy, it may be assumed that as those subjects turn up in life the boy or man will regard them as acquaintances, and therein lies the beginning of knowledge. Interest is that "better acquaintanceship" to which boon companions drink when they first meet. Its secret lies in the pride which all feel in knowledge. We may converse with a man on any subject, and he may assure you he knows nothing about it, and takes no interest in it. But if we have given him any information on it, and he remembers it, he will be very glad to display it; and if he does so with success, he will probably carry it further, and end by avowing a great love for it, and intimating that he has a genius for that very thing. In this the boy is the father of the man. A sure way to persuade people, young or old, to take up any art or study with interest is to get just enough of it into their heads to induce them to talk about it, or explain it to the more ignorant. To adroitly induce a preliminary acquaintance with a subject or attract the attention is therefore an important element in the art of inducing interest.

There are a great many people who declare that it is not in them to learn any art or language, or to take any interest in culture, who would however acquire it all without delay if a large fortune awaited their passing an examination on it. A London physician once said to me that a legacy of a hundred thousand pounds would at once cure most of his patients. It is not in the power of the teacher or of society to awaken ambition by such rewards, but the mere admission of the fact that there is in most or all a power to learn which *might* be drawn out is a tower of strength to all who hold the affirmative in this question. Reward in some form is a great aid to interest—not as a *premium* for competition, but as a condition of learning. I once went to a school in which on Saturdays those who had tàken the highest mark during the week for studies were allowed the first choice of certain minerals. This was all very well so far as awakening an interest in mineralogy went, but it was soon found that the same boys continually took the prizes, so the majority would not even wait to receive their less valuable specimens.

At another school near Boston, and in an exceptional winter, when the thermometer was very far below zero, the boy who got up first in the morning received an apple. The result was that to contend for the apple was regarded as a reproach, and the majority remained abed much later than they would otherwise have done. The principal of this school was a kind-hearted, easy-going old gentleman, who having failed as a merchant, yet having many friends, and being unqualified for anything else, was set up as a schoolmaster on the principle of the *inutile ficus* of HORACE—the bit of timber being fit for nothing else, they made a god of it, "even a graven image." This graven image of whom I speak might have acted wisely had he given apples to all who were down before eight o'clock, but there was in him a feeble or silly vein of eccentricity which inspired him to mismanage his boys morally in many ways. Having altogether nearly a hundred pupils, many of them from sixteen to twenty years of age, he adopted for them all a petty goody-goody system which would have suited an infant school, but which developed no manliness, no vigour, and no interest. There was no cruelty or unkindness whatever in his rule, but there was nothing in his teaching tending to awaken interest or to make scholars, or anything else. He was not learned, and his school was carried on by hired assistants The studies were conducted in that shift-less, aimless way which too generally characterises the teaching of those who have taken up as a trade a calling for which they have no qualification and have had no training. As a reward for good conduct, or as a favour, the boys were allowed to undertake different kinds of menial, ungentlemanly, or dirty work, *a la* Squeers, for which they received from two to three cents (half-pence) an hour. As this was in its time perhaps the first school in New England, both as to expense and respectability, it has always seemed to me that this tendency to train boys as if their future life was to be that of under-servants was as great a mistake as fagging in England. It withdrew their minds from interest both in books and healthful play. As regards the latter, or physical culture in any form, it was considered as a great indulgence of a necessary evil. To prevent it as much as possible, all boys having bad marks were prohibited from play or exercise of any kind or even taking a walk, it being usual to send offenders to bed in the day-time, during play-hours. But at the time of which I speak the idea that physical exercise was a duty had no more entered the heads of parents or teachers than that play was not in some way wicked, or that study could be anything but disagreeable.

I am confident that examination of the subject cannot fail to convince the reader of the great disadvantage of the private school when conducted in an irresponsible manner and as a mere business. When the teacher regards his calling as something worse than what he might have had or would have, he is to be respected as the Western preacher was who always thought it would have paid better if he had gone into the clock business. There is no profession in which a man can exert so much influence for good as in teaching and training, and he whose heart is not in it should leave it at once. If we were awake to our duties, the teacher would be regarded as far more valuable to the community than the military man or politician. It is a melancholy sight in reviewing the lives of American professional politicians to read that so many of them have "risen" from keeping school to being lawyers, and from law to the Legislature! This ascent seems like that of the dough of Paulding's Dutch baker, which rose downward.

I retain vivid and very numerous feelings and memories of my school-days. Owing to certain causes

and influences which I can accurately recall and explain,
I became at a very early age a great reader.   One of
my teachers [1] was in the habit of reading passages from
SPENSER'S Faerie Queene to the boys, and of describing
scenes which he did not read. So before I was ten
years old I borrowed the book and read it all   I can
remember that looking out the hard words in the
glossary was rather a pleasure   I think that some of
the other boys did the same. What I remember very
distinctly and *apropos* of this reading, which was in
extent and character far beyond my age, as such reading
is generally rated, was that once when I was complimented on it, I reflected that most of my companions
could and would have done as much or more if they had
only been directed that way, and that I myself could
have exerted that influence   I think that BENJAMIN
WEST said in his Life, that when his boyish efforts in
art first began to attract attention in his rural circle,
many other boys began to draw and paint also, and
that some of them were cleverer than himself
Now the teacher of whom I spoke, though he had
several great disqualifications, at least knew how to
make his pupils take a remarkable interest in all such
books as interested himself. Of the four of whom I
have given descriptions, two evidently had no gift or
inclination whatever to inspire any interest in their
scholars in anything, the other two inspired it uninten-
tionally as regarded miscellaneous and curious culture,
poetry, and the beginning of what in later days led to
philosophical and æsthetic studies   And in all these
cases there was of course a direct and very perceptible

[1] This was T B ALCOTT, whose singular school is mentioned by Miss
MARTINEAU in her autobiography.

result on the pupils. Be it specially remarked that the two who thus awoke an interest in their pupils for general reading and a wider range of thought, though they had not one-third of the number of pupils of the other two, had three or four times as many who distinguished themselves when grown up. The one who was by far the most learned and the most severe had almost no pupils who have ever since been heard of in the world "for any good." He punished boys for very trifling offences by "keeping them in" all day from 9 A.M. to 5 P.M. without food. I can well recollect, when this happened to me, how terribly hungry and irritable I became in the afternoon, and how I often chewed pine-wood sticks and paper to alleviate my sufferings. But how the intellect or the morals can be mended by such treatment is difficult to understand. A single piece of bread would have done much more to enable me to study my lessons.

There is a class of critics whom one may call extremists or exaggerators, whose method is to immediately assume the last stretch of possibility or probability as the legitimate scope of an argument, and who defend themselves on the ground that logical deduction demands perfection. These men should read that great and good work, the *Baital Pachisi*, or "Vikram and the Vampire," from which they may learn that the last lesson of wisdom is not to be too wise, nor to expect the last grain of perfection from anybody. Such men oppose a small objection to a great reform They are like the Arab who, when starving to death, declined a cucumber because it was crooked. They do much harm in the world, and little good. As critics they depress and destroy, and they help little in developing.

Many of this kind inquire where the teachers are to be found who can inspire *interest* in the youth in anything, still more awaken the faculty of inducing self to endeavour to be interested in all things. They say we must wait till the world is more advanced; that we must *laissez faire*, or let things work themselves. They are prompt to carp captiously because vanity is far more easy to gratify by fault-finding than by appreciation. Now it is unfortunately true that in the whole range of effort to aid man there is not one in which so much unkind and petty criticism is exerted as on any reform in education. Such changes as are here suggested do most certainly involve more thought and study from both parents and teachers than they have previously given to such subjects. All of this will involve trouble, and nobody likes to take trouble. So when Ross BROUNE suggested to YUSEF in Syria that a great idle Arab who lay lounging before him could in America earn a dollar a day, his guide replied, "But to do that would he not have to *work?*" And that ended the question. Truly both parents and schoolmasters will have to work not a little before their children and pupils can be properly taught. That is not to be denied. Among all teachers those are rarest who endeavour to interest their pupils in school or studies, and yet such experiments, wisely planned, rarely fail. There was a master whose pupils persisted in coming late to school. He made it a matter of reward or privilege that some should be allowed to attend an hour before the regular time, during which extra-time he conversed with them or aided them in their lessons. The result was that before long they all came early. To this schoolmasters may object that they are not so well paid or so highly esteemed that they should give so much time and pains to work, and they are quite right. At present teachers are not as a rule able to do what they should, nor would they be properly paid if they could. The city of Philadelphia, which expects to pay fifteen millions of dollars for its Public Buildings, which will be, when finished, the most misplaced architectural monstrosity in Christendom, does not pay its public teachers one-half what they should in decency receive. The fault is not with its School Board, who perform their duties most honourably and intelligently under great difficulties, but with the many who complain of school taxation, as if every dollar which went for such purposes were a dead waste. In which this city differs little from any other, since that in which the school tax is not the one most grumbled at is indeed a rarity.

The keepers of boarding-schools and parents all have it in their power to do much to awaken in children an interest either in their studies or in that which will tend as much as study to improve their minds. I shall have written to no purpose if the suggestions which I have given in this work cannot aid in this direction. I can well remember that at a boarding-school where I passed a portion of my boyhood there was time enough and readiness and cleverness enough among the boys to have easily become apt at hand-work had there been anybody to teach it. Such work would open many doors of interest in many a branch of culture.

When the habit of making the will arouse the memory shall have been induced until the scholar finds no difficulty in learning, and this faculty in turn is balanced by increased quickness of perception, it will not be difficult to awaken interest in anything. These are sure steps to the highest culture. The last and highest is that of teaching the pupil that he can *will himself* to take an interest in whatever he pleases Many great scholars never discover that they have such a power. And yet the whole history and tendency of civilisation lead to it Happy is the man who can read every or any book and find something in it There is no such thing as a dull book written by any one whom Time has approved as a genius. Dulness as regards it is in the reader. But the last thing which I would urge is that on this ground there should be much reading of inferior books Minds, when not of the very strongest nature, can be hopelessly enfeebled by much reading of second-class novels, most people lose themselves in far lower grades of worthless fiction. Genius is so effective that many books which contain much that is bad really do no harm in proportion to the good which they inspire, for true ability is, as I have said, like a running stream which washes itself clean—the stronger it runs, the sooner it is purified. Those who doubt this may mark with a pencil in a Bible all the passages which they would not like their children to notice I never knew a commonplace youth, however prurient his tastes might be, who ever succeeded in reading more that a few chapters in "Rabelais;" I never knew a clever one who was in the least injured by the great humorist. This is beyond my subject, but I mean to say that even schoolboys may be wisely encouraged in the faith that they are capable of being interested in what they will. For appetite comes with reading as with eating, and he who has learned A can master B.

As a recapitulation, I may remind the reader that a great development of the power of simply memorising may be attained by practising the young in perfect *lessoning* This is to be balanced and aided by training quickness of perception, the two being greatly aided by hand-work and the development of eye-memory When all of these faculties or accomplishments shall have been educated out of or into the pupil, the teacher or parent will find that it is no difficult matter to awaken interest in anything that can be studied or performed. All the processes are mutually helpful, mutually strengthening Every one makes the others easier. The possibility of each has been proved by experiment. What I suggest is their combination.

There is a principle which underlies all mental effort. It is attention. On this MAUDSLEY has written wisely and well. The art of awakening attention depends on the sympathetic or magnetic power of the teacher. He who can induce a pupil to *attend* to anything, that is, to really remark it, has gone half way in awakening an interest in it. There are very few who cannot do the former if they will, and when this is done all can develop the latter. The art of attracting the attention is one with that of awakening quickness of perception.

CONCLUSION.

THERE is a disposition among many critics to point out as defects in a system of education the neglect to specify details which in practice must really depend upon the teacher or on circumstances. On the other hand, the author of a scheme, if he attempts to previse and provide for every contingency, is sure to overwhelm his readers with an excess of matter which few can master, and very few will read. I have already said that if I had in my experience begun by advocating an entire reform in industrial training, including a preparation for agricultural, commercial, or industrial pursuits with housekeeping, I should have been still in the position of a mere theorist, and could never have got a school. I preferred to prove by experiment simply a portion of my principles, and now that it is proved, I can see no reason why the rest may not be admitted. It cannot be harder to make a farmer or shopman of a boy than an artist; in fact it has hitherto been universally assumed that it is much less difficult

But there is a more serious objection which may properly be urged, should I rest here, and that is that while I have given tolerably full and practical detail of *industrial* art, I have merely sketched in outline the rudiments of teaching the other branches. This is true, because the obvious methods of teaching them seem so simple that one is inclined to leave them to the

" practical" people who assume to understand how eveiy-
thing should be done so much better than the "mere
theorist," and who will not fail to appear in swarms as
soon as the method shall have been universally recognised. They are always to be depended on, as surely
as the wake follows the vessel. Another and far more
serious objection may be found in the fact that I have
not arranged and carefully co-ordinated the different
branches of a reformed education, that I have not
shown how, for instance, memorising and quickness of
perception are to be adopted to the course for a farmer
or shopman; and finally, that all my system as set forth
is limited to children under fourteen years of age.

In the hands of any man fit to be a teacher the hints
which I have given should abundantly suffice to enable
him to practically develop an entire system to its fullest
extent. But, as I have said, while teaching children
continues to be a half-paid, inferior profession, clever
men, if they happen to be in it, will not exert themselves to the utmost to excel. Therefore it will be
necessary for those who may think there is something
in what I have said to consider seriously how and in
what manner industry may be made a branch of all
education, that is to say, of the education of every
child, with reference to some special career if possible,
if not to teach such general principles as may in any
case be applicable to every calling. There are countless
instances in which circumstances change intentions:
it will often happen that the boy who meant to be a
farmer turns to a merchant. Now it will accordingly
be an object to educate these children in such a way
that even if changes occur they will be ready for them,
and not have lost time. And this can be done.

We will assume that a boy having left the Kinder-garten or infant school, begins by being trained to merely memorise, and then to exercise the memory until it is perfect. In the East this stage of education begins at the age of from six to eight. This should not form a branch . it should be for a long time the only study. When the memory begins to manifest great strength, then exercises in quickness of perception may be introduced. Now I would call attention to this, that if these two faculties are *really* developed by careful teaching, they will give great power to learn and under-stand anything, and improve or create intellect. If they do not, then there will be nothing in it all. Fortunately they do not require genius to teach them · only a clear comprehension of the method and patience. For it must be distinctly understood that although a child under fourteen can be so trained as to make a living when that age is reached, this should not be the object of its education, unless dire need and manifest poverty are before it. In other more favourable cases the edu-cation should be such as to prepare it for the factory, or farm, or counting-house, or family, so that it will be perfectly at home in them on entering. There is a war being waged at present between those who wish to have every child so schooled that the parents need pay out no more money for it after it is fourteen years old, and those who doubt whether childhood should really be turned into a kind of factory-mill life There is a certain truth to be ever borne in mind. Childhood is *ideal* or unreal : it is a season for play in animals as with mankind. Take away its idealising, its play, its romancing—you can do it if you will—and the result is a hard and selfish, if not cruel and wicked manhood.

One can see such children every day among the lower classes: children in whose miserable little faces greed and sin and shrewdness, vulgarity and harshness, have set the sign of evil thoughts. Yet these children who have been trained to make their way in life will never lead lives such as any human being ought to experience. It is very true that among vulgar Americans or Britons, as among those of many other races, there is a melancholy majority of people who would be charmed to have sons who would "succeed in life" at any cost, independently of principles or poetry, culture or humanity, according to the wisdom of "business first, pleasure afterwards." But I assume that childhood, like womanhood, is, or ought to be, instinctively fond of the ideal or imaginative, and that instead of repressing this tendency we should employ it to practical purpose in its time.

Now the boy who has got a general idea of design, and sees the possibility of mastering all the minor arts, does not feel, on acquiring this power, as a man of thirty would. He is still in fairyland: it is droll or wonderful that he, a boy, should be an artist. Play is still a part of his soul: it is his nature, as it ought to be. Take it out of him, and you will take the humanity out of his after-life. When lessons are given to children simply as work devoid of the *ideal*, they may learn them, but not with love. Present these same lessons, not precisely as sports, but as employment which gives them a consciousness of being beyond what they are, of playing a part in life or of acting, and they will master them with great facility. It is as if one were to offer any ordinary man a fortune as soon as he could speak any given modern language. He will be *sure* to learn it.

I do not wish to be understood here as advocating the ridiculous French socialist theory that work can or ought to be turned into play   I do urge, however, that play may be turned into or made to tend towards work without losing any of its charm   Now a boy told that he is to be a farmer, and talked to and treated as if farming were quite an art, and familiarised with its simple details by means of a manual, or perhaps seeing a farm and such extra information as every teacher should be able to impart, would, I am sure, advance in proportion, in his interest in and knowledge of farming, just as my pupils advanced in minor arts.   In every village these pupils, as they get on, could be made more and more practically familiar with farms   There would be no want of advice from farmers.   If memorising has succeeded at all, it will show itself with quickness of perception in agriculture.   The pupil having learned the DESIGN—that is, that industry is a part of education, and that his first act in it is agriculture — will, with memory and quick grasp of details, progress rapidly   And the idealising tendency peculiar to youth will, when allied to these powers, produce genius—that is, the power to awaken and apply the will.

If my theory is worth a rush. when this *genius* is once awakened, it will master the details of any calling very rapidly.   If a boy is to be in business, the idea of industry must be set before him in a handbook of trade, to be followed by the course of a commercial college.   For this, as for farming or art, there is the period before fourteen years of age, which should be rather preparatory practical than purely practical, and that after it, which should be serious.   As yet men have not learned to distinguish between preparing for a career and beginning to prepare for it. They do not draw the line between learning the alphabet and learning to read. In early youth the preparation should not be too extensive or too difficult. Boys are not taught in my industrial school as yet to sculpture statues, but simply to carve flat panels. It will be enough if, while boys, their attention is attracted towards farming and commerce and art, and that they shall be practically just so much instructed therein as to feel at home in them, though only as apprentices.

Everybody will not grasp in all its fulness what I mean by the ideal or unreal nature in children, but those who do will agree with me, that far from extinguishing it, as men have generally sought to do, it should be cultivated, for in it lies the germ of generosity, nobility, honour, and poetry, as well as more practical qualities. I am quite sure that all my cleverest pupils have the keenest sense that there is a kind of fun in their being artists, able to do such work as is popularly associated with the efforts of grown people, and "geniuses" at that. They feel as if they were on a stage playing a part. And when visitors come in and exclaim, "How wonderful!" "What talent!" and the boy or girl hears it, and knows very well that there is nothing so remarkable in it after all, since all in the school can do as much, it is not strange that he or she feels that it is only applause for a part well played. It is difficult to make a child (and some grown up people) believe that life is worth living for unless it *is* "acted." Now the task is to train this tendency to play to practical ends. If it be allied to great memory and a highly cultivated quickness of perception this instinct will literally work wonders.

It would be impossible to keep a boy so trained from being an excellent arithmetician, for quickness of perception is almost in itself quickness in numbers, which are only the relations of things. Bookkeeping is the record or memory of numbers applied to things Arithmetic is to bookkeeping, mensuration, navigation, and technology what design is to art. It can be readily understood that after fourteen years of age a career will be easily found for a boy who has been trained to a beginning. As for further education, there is the industrial school proper, the technological institute, and the higher art schools. It must be admitted that these require much reform, but it will come. Perhaps after all is shaped, last and least, the universities and colleges will awake from their slumbers and also begin to prepare pupils for a practical life. As the magazine which sets forth the views of one of them has within a very few years passed through the stages of declaring that "Darwin is atheistic"—"Darwin is doubtful"—"Darwin may be reconciled with true Christianity"—so it will perhaps say that these views are Utopian and irreligious—they are possible—they are practical. *Non possumus* depends on circumstances.

If children can be educated in the way I have indicated before the fourteenth year, if the public try the experiment, and it should succeed, there need be little inquiry as to how it is to be carried on through the succeeding years. That it will succeed is rendered certain by a few facts

I. During centuries before the invention of printing, *memory* was millions of times developed to a degree which at the present day would suffice to silence all complaint as to over-cramming with too many studies.

II. *Quickness of perception* has also been shown to be susceptible of development in children by culture. It has been declared to be a fact, and it is one.

III. *Industrial art* is also within the reach of all children. Thousands are now practising it in America and South Germany, and going to school at the same time. All of these exist as wild plants The question is, Can they be cultivated ? If I have done or written aught which induces the reader to believe this, my end is attained.

APPENDIX.

———+———

I.

KARL WERNER ON THE AMERICAN SYSTEM OF ART EDUCATION IN SCHOOLS.

THE following review of the pamphlet, "Industrial Art in Schools," by Karl Werner, Government Inspector of Schools at Salzburg, appeared in the *Literarische Beilage der Montags Revue, Vienna*, April 23, 1883.

The opinions held at different stages as to the object and aim of public schools made or followed the currents of the stream of Time. One of these currents runs deeply at the present day, and the practical interest which influences society is making itself felt in education.

While people were contented at an earlier period with giving in schools only such branches of knowledge as might form the basis of a more extended culture, the requirements of life demanded practical training for the people and industrial education. The child should, in addition to reading, writing, and arithmetic, also learn those things which exercise a determining influence on life, and knowledge derived from natural science, geography, and history should give the future citizen broader views to qualify him the better to fulfil his mission

But the teachers did not rest here. It was desired to introduce work itself to the school, and this is what is treated of in a pamphlet by CHARLES GODFREY LELAND, Director of an Industrial School in Philadelphia, who seems

to have practically solved a problem for which Europe is
yet hardly prepared.   This document, which is warmly
commended by the Commissioner of Education in Washington, General JOHN EATON, has three divisions—the introduction, the practical portion, and general remarks, which we
will briefly sketch before commenting on the whole

According to the precept that flowers precede fruit, the
writer is of the opinion that during the childhood of an
individual as well as of a race, the production of ornament
precedes that of the merely useful   And on this truth the
education of children should be founded   Schools have
hitherto certainly given what is popularly called culture, and
yet youth left them quite as unfit for practical life on the last
day as the first.   For it is practical preparation which children
require ; not indeed that public schools shall become mere
trade schools, since that is unreasonable for children under
fourteen years of age, but that the pupils should be at first
accustomed to agreeable or ornamental work, or the exercise
of the minor arts.   What these are will be described in
another place   Suffice it to say that by their practice the
regular studies, far from being disturbed or interrupted, will
be directly aided, since by exercise of the hands and eyes
quickness of perception is awakened   If a child can learn
in the Kindergarten of FROEBEL to sew, sing, braid, draw, and
model, it can in a more advanced school study more advanced
branches, and all the more so, because the whole system
does not depend on learning different branches, but because
the necessity of design and modelling is the same for every
art study, be it in wood, clay, sheet brass, paper, or even
embroidery.   In fact the establishment of schools where
such arts are taught must be regarded as absolutely necessary,
since it naturally fills the time between the infant school
or Kindergarten and the learning a trade.   And there is no
real difficulty as regards establishing such public schools if
the teacher can only draw a little, since what remains can
be easily learned from good practical manuals

That which is most important for such schools is drawing, and that free-hand, which, however, is not the kind
mechanically taught by copying, but in such a manner that
from the first lesson in which the children are shown how to
throw lines freely and accurately, they are made to exercise

their inventive faculties, or to *design* As by the ordinary system the child too frequently wearies of drawing, by this it is step by step made familiar with variations upon given motives or patterns, so that it can in a few weeks or months develop entirely original patterns

If painting is to follow design, it is not begun according to the old method, with many colours and the favourite flower-painting, but merely with monochrome The author has tested both methods, and found the latter alone practicable. Drawing, as has been fully established, is very important even for girls who are to learn any trade: it is much more so for children who model in clay. Of course all designs should be on a large scale, and must neither descend to pettiness nor be lost in mere imitation.

The practical part is devoted to details. We are told what materials are required for drawing, in doing which the author declares that drawing-boards are useless when flat table surface of sufficient breadth can be had As for drawing, it is required for almost every trade, and it bears to modelling almost the same relation which the latter bears to all the minor arts which require taste Drawing is decidedly the key to all arts, but it must not consist of petty detail, but every effort should be made to acquire the art of making every line and curve at a single sweep, and to attain a certain freedom in the motion of the hands and arms For most beginners fail especially in paying too little attention to this command of the pencil And as the painter TURNER worked without a maul-stick, so should every pupil attain perfectly free-hand. Pupils too should never be allowed to draw with short pencils, as they, oddly enough, are fond of doing, so that they often cut whole pencils in two. The paper must be of good quality, smooth, thin, and hard, which, however, entails no great expense

There is no literal copying. What copies are given to the children are simply intended to serve as motives to be varied. This awakens invention, and better designs for wall-papers and carpets are called forth than those manufactured by the old processes, in which the same ideas are continually repeated. The whole secret of design consists in this, to begin with the simplest and easiest patterns, and to continually advance; but for this no "gift" or "talent" is required but constant industry, and it cannot be too frequently or too clearly declared that the object of the school is not to make works of art, but to *learn how to make them.*

MODELLING is the next branch of industrial art. Any teacher who can draw can with the aid of a manual teach modelling in clay, since it is for children really easier than drawing. Clay and the tools for modelling are very cheap, the fingers being in fact the chief aids. Cylindrical vessels can be shaped on a tube of pasteboard, and baskets, vases, and the like made of beautiful form, and then baked at the pottery

As the practical result of this union of drawing and modelling, LELAND indicates the practice of eyes and fingers, by which pupils are prepared for every practical occupation, and the direct qualification of such pupils for branches of industry where there is a constant demand for employés who have been thus trained. On the other hand we are told of a reformer whose name is known to every newspaper reader, and who professed a great interest in art, who wished to know the "market value" of the children's work, and of another who asked if all the pupils did could not be more cheaply manufactured by machinery It is evident enough that such remarks, in spite of their extreme "practicability," are simply idle, since they do not grasp the real object of the school. It is as irrational as if one should require that reading and writing should directly "pay."

As a third branch—especially for girls' schools—embroidery is commended, and in this patterns after original designs are of extraordinary value. These three branches can be introduced to any common school In many places, as, for example, in England, wood-carving is preferred by parents to modelling. It may be added as a fourth study to the three already described. For this, wood and a few tools are all that is required. It is also important that the children shall not be set at difficult or advanced work.

If these four things are provided for, the school is fitted for work, and the pupils may in time be properly prepared for advanced industries And such a provision for work may be made in every country school.

To this beginning our author adds the designing and

cutting out of stencils for ornamenting rooms, an art as
yet little practised, yet by which thousands might make a
living The expense which it entails for cardboard, brushes,
pencils, colours, and varnish is trifling   To this succeeds
papier-maché, which has much in common with modelling in
clay, and offers a wide field to inventiveness and industry.
With these are included leather work, by which very beautiful and attractive objects are produced

Less directly related to such work is ceramics, with the
allied painting, which is, however, not of great importance
for elementary schools ; and then repoussé or hammered sheet
brass work, which requires a good knowledge of drawing and
great dexterity in the use of tools ; and finally painting, which
is the most popular branch with children, but which, in proportion to its expense and trouble, is of the least practical
value.   It is not therefore to be introduced to common schools
without consideration, though it naturally is included among
the studies of those of a higher class.

Now since all that pertains to establishing and carrying
on such branches may be readily obtained everywhere, and
as by their practice a sense of the artistic and beautiful is
awakened in children, it is but rational that they should
form a part of school studies   The teacher too, learning while
teaching, and deeply interested in his work, will exercise
withal a decided influence on national culture and industry,
and find in it all a relief from his severer duties.

The introduction of this practical apparatus to schools will
of course arouse opposition, but if those who oppose it can
be induced to visit the classes and see the children at work,
with the room ornamented with its results, they will soon
change their opinion, and be the more easily persuaded to
permit the expense   Moreover, their outlay need not be
very great.   Care must be taken to supply good models, and
this can be done by publishing illustrations of the treasures
of the museums of different countries   These can of course
be adapted with variations to any of the arts above described,
and it follows that the work will vary in different places
according to the expense or difficulty of obtaining certain
materials.   It must be established as a principle that teacher
and pupils, in whatever they work, be it stone, clay, leather,
or aught else, shall take pains to make the result truly good

and tasteful, and not such trash as is generally seen at fairs (*Jahrmarktsplunder*).   For when sale or money-making is not definitely the aim of the school, excellent work may still be produced, and the permanence of the institution still further guaranteed   By further applications of these arts, such as painting on stone, artistic rag-carpets, mosaic, &c., a whole house may be cheaply furnished.   The furniture may be simply and solidly shaped, the floor laid with mosaic, the windows hung with tapestry, and walls, ceiling, or doors bedecked with papier-maché and repoussé brass All of these may be made in the house or in a school.

We shall hear, of course, that it is useless to adorn houses in this way for people who do not understand it, and there will also be wailings that maidens learned in minor arts will make bad wives for workmen.   As for the first indictment, one may plead that everybody is not a bush-whacking back-woodsman, and that half the world spends money on machinery-made trash, when they could get something better for less money, while, as to the second, young mechanics, like other people, always choose the best educated girls when they can get them   As the aristocracy of old cried out against reading and writing for the people as the ruin of all social order, so to-day we hear the protestation against teaching industrial art to the people.

This education is not to take the place of trades, but by educating pupils in minor arts to train them to mechanical dexterity, and it is by means of such schools that a desire to learn trades is to be awakened.   LELAND boasts that he was one of the first to declare the fact that the overthrow of our whole present decayed system of teaching must lead in its fall to industrial training in schools   In earlier times the apprentice system had a far greater significance, since then by it the child learned a whole trade, while by the present subdivision of labour a modern workman makes only the sixtieth part of a shoe, and is only the serf of a capitalist. And it is by the tendency to true art by teaching it in schools, and by the reaction of true taste against machinery manufactures, that a remedy will be found against the error of the age.   Here ends the practical part of the pamphlet.

In the general remarks which follow, the writer remarks that boys and girls show equal capacity in design and modelling, but that in brass-work and wood-carving the males are masters One of the greatest impediments which tasteful industry meets is the extravagant and be-puffed work popularly called art. Every one at this word thinks of statues and pictures, and even eminent men believe that artists are gifted ,with special inspiration, and that education must begin with a refined appreciation of great works Yet true art for home decoration need be a mystery for none. The æsthetes preach how desirable it would be to bring the renown of RAPHAEL and of MICHAEL ANGELO down to the people, but they do nothing at all to make them understood. Now these artists were children of their time— a time when every object was a work of art And when this shall be the case with us, we too shall have again a RAPHAEL

Art training is conducive to morality Boys trained in schools of which they love the work, and where they learn to get a living, will be kept from much idleness and mischief. Even men may learn, instead of talking petty politics or mere loafing, to converse on more sensible subjects. Young girls will be even more benefited by such occupation, by more readily obtaining places in factories or shops, or similar industries, or else as married women finding occupation for their leisure

In such an education there is also an economical factor, since by it every one can assure self-independence. This is the more accurate, since it is shown by the small cost of teaching design and modelling in the smallest schools There can be no regular rule or system established for the sale of work, but nothing should be offered for sale which is not *good*, and the delight of pupils over their first productions should be checked, to prevent an overestimate of what is worthless.

But the most striking remarks made by LELAND are to be found in the last paragraphs of his pamphlet, and it must be admitted that what he says is as applicable to old Europe as to young America It is by introducing hand-work into schools that the popular prejudice against the " vulgarity " of "work" can be most effectually destroyed Hitherto one has been regarded as a gentleman who had soft hands, and it was considered a sign of social superiority when a man declared he had never done a day's work in all his life. Millions are still influenced by this idiocy. And this is so, because hand-work is really not as yet inspired or guided by culture and education. But by the application to it of art, and by its union with school studies, work will become honourable. The minor arts as practised are most intimately allied to the highest art, and to all that pertains to the most refined culture. Those who know them will also know the names of BENVENUTO CELLINI, of ALBERT DÜRER—in a word, of all the great men who won the greatest fame in the most glorious of ages. Moreover, the practical knowledge of art which children thus acquire has this result, that they visit museums and collections with greater intelligence, and understand the bearings of the subject better than any amateur. LELAND made this experiment in person. He had read all that he could find in books on wood-engraving, but two days' work over a block taught him more than a library had done. "For of all learning since books were invented there was never aught like experience, and of all experience there is none like one's own."

The introduction of these arts into schools is truly a question of the time, yet clubs and societies should everywhere be founded, and even ladies' clubs formed in the smallest villages, to advance culture and become a source of profit. Last, not least, it must be admitted that the work is agreeable and easy to a degree which none would suppose who had not tried it; and the author answered, when asked, as President of a Ladies' Art Club, what was the most remarkable in it, "The love of the students for their work."

It is before all especially satisfactory to us to be able to prove that the idea propagated by the American LELAND of introducing work to public schools is of German origin. Apart from the views of AMOS COMENIUS and RATICH, PESTALOZZI was the first who made the experiment in his pauper-school at Neuhof in 1775, to busy children in summer with garden and field work, and in winter with spinning, weaving, and similar occupation. He was followed by FELLENBERG, SALZMANN, WEHRLI, and many more. Schools for poor and orphan children, above all for girls, were especially established, as for example in Belgium, in the Saxon Erzgebirge, in Wurtemberg, in Schleswig-Holstein, in which latter country care was taken by means of the KLEUTER schools to train boys to a trade Yet these were all rather tentative experiments than well organised and complete establishments.

Since that time an abundant literature has been developed on this subject, unions have been established which devote all their energy to "instruction in manual dexterity and domestic economy," and whoever will read through the interesting proceedings of the Congress, held in Leipzig in June 1882,[1] will clearly see that much work and many sacrifices must yet be required ere the full and proper results can be obtained

Among those men who in recent times took a leading part in making work a part of education we class Professor BIEDERMANN of Leipzig, whose important work appeared under the pseudonym of "KARL FRIEDRICH" in 1852. To this may be added the important aid in Austria of Dr. GEORGENS, who set forth his ideas in a newspaper in 1856, and Dr. ERASMUS SCHWAB, who published in 1873 and 1874 his views as to work schools and school workshops.

As regards BIEDERMANN FRIEDRICH, he requires that his method shall be entirely attached to the domestic home, "since an education without parental co-operation is irrational." The school itself is accordingly rather a support than independent In the first year there is only manual work instead of study, and the abstract "pursuits of reading and writing are followed until the eye and hand are made accurate by practice." But practical instruction should be balanced with theoretical branches of knowledge So there should be a garden with every school, which the children are to cultivate, while they receive lessons in natural history and philosophy, chemistry, &c. The older pupils shall subsequently aid in work to be supplied by the local municipal government As for housekeeping, the Kindergarten is to be simply continued and extended, those things to be especially made which are of direct use in domestic economy or in the school. In its result, through this practical education of children, the system is very intimately connected with the social life of the community.

[1] Verhandlungen des Congresses fur Handfertigskeitunterricht und Hausfleiss von Dr W GOTZE, GERA, ISSLEIB, und RIETSCHEL, 1882

GEORGENS would establish the school on a similar basis. The problem is with him on a far greater scale than with FRIEDRICH, but differs as to the co-operation of the family in education, knowing very well that in general home gives but little aid to the school.

SCHWAB has in common with both the principle of regarding work as an element in the course of public schools, but he sets it forth in a much clearer if far narrower and pettier manner than his predecessors, thereby showing himself as a real and practical schoolmaster. Work is for him the main motive in moral development, and the "mother of moral force in thought and deed," which ennobles the soul and matures as the best fruit independence and serene self-confidence. In the school there is to be that well-regulated work in common which tends to familiarise children with the social virtues. When this work in common is at present applied in the Kindergarten, with the best result, it ceases however in the seventh year, and is not resumed till the fourteenth. Yet this is the age when all energies are in most active operation, though they are not exercised, with the exception of the instruction of girls in sewing and similar pursuits. This is done with the purely practical intent that they shall help in the house, yet in the right hands it may be made a means of far higher training, since it need not be limited to theoretical knowledge of materials, implements, and the like, but may also lead to a love of work and habits of industry. Attention and patience, order, neatness, and economy may thus be obtained, and much frivolity and folly worked out of the mind.

In like manner SCHWAB would establish a division of practical teaching for boys, or a school garden and a school workshop. In the latter the "minor arts" are to be taught, such as LELAND requires for his industrial school.

And here we return to the American and his system. It must before all be regarded as a great deficiency in his system of education that he pays no attention to the rural-industrial (*landwirthschaftliche*) or agricultural needs in education,[1] and so provides practically only preparation for

---

[1] Professor KARL WERNER is quite right, as regards so much of my system as I have as yet published. But as originally conceived, and as it has been set forth in this book it will be seen that it must neces-

trades. And yet if we consider that there are more country
than town schools, the employment of children in gardens
becomes of almost paramount importance. One is not, however, to suppose that the school garden is of one whit less
importance for city children than for those living in the
country,[1] since it is exactly for them and for their unnatural

sarily have been based on an entire and comprehensive theory not only
of all industries, but of a far deeper reform Had I begun in so practical a country as America with preaching so much, I should never have
succeeded in teaching ever so little I have had in common with my
friends of the School Board trouble enough to persuade people that there
is any sense in showing children how to prepare for trades : if I had
offered to include agriculture, commerce, and housekeeping, it would
have been entirely too much It was not by writing books, but by
putting my hand to the work, and practically teaching boys and girls
in person, and showing the results, that I made that teaching known.
When I first proposed to offer my system to be put in practice in the
city of Philadelphia, a gentleman who had for many years been a leader
in education and in the Board said to me, "There is no use in your
preaching any theory of reform It will all depend on your own personal skill as a designer, a worker in brass, a wood-carver, and so on
Get up a lot of specimens of your work to show people It is only as
a man who can do these things practically and better than anybody
else that you will be judged" This was effectively the same as if a
man preaching a new religion had been required to prove its truth
by sweeping out the church or taking up collections But my friend
was in the right, and it was by such work and personal teaching only
that I succeeded in establishing the school Fortunately aid came to
me, "wie berufen," or as if invoked by the spell of need Yet it was
difficult, for it is a hard thing to theorise and prove by practice at the
same time —C G L.

[1] The bringing up of children in the country is destined to become
a question of national importance when the nation shall pay as much
attention to education as to the petty schemes of politicians The
old French nobility was probably preserved from utter deterioration
by the keeping its children on farms under peasant foster-mothers
until they were seven or eight years of age The *New York Tribune*
has of late years made a noble beginning in this reform by sending
thousands of poor children to pass the summer in the country. The
testimony which Mr JAMES GREENWOOD has borne to the beneficial
results of the "hopping season" on London children—which I can
confirm from personal observation, having known many London hop-
gatherers—is in this regard of great value It is hardly possible to
exaggerate the importance of this subject, since one-fourth, perhaps
more, of all the deaths in New York city are of children under four
years of age, and this could be reduced to a minimum by keeping the
young out of the slums How it is to be done is as yet among the
problems, but it is simply a problem of life and death. Nearly allied

physical education that rural occupations are of the utmost importance. It is only during the pleasant part of the year that work can be carried on in the school garden, in winter instruction may be given in the minor arts

And here it is to be advanced as of the greatest importance (*als das Wichtigste hervorzuheben*) that LELAND lays far more stress on design and drawing than is to be found in the German and Austrian programmes. Not that drawing is really neglected here, but with the American the further development of the children is based exclusively on this, which in the European schools referred to is not to any such extent the case In the latter it is only the means to an end, while with the former it plays an independent part, and is meant not only to develop freedom of hand and eye, but to lead to invention and to art itself And in this we must decidedly give the preference to *this* system. Drawing thus enters into the ideal efforts of the school, as into the rest of its system or discipline, and so through this idealising tendency in all the branches of education the formation of the children's character—to which so much importance is universally attached—is alone made possible. And as the practical realisation (*Praxis*) which the public school requires receives through this ideal the right beginning and the proper turn, and is thereby prevented from sinking to mere materialism, which is for a child's heart utterly depressing.[1]

From such a beginning a limitation of merely practical work results as a matter of course, and the saying that in school the pupil is not to learn to make works of art, but

to it is the question as to whether it is a municipal duty to exterminate pestilential slums and rookeries, in which poverty forces weakness into vice. The coming generation will find much to amuse it in comparing the philanthropy of this age and much of its expenditures with the hideous truths of our neglect of the simplest and most apparent home duties —C. G L.

[1] Whatever power a boy above fourteen may have to grapple with the stern realities of life, it is absolutely impossible to train mere children to their full capacity without allowing play for the *ideal* or the imaginative Teach a child that agriculture, commerce, housekeeping, or art is a *whole*—a great and marvellous thing, yet really within his grasp—and he will grasp it It is as if he were told that he could be a doctor or a farmer almost in play, and yet in earnest truth. I can stimulate pupils to their utmost effort by gravely addressing them as if they were skilful adult artisans.—C G L.

how they should be made, becomes a truth. The school workshop is here no mere shop, and the industrial developments are far from mere trades. In fact no mere trade would be taught at all, but simply the mechanical faculties exercised and developed, and the soil, so to speak, prepared for work. The impulse to some practical occupation, which is innate in every man, and which in the FROEBEL Kindergarten is awakened in tender years, must and shall be satisfied, but taste at the same time must be developed and the intellect ennobled

And on this very ground we should consider the question so often put by "people of quality." "Why need our children learn design and modelling, wood-carving and stencilling, and all these arts? They will never earn their bread by these or by any hand-work, for they are meant for higher studies" Now it is precisely because they will *not* have the opportunity later in life of developing this instinctive impulse that their taste and touch should be trained in childhood, and therefore they ought to learn betimes.

A much more natural objection to the whole system is to be found in the obvious question, " Well, if this education to work is really so extremely necessary, why was it not long ago practised." One cannot escape by saying that we now for the first time see into its importance, since teachers have now for nearly a century studied the subject In fact we have long had schools for teaching feminine arts to girls

But there are many reasons why we were not so ready to introduce innovations of such a deeply searching nature *to public schools.* Firstly, we do not as yet see clearly into the object and scope of all that is to be taught, or how far we can carry out the theoretical pursuits indicated, because the time and local circumstances must be studied or determined. It was soon and easily discovered how to prepare and equip schools for girls' work. The scope of what is necessary or useful for future life is here far more limited. It is much harder to make a choice as to what work shall be taught in boys' schools, for there are a thousand directions in which men labour Here there is no equal uniformity as with girls, for the field for masculine labour has indeed almost infinite sub-divisions. Now we cannot precisely determine the future calling or trade, but we can teach general practical principles, and these in such a manner that the teacher cannot miss nor the pupil misunderstand them. Therefore we cannot lay down an exact course for every school, because the teaching of the minor arts depends on the materials to be obtained in certain places, or on the tastes or occupations of the people around, and on a hundred other conditions Yet where the codification is difficult or almost impossible, the deliberate German who likes to advance securely, and does not plunge headlong into new experiments, is not so easy to initiate

And again, it may be asked, where does school training cease and family training begin? How far can or must the home be made to prepare for the school? And, in further consequence, how far shall the municipal authority take part in establishing and supporting schools for teaching trades to boys, since thus far there is so little general and primary occupation for them. Would it not be better to leave it entirely to the parents to prepare for the future calling, and leave the special training to the school [1]

[1] *Apropos* of choosing a calling, I had a pupil familiarly called SAM who distinguished himself by good behaviour and cleverness He soon learned to design so well that I sold some of his patterns He also worked in brass I did not fail to impress it on his mind that he had become in fact a practical workman, since he could produce something by which he could live When he was fourteen years old he left school, and a few days after his father asked him what he intended to do for a living "I intend," said SAM, "to be an apothecary. I have thought it over, and it is a good business" "I don't know about that," replied his father ; "I am afraid that I cannot afford the expense" "It is too late to consider that, father," replied SAM "You know that I had saved up forty-five dollars to buy a watch Well, I took my watch-money and paid the matriculation fees, and have entered myself for a course of chemistry To-morrow I am going to try to find some druggist who will take me in his store for practical education" Now it was not because SAM had learned to draw or beat brass that he developed so much young American independence, but I am sure that the consciousness that he could take care of himself as a practical artisan had been partially brought out by work This was the view which his father took of it He said I had given SAM confidence that he could take care of himself The industrial school does to a certain degree make boys and girls think of themselves as possible future independent workers Girls who would not have thought much in the ordinary school about an occupation often hazard the conjecture or form the determination to become teachers of art I have observed numerous instances of this —C G. L.

That this is not the method to be adopted is sufficiently shown by what has been said, but the difficulties refer in the main to the establishment of such industrial schools, and it may be definitely said that thus far in Europe we have only made experiments with such institutions. Wherever we look, be it to Sweden or Denmark, to Switzerland or Germany, we find different arrangements and different views as to the kinds of work and the order in which they are to be taught. Thus, for example, in the Gorlitzer School of Ready Practice (*Handfertigkeitsschule*), which consists of a course of one year, there are united pupils from the most different schools, and of the most different ages BEUST in Zurich teaches by groups, while GOTZE in Leipzig advocates teaching work in classes.

As for Austria, such institutions are as yet unknown to her, but every day there is more discussion of the subject of industrial teaching, and whoever has read DUMREICHER's brilliant pamphlet "On the Problems of the Policy of Education in the Industrial Towns of Austria," and paid attention to the latest message of the Minister of Culture and Education on schools for training to callings and trades, must admit that we can no longer put aside the "education to work," but that we must soon organise it But we are taking a roundabout way to our work. Here we are establishing "great trade centres of education, in which the progressive school system (*Fortbildungschulwesen*) of each province may find its intellectual point of support." From this basis of operation the minor institutions for teaching industries may be organised With regard to our present condition, this seems to be the best way, "since all educational institutions which are open to voluntary pupils are formed by the natural development of culture in the people, and therefore they grow like all other forms of social life."

That is accordingly the present predominating practical principle which will tend to spread the material of culture into wider and wider circles, and which aims at a substantial calling as well as a substantial social condition corresponding to it. This has, however, less to do with the actual school basis, as it is especially shown in the public schools, at most only so far as there is also "an education of the industrial classes." The problem of the popular schools consists however in the education of *all*, not merely of the working classes, and it may, according to what must be called "educating to work," be formed at the same time with the organisation of industries, since the dexterity acquired in the lowest classes will be of avail in the upper. There will be indeed a vacancy filled in our public education, for as SCHENKENDORFF of Gorlitz correctly remarks, "the present generation is beyond all things being *intellectually* educated, while all that could lead men to *action* is left aside. Hands and eyes remain untrained, so that we find everywhere want of tact or dexterity and of practical common sense, yes, even as regards simple sanitary relations, there is fault to be found, since, as HARTWICH says in his monograph, "What we suffer in," "If we overload the brain in the years of growth, and thereby chain the body to the bench in the schoolroom, the natural result will be intellectual smattering and bodily weakness"

But the greatest difficulty which we shall encounter for such work in the public schools is the want of properly prepared teachers. It seems therefore a little sanguine when LELAND simply requires from the teacher that he shall be able to draw a little,[1] because he can then with the help

---

[1] It is enough that the teacher shall be able to draw a little, if he has the ability to learn, and that rapidly   An intelligent class of adults with a good handbook, or manual, and copies, may even dispense with a teacher   It is not generally advisable, but it may be done   It was precisely because I was confronted by the difficulty which suggested itself to Inspector WERNER, that I said this, to encourage the vast majority of people who, especially in the United States (it is less the case in Germany), ignorantly believe that to draw at all, much more to design, requires either innate "genius" or extraordinary labour   It is hard at present to find teachers for industrial schools, but it is not hard for those who are fit to teach at all to form elementary art classes and teach and learn together—even drawing It is hardly worth saying that for the higher and better endowed schools the teachers should of course be able to draw not a little, but *well*   Experience has however taught me that by the system which I follow, and which has been briefly explained in the preceding pages, a mere child who has drawn very little indeed often makes as rapid progress in *design* as a grown-up teacher who has passed through all the years of a regular course in a first-class art school   And it is design, not simply very good *drawing*, which is required for proficiency in the minor arts   If it be true, as I have asserted, that decorative design and these arts are easily learned by mere children—and all the East and the Tyrol and Spain prove it—is it not reasonable that they can be as

of good manuals easily master the other branches. We believe that the teacher must not only be able to draw very well, but that he should know exactly in teaching drawing what method to adopt, and what the results are to be. For he must take an active and practical part in the minor arts which he is to teach. He must be a master of the material with which he is to deal, and all this is not to be done in a hurry, or without previous preparation.

On this account care has been taken here and there to practically educate teachers At Naas in Sweden, at Emden, where Rittmeister CLAUSON VON KAAS teaches, in Dresden, and even in Gorlitz, there are such courses for teachers, since it has been understood that only real teachers can take boys in hand, and that there is not much use in setting even an experienced workman to teach, though he should do it under the eye of the master [1] In Austria such a course for teachers could be established at small expense in our admirably organised and generally well furnished normal schools And this the pupil could further develop in the public school.

Of course the establishment of work-rooms in the public schools would entail expenses which would fall on the com-

---

easily mastered by a teacher, who, though he may be but a little in advance of his pupils, can still lead them If I had begun by telling the world that no classes or elementary schools could be carried on without teachers who could " draw very well indeed," it would have been many a year ere the hundreds of schools and classes which " Circular No. 4, 1882," called into existence would have been established. Such a system, however, works more promptly in a country where the people act for themselves. What effectively settles the question is the fact that hundreds of classes *have* been formed and successfully conducted by ladies and gentlemen who had a slight or amateur knowledge of drawing with the aid of my Manual of Design and Drawing. It is intended that a greatly enlarged and very much simplified and improved version of this Manual shall appear with this work on Practical Education. It will be arranged in series of easy consecutive lessons.—C. G. L.

[1] This does not agree with my experience. But be it observed that in the two hundred schools or classes of the Home Arts Association in England, the teachers, and able ones at that, have always been found when they were wanted. This has been fully proved by the remarkable excellence and great variety of the work shown in the annual exhibitions held in London of the work executed in classes in all parts of Great Britain.—C. G. L.

munity. But when we read the list which LELAND gives of objects required for equipment and study, or the demands made by SCHWAB in this matter, it is evident that the expenses are by no means so great but that an intelligent municipal government, or where this is too poor, societies or private benefactors, may aid in the need[1] It is not impossible that these schools can be self-supporting, since such work as is worth anything can be sold, and the profit appropriated to the school fund. Certain communes can adopt the system and try the experiment, and from these roots branches may extend in every direction.

We miss one thing in LELAND's programme, as well as in that of Germany and Austria. How, for instance, the art schools are to be brought into accordance with the public schools, as they have hitherto existed; how much time should be given to each theoretical or practical branch; and how many pupils can be taught in a single class, &c[2]

This union of the industrial with the public school as it has been is, however, the head and cardinal question of

[1] It has been found in the hundreds of schools and classes for industrial art work established in England and America that societies or private benefactors have always come forward to aid the work, and that so generally that this aid may be always confidently relied on Very recently the Home Arts Association received an anonymous gift of £650 I avail myself of this opportunity to thank the giver in the name of the Association.—C G L

[2] I have stated in the pamphlet under review that my classes accord with the public school in this way the pupils are excused from two hours every week of the regular course of study in order to attend my school They make up this lesson at home I have also stated that about one hundred hours is the minimum in which pupils can attain sufficient knowledge of design for practical purposes, and also become familiar, e g, with modelling or wood-carving. I do not mean by this that the boys and girls become artists at all, but that they do in this time learn to produce designs fit to work out, and panels or ornaments which will compare with common work and sell, may be seen by any one who will visit the schools, or examine the engravings after photographs of our school work which were published in The Century I have received a great many orders for designs for brass work, and these have been in every instance executed to the perfect satisfaction of the purchaser by pupils from thirteen to fifteen years of age For these designs they have received from 50 cents to $2 each. As for the number of pupils which can be taught in a single class, it depends on capacity, circumstance, and age, to say nothing of the teacher.—C. G. L.

the whole affair, if it is to be represented as capable of existing The entire overthrow of the present system and a complete renewal will provoke absolute opposition among the public, which is with difficulty brought to understand anything new As it is, especially in one or two-class country schools, difficult in the limited time allowed for teaching to get through the appointed studies, or do anything in addition to the regular reading, writing, and arithmetic—how much more impossible does it seem to add to these other branches, or, as they may be called, "practical hours of practice" Where the children live near the school it may be done, but in the country, where the childien often go four or five miles over a bad road to school, say in mountain land, where the days in winter are still dim at eight in the morning, and are dark at four in the evening, there can be no increase of school hours Nor is it much better in summer, when the days are long, for the school garden, since then the parents need the elder born to aid in thrifty home work or afield.

It is in this that the greatest difficulty lies—how to practically carry out the idea of the industrial school. Yet this "time question" is after all only a question of time, and presents no difficulties that will not be overcome Work will be introduced to schools, and children become familiarised with it, for whoever has learned to love it in youth in any form will never in later life yield to idleness, be his rank or station what it may And then the moral and æsthetic gain of the individual in the strife of life will show itself in the progress of the whole.

CARL WERNER.

II

REPORT OF THE COMMISSIONER OF EDUCATION IN THE UNITED STATES ON THE LELAND SCHOOL IN PHILADELPHIA.

From the Report of the Commissioner of Education (General JOHN EATON) for the United States for the year ending 1883.

THE PUBLIC INDUSTRIAL ART SCHOOL OF THE CITY OF PHILADELPHIA [1]

This school was established under the direction of CHARLES G. LELAND, and opened on the first Tuesday in May 1881 It was maintained by an appropriation from the funds of the School Board, under control of the art committee, Messrs WILLIAM GULAGER, WRIGHT, SHEDDON, and COOPER This appropriation for the first two years was $1500, but only half the sum was spent by the school, the rest being devoted to teaching drawing in other schools, to an exhibition, &c [2]

The school began with 150 pupils of from twelve to fifteen years of age, all sent from the public grammar schools, each teacher of which was allowed to select a limited number of applicants Nine-tenths, if not more, of these were from thirteen to fifteen years old They were divided into two classes of about seventy-five each—one attending on Tuesdays from three to five P M ; the other on Thursdays, at the same hours A class in brass repoussé was held on Saturday afternoons from two to five

All the pupils were obliged to begin with lessons in design,

---

[1] In America the word *industrial* is always used in its literal and correct sense, and does not suggest the reformatory or penitentiary

[2] Subsequently increased to $3000, when the number of pupils was raised to 200 Of this appropriation only about two-thirds was taken by the school. Apart from rent and warming the rooms the expense for each scholar did not much exceed at any time $5 (or £1) annually. Out of this all the teachers, except myself, were paid salaries after the first year, and all expenses for materials, &c , defrayed.

according to Mr LELAND's method of simple outline decorative work in curves. As soon as a boy or girl could make a design fit to be " put in hand " he or she was allowed to take up any branch of work taught in the school.

These other branches were embroidery, modelling in clay, with colour and glaze (or barbotine), and rudimentary decorative water and oil painting—subsequently increased by carpenter's work, turning, inlaying in wood or marquetry, fret-sawing and cabinetmaking, mosaic-setting, and sheet-leather work (for covering furniture)   There is no definite limit, however, as to the branches taught, the principle tested being this, that any pupil who can design and has learned to model in clay can turn his or her hand almost at once to any kind of decorative art   This has been fully tested, as there is no pupil in the second year who cannot turn his or her hand successfully to anything taught in the school.   The seeing others work, the being in an atelier where many kinds of work are going on, teaches them to regard them all as one

The business of the school (i e., purchasing art-materials, paying all bills, keeping the accounts, calling the roll, and looking after the children) was in the hands of Miss ELIZABETH ROBINS, who was also treasurer of the Ladies' Art Club.[1]

The general direction of all branches of study, except design, which was taught by Mr. LELAND, was under the charge of Mr. J. LIBERTY TADD.

The teacher of brass repoussé was THEODORE HEUSTIS , that of wood-carving, BERNARD UHLE , of embroidery, Miss L. Moss, who also gave her labour gratis for more than a year. Being obliged to leave on account of ill-health, her place was filled by Miss ANNIE R. SPRINGER.   Mr. LIBERTY TADD teaches modelling, painting, mosaic, and practical pottery, a throwing or potter's wheel, or apparatus for making vases, &c., having been provided. Carpentry, scroll-sawing, cabinetmaking, and inlaying or marquetry are taught by EUGENE BOWMAN (coloured)

---

[1] Another institution, consisting of 200 ladies, who pursued the same branches as those taught in the school, with the addition of oil and china painting as usually practised, sketching from nature, and repoussé on pitch. There is such a club in most American cities and towns. Miss E. ROBINS is now Mrs. JOSEPH PENNELL.

The school was from the beginning, an experiment to fully ascertain what children could do, and not simply an institute to teach art. A want of appreciation of this fact on the part of the public has been the source of the only troubles which the school has experienced. The general outcry has been, "Teach *boys* while at school a practical trade by which they can get a living." The LELAND experiment was made solely to find out what *boys and girls* are capable of learning. The result has been to prove beyond doubt that all children taking one or two lessons of two hours each in a week in an *atelier*, can in two years' time learn not one but several arts so well that they can obtain paid situations at almost any kind of employment.[1] On one occasion the head of a factory offered to take forty of the designing class at once into paid employment.

No effort was made to sell the work of the pupils, but much valuable and beautiful glazed and coloured pottery was made, which had a high market value. The panels produced by the wood-carvers, owing to the ability of the teacher, Professor B. UHLE, are decidedly superior to the average work seen in cabinetmaking or furniture. There are thirty boys and girls in this class (three coloured), and there is not one who could not earn by carving $9 (£1, 16s.) a week.[2] All of the pupils in this class can design a piece of work, model it in clay, and then carve it. All the wood-carvers are encouraged to make their work up in the carpenter's shop.

Orders are sometimes received and executed. These are for designs, repoussé, &c. It has been fully proved that if the rooms or building could be provided with an outfit, the school could be made to pay its expenses, as is the case with the MIDHAT PACHA School in Damascus. This would

---

[1] The quickness of perception or intelligence awakened by industrial art work has an immense advantage over a single trade or merely mechanical work, in this, that it enlarges "the capacities" to such an extent that the learner easily masters *any* kind of calling or occupation. This truth is one very little appreciated by the public.

[2] One of the pupils a coloured boy, obtained a paid situation as carver in a factory while he was still working in the class. The carving executed by these pupils was of a much higher character and very far superior to any work of the kind by children in the London Health Exhibition of 1884.

require a special out-of-door agent to solicit orders and sell goods

A close study of the pupils individually, and many inquiries by the director, developed these facts

(1) That one or two afternoon's work in the week at the art school, far from interfering with the regular school studies, aids them materially. This is the opinion of the teachers in the grammar schools.[1]

(2) That the pupils in the art school began to take a greater interest in reading, and that in visiting exhibitions, or when seeing art work or tasteful manufactures, they criticise what is before them with more ability than grown persons display who have not been trained to understand design and its applications

(3.) That the children all regard the art work as being attractive as an amusement, and as the drawing is not mere copying, but original design, they regard it also as agreeable employment. If the bell did not ring to summon them to cease, the pupils would apparently never leave off designing, modelling, mosaic-setting, wood-carving, &c In one school of 87 pupils every one entered his or her name for a place in the industrial school.[2]

From the same Report.

PREPARATION FOR INDUSTRIAL ARTS.

Two circulars of information were issued by this office in 1882 in response to this popular feeling and demand. One prepared by CHARLES GODFREY LELAND of Philadelphia discussed the subject of industrial art in schools from a practical standpoint. The experience of the author enabled him to speak clearly on the topics presented, and to engage the attention of readers to unusual interest. About 50,000

---

[1] The intermediate relaxation and change to hand-work is a relief and a healthy mental tonic One needs to be personally employed in such a school for years, closely studying meanwhile the results, to realise the truth of this and of other statements in this work

[2] In every one of these cases the parents preferred requests that the children should be allowed to enter the industrial art school This was after some understanding of its real nature had spread in the community.

copies have been distributed to correspondents and applicants, and have produced marked results   The circular has been reviewed and warmly commended by educators in foreign countries   Thus KARL WERNER, Government Inspector of Schools at Salzburg, presented a review of Mr LELAND's circular and an outline of industrial efforts in European schools in the *Literarische Beilage der Montags Revue, Vienna*, April 23, 1883, in which he remarks that "it was desired to introduce work itself to the school, and this is what is treated of in a pamphlet by CHARLES GODFREY LELAND, director of an industrial school in Philadelphia, who seems to have practically solved a problem for which Europe is yet hardly prepared"

III.

THE BRITISH HOME ARTS AND INDUSTRIES ASSOCIATION

In the year 1880 I published a little work, entitled "The Minor Arts" (London, MACMILLAN & Co), setting forth the methods for self-instruction in leather work, woodcarving, repoussé, mosaic-setting, designing, and other branches of industry.   The preface contained the following suggestion —

"It is greatly to be desired that in every village, or in every district of the larger towns, ladies or gentlemen, able to draw, and who are interested in providing employment or in advancing culture among the poor, would found little societies or schools for teaching the arts set forth in this book, or similar ones   It would not be an expensive undertaking.   A room with tables and chairs, a supply of cheap leather and leather waste, old newspapers, wood, sheet-brass, paste, glue, and tools would be easily provided, and the school, if properly managed, soon pay its expenses, and prepare and qualify with taste applicants for many trades and callings.   Such schools would supply both amusement and instruction for old and young, and effectually promote an elementary and general knowledge of art.   Drawing alone is not sufficiently attractive for the ignorant and uneducated, but there are few who will not practise one or more minor arts It would be well if circles, clubs, or societies could be formed among young people of every class for the same purpose, and for mutual instruction. I venture to assert that with the instructions given, and a little knowledge of the simplest elements of drawing, the majority of pupils would in a few weeks attain a practical mastery of all of which it treats I shall only be too happy to communicate by letter with any one forming such schools, classes, or circles, and give any advice in my power as to their organisation or minor details "

It was in accordance with this suggestion that Mrs. JEBB, of Ellesmere, Shropshire, established, firstly, a class in art in her own village, and then others by the aid of friends All of these formed a league or union for mutual aid and support In time ladies and gentlemen in all parts of Great Britain joined in the undertaking, and in November 1884 it finally took the form of the Home Arts and Industries Association. This society at present has two hundred classes in different villages and towns, and the number is rapidly increasing. The association consists of honorary members who contribute each a guinea and upwards annually, working members paying only half-a-crown.

Training classes for voluntary class-holders and other members are now being held at the rooms of the association, 1 Langham Chambers, Langham Place, London, W. In these classes instruction is given in the various minor arts Readers are invited to visit them. Any one wishing to join them can do so by paying one pound a month for instruction in two branches, or on other terms by arrangement

Independent art classes, wherever they exist, are invited to join, or correspond with the association. Those who wish to establish new ones of any kind may do the same very much to their advantage. They will receive advice, be supplied with the leaflets or brief manuals of instruction, and with designs and models for teaching, either gratis or at cost price, and they will also have the right of exhibiting the work done in their classes at the Annual London Exhibition, the first of which was held in July 1885, at 3 Carlton House Terrace.

Ladies or gentlemen who will form clubs of five full paying subscribers will be admitted as working members, and empowered to act as associates to establish classes, and receive all aid needed. All members will be cordially received at the weekly meetings of the association.

There have been held three annual exhibitions of the work furnished by the classes from all parts of Great Britain. They contained specimens of carved wood-work, embracing much furniture of a superior description, a great variety of very beautiful pottery, embroidery, repoussé metal work, spinning, weaving, carpenter's work, admirable specimens of mosaic made from broken china ware (an art first practised in the H A. and I Association), and of many other arts. It is strictly true that all of this work was such as to do credit to good artisans, and not of that fancy amateur kind generally seen of old in ladies' fairs It may be here mentioned that through the teachers of the H A and I. A. the minor arts were extended to the People's Palace, the East of London working-men's clubs, and to many similar institutions in many places.

I add to the foregoing a list of the officers of the Home Arts and Industries Association, with some extracts from its circular. It is by far too modest, in the fact that it gives no idea of what it has done since its classes (now nearly two hundred and fifty in number) were established. I venture to say with the utmost confidence that there is not an association or society, charitable or otherwise, in Great Britain which has, in proportion to its means, done so much practical good during the same time, i e., during the three years which have elapsed since its establishment.

President.

The Earl BROWNLOW.

Vice-Presidents

Maurice Adams, Esq	J Comyns Carr, Esq.
The Lady Marian Alford	Mrs. H T Clements.
The Lady Ardilaun	Lady Colthurst.
Mrs Richard Bagwell.	Sidney Colvin, Esq.
Eustace Balfour, Esq	The Countess Cowper.
Hon Mrs. Richard Boyle.	The Lady Elizabeth Cust.
The Countess Brownlow.	The Archbishop of Dublin.

Albert Fleming, Esq
The Lady Hampden
The Lady Fitz Hardinge.
Miss Holford
T. C. Horsfall, Esq
R C Jebb, Esq
The Countess of Kenmare.
Sir Frederick Leighton, P.R A.
The Lady Louisa Hillingdon.
The Lord Monteagle.
The Lady Georgina Drummond Moray.
Lady Musgrave.
The Lady Dorothy Nevill
The Countess of Pembroke
J Hungerford Pollen, Esq
E J Poynter, Esq , R.A.
Val Prinsep, Esq

W B Richmond, Esq
Lady Sitwell
The Lady Sarah Spencer.
Lady Stanley of Alderley.
Rev. F Sutton.
Hon Mrs Alfred Talbot.
The Viscountess de Vesci
The Marchioness of Waterford
Louisa, Marchioness of Waterford.
G F Watts, Esq , R A.
The Countess of Warwick.
The Lady Wentworth
The Duchess of Westminster.
The Countess of Wharncliffe
The Countess of Wicklow
Hon Mrs Percy Wyndham.
The Dean of York

Council

*T R Ablett, Esq
Eustace Balfour, Esq
*W A S Benson, Esq
*Bernard Bosanquet, Esq
*The Countess Brownlow.
Richard Bourke, Esq.
Miss Fanny L Calder
*Rev. J O Coles
*Albert Fleming, Esq.
Alfred Harris, Esq
T C Horsfall, Esq
Mrs A T Jebb
E. Hay Murray, Esq
*Miss Louisa Jebb.

*Charles G Leland, Esq.
*Mrs Kellie M'Callum
Miss E Herbert Noyes
*The Countess of Pembroke
Hon Emmeline Plunkett.
*Gilbert R Redgrave, Esq
Mrs W Le Fleming Robinson.
Miss Rowe
Claude Vincent, Esq
Mrs G F Watts
*The Lady Wentworth
Miss Anna Hogg
W Bliss Sanders, Esq

* Members of Sub-Committees

Hon Treasurer
WALTER BESANT, Esq.

Secretary
MISS DYMES

Office and Studios of the Association
I LANGHAM CHAMBERS, LANGHAM PLACE, W,

The object of the association is to spread a knowledge of artistic hand-work among the people, the instruction to be given in a manner which shall develop the perceptive faculties and manual skill of the pupils, and prepare them

for entrance into trades, whilst also increasing their resources
and enjoyments. The methods employed by the association are —1 The organisation of classes in Great Britain
and Ireland, in which attendance is entirely, and teaching
almost entirely, voluntary   2 The distribution to these
classes of selected designs and casts, and leaflets of information   3 The employment of Honorary Local Secretaries to
carry out the work in country districts   4 The maintenance
of a Central Office and Studios in London, where both voluntary and paid teachers can be trained.   5. The publication
of a yearly report, in which successful experiments in class-
holding will be described   6. The holding of a yearly
exhibition and sale in London, where the work done in
the various classes may be compared and criticised, and
certificates of merit, bronze, silver, and gold crosses awarded
for progressive attainment amongst the pupils

The association differs from any other in its power of
assisting isolated workers in remote and poor districts, where
neither pupils nor teachers could conform to the regulations
enforced by existing agencies

It is hoped that local classes, when self-supporting, will
become the germ of revived village industries.   It has already
effected much in this respect   The following minor arts
are at present being taught in the local classes —Drawing
and Design, Modelling, Casting, Joinery, Carving in Wood,
Chalk and Stone, Repoussé Work in Brass and Copper,
Hand Spinning and Weaving, Embroidery, Pottery, and
Tile Painting, Embossed Leather Work, Mosaic Setting, and
Basketmaking   Others are practised to a smaller extent.
Owing to the continued and rapid development of the work,
and the consequent increase of expenditure, funds are greatly
needed at the Central Office

The conditions of membership are that members contribute £1, 1s. and upwards per annum, while working
members, that is, all who hold classes, or otherwise in any
way give their services to the association, contribute 5s.
and upwards.   This entitles working members holding
classes to receive designs, leaflets, models, &c., in any one
subject.   Working members who conduct classes in several
localities in the same subject may be called upon to pay a
separate subscription for each class.   As working members'

fees do not cover the cost of the office, studios, printing, and supply of models and designs, the association is dependent on donations and subscriptions from other members. When desirable the Council appoints Local Secretaries, who organise the classes in their districts Rules are supplied to them. Local Secretaries sending subscriptions to the General Fund to the amount of £9, 9s. per annum can nominate a student who will receive instruction gratis in five branches during one session

Classes are of two kinds.—1st. Training classes held at the studios, or under paid teachers in any part of the country, for the purpose of instructing amateurs who intend to assist in the ordinary classes To defray the cost of such a course of lessons other amateurs are allowed to join unconditionally 2nd Ordinary classes in which amateurs give voluntary instruction to boys, girls, and sometimes adult working people, and thus carry out the scheme of the association.

The question whether pupils in ordinary classes are required to pay for their lessons or not must be decided by local considerations, but the classes are eventually rendered self-supporting by means of a percentage charged on the work sold. The first outlay is met by local subscriptions Ordinary classes can be held in clubs, or in any available public or private room or workshop

Students are admitted to central training classes at a fee of 2s 6d. per lesson, and are allowed to work in the studios between their lessons when there is room. A list and time-table of training classes is issued at the studios, classes being formed for the various arts according to the number of students applying for instruction. All communications to be addressed to the Secretary, Home Arts and Industries Association, 1 Langham Chambers, Langham Place, W.

www.ingramcontent.com/pod-product-compliance
Lightning Source LLC
Chambersburg PA
CBHW030343270326
41926CB00009B/936